Praise for Gates of Power:
Actualize Your True Self

"Inspirational and action-oriented, *Gates of Power* presents a set of ambitious challenges and practices, to create the life we desire, to be successful at work, to be true partners in our homes and to have caring relationships. Bachar provides us with a how-to guide that is both spiritual and practical so that we can become who we are meant to be."

Catherine Kaputa,
author of *You Are a Brand!* **and** *Breakthrough Branding*

"Nomi Bachar shares a solid body of hard won wisdom. Her work encompasses knowledge to inspire the mind, body and spirit. It uplifts and transforms those who journey through the Gates of Power."

Joyce Z. Meyers,
LCSW, CRT, CHT

"Nomi Bachar is exceptional. Her book addresses one of the most important yet elusive issues of our time: how to create "success." Not the accrual of material goods, but our mental, emotional and spiritual success! I highly recommend Bachar's brilliant book to all who honestly seek the powerful and exciting success within themselves."

Al Cole from CBS Radio,
host of the syndicated talk show "People of Distinction"

"This book, one of the best I've read, delivers insight and freedom that will help the reader live a life of mindfulness and purpose. Whether you are a beginner or continuing student, "Gates of Power" will guide you into understanding your heart, the world, and the portals through which your True Self communicates."

Carole McDonnell,
author of *The Constant Tower*

"The Gates of Power Method and Nomi have given me the transformative techniques necessary to function and succeed both personally or professionally. I use some Gates of Power techniques to assist my singing students with the insights necessary to blast through emotional impediments that prevent them from reaching their singing potential. Personally, Gates of Power techniques provided me with the ability to lead and to love in ways I never thought possible."

Lenora Eve,
vocal instructor, New York City. Artistic director and founder,
Opera Breve

Gates of Power

Actualize Your True Self

Gates of Power

Actualize Your True Self

Nomi Bachar

© Nomi Bachar 2018

The right of Nomi Bachar to be identified as the author of this work has been asserted by her in accordance with the Copyright, Designs and Patents Act 1998.

ISBN 978-1-946978-76-9

All rights reserved.

The contents of this book may not be reproduced in any form, except for short extracts for quotation or review, without the written permission of the publisher.

A CIP record for this title is available from the British Library.

Edited by Nicky Leach
Front cover design by Crystal Joy
Interior design by Crystal Joy
Printed in the USA

Contents

Acknowledgments 9
Introduction My Own Journey and How to Use This Book 11

1 An Invitation to Be 15
2 On Suffering 25
3 The Gates of Power 37
4 The Four Commitments 47
5 The Inner Aspects of the Self 53
6 The Gate of the Body 65
7 The Gate of Emotions 109
8 The Gate of Dialogue 139
9 The Gate of Creative Expression 167
10 The Gate of Life Path 185
11 The Gate of Silence 207
12 The Gate of Knowledge 221
13 Creating a Personal Practice 233
14 In Their Own Words: Clients' Stories 245

About the Author 261
About the Gates of Power® Program 263
Bibliography 265
Endnotes 267

Acknowledgements

First and foremost, I thank my parents who have dedicated their lives to providing for us. Your love and loyalty are etched in my heart. I thank my wonderful siblings—my brother Baruch and my sister Ora—for being my forever loving companions.

I thank my spiritual teachers: Shri Brahmananda Sarasvati, Lillian Shwabe, and Rav Michael Laitman. Your wisdom and compassion illuminate my path.

I thank my good friends. You are my playmates and my confidants, and your company is a joy to me.

I thank my clients. You inspire and move me every day.

Thank you, Ron Kopp, for your wise remarks and guidance in writing the book. Thank you, Nina Pollari, for helping with the typing and editing of my first chapters.

Thank you, Jackie Arellano and Talya Cousins, for your help with the design of the cover and the diagrams for the book.

And last, but not least: thank you, Theodore Poulis, for helping with organizing the final touches of the book.

You all inspired and supported the birth of this book, and I am grateful for your presence in my life.

— Nomi

Introduction
My Own Journey & How to Use This Book

This book was born out of my own personal journey and years of witnessing my clients and counseling them through their journeys. I feel deep gratitude for the inner courage and tenacity, theirs and my own, that keeps us traveling through darkness and light. I am deeply moved and inspired by my clients and all of us who are committed to our transformation.

I was born and raised in Israel, and like most young Israeli women, I served two years in the army after completing high school. I was stationed at a border kibbutz under the Golan Heights. There was beauty in the simple life in nature and in working the fields—until the war interrupted it. Then there were the long nights and the two thousand bombs that fell on that kibbutz. When the war and the service were over I could use a long vacation, but the pressure to choose a career was mounting. It came as a shock to me, as well as to my parents, when I decided to audition for Bet-Tzvi, the Academy for the Performing Arts. I did not exhibit any acting talents, so my decision was puzzling. My father considered my decision very frivolous and irresponsible. He proclaimed that he did not raise me to be a gypsy, and had no intentions of supporting my studies. He expected me to enroll in the university and become a respectable scholar.

I actually expected that from myself, too, but some other force within me was driving me toward creative expression. That inner voice seemed to know better than I did what I needed. Now in hindsight, it is clear to me that my enrollment into the academy started my personal journey toward reclaiming my aliveness, inner freedom, and creative expression—a journey that became my life path. I was a young woman restricted, bound, and even imprisoned by her fears, insecurities, and defensive patterns. Unknowingly, I was guided by a deep need to experience inner freedom.

To my parents' surprise, I was accepted into the academy and received a full scholarship. In the academy, I was surrounded by some very expressive young people, and there *I* was—painfully shy, awkward, and inhibited. "Open up!" my frustrated acting teacher yelled at me, time and again. One little step at a time, and with an intuitive dedication to my sense of freedom, I proceeded and successfully graduated. One month after graduation, out of the blue, I received a call from an artistic director who had seen me in one of the academy's final produc- tions. I was invited to audition, and as a result, was offered a principal role on the national stage as Nastia in Gogol's *Lower Depths*. My performance was a success, doors were opened, and I enjoyed years of performing, and later, directing, chore- ography, writing, and producing. At a crucial time in my life, when I was already living in New York City, I decided to train as a psychotherapist. The same path of healing, expression, and growth continued, albeit in a different form.

My personal journey has been one of many sheddings. Layers of defensive and protective shields needed to melt away to first uncover a sense of deep despair and hopelessness. It took self-awareness and much self-nurturing for the darkness to slowly dissolve. I needed to understand the roots of my suffering and to discover the real needs and desires hiding within them in order to grow beyond the pain. The gift is a passionate, vibrant, creative spirit, whose company I enjoy today.

This book is a road map to the art and craft of full aliveness—the pleasure and fulfillment of being true to the best and highest in you. The book presents the principles and philosophy, as well as the many practical processes, of the Gates of Power® Method. Gates of Power® developed slowly and organically throughout the years of my own inner work, and from 20 years of counseling others.

When reading this book, you need to know that it is not necessary for you to agree with, or even emotionally understand, everything presented, in order to glean insight, inspiration, and practical tools. Give yourself the freedom to take what feels right and useful to you personally; keep an open mind. Question, discuss, and allow for discovery. Do not rush your reading. Pause, taste, savor, feel.

I do recommend doing the exercises and using the Reflection Pauses to go within. A few words about reflection. To me, reflection means feeling into a question, using your intuition, imagination, and emotional association. It is a deeper level than just thought; therefore, it might take you some time to fully and truly answer each question. Please do not hesitate to revisit the Reflection Pauses and to change your answers if need be. At the same time, trust your instincts when answering the questions, and move through them with an ease and a speed that feels natural to you. The few lines that are present after each Reflection Pause symbolize a space for thought, but they are by no means there to limit your answers.

If you wish, feel free to work with a notebook and develop your answers as you go along. As you travel with me on the paths of this book, take yourself on an adventure. Keep in mind the Four Magic E's: Experience, Explore, and Express, so that a natural sense of Empowerment emerges. Let the book become a mentoring companion; we can all use inspiration and a bit of mentoring. I am forever grateful for all my mentors—past, present, and future. In order to open ourselves to joy, pleasure, and true expression, we need to find out what holds us back and binds us. The book explores the roots of suffering and the "Gates" to our inner power.

I believe that we are innately wired for happiness and fulfillment. The pursuit of bliss is our sacred right and our deepest blessing. We're meant to relearn how to be present in the moment and naturally intimate with ourselves and life. We can learn to have fun and engage in pleasurable activities, as kids do. We can learn to love with abandon, likewise fools; express ourselves like the inner artist that exists in each one of us; and be as caring and responsible as a great parent. What's more, we can enjoy all of these facets of ourselves simultaneously. The book offers you guidelines to create a joyful discipline for inner freedom and fulfilment.

1

An Invitation To Be

I invite you on a journey to full aliveness. "Full aliveness" is not a real expression, per se, so you won't find it in a dictionary; rather, it is my shorthand way to express the idea of being fully alive, and I will be using it from here on. If you are already on the path to full aliveness, enjoy the information and any new ideas or tools presented to you.

To me, full aliveness means self-expression, creativity, capacity to feel all of our feelings, openness to love, adventure, and learning, and the ability to actualize our vision and deepest desires to create a life of contribution. I know it seems like a lot, but why not go as far as we can? Nature intended us to be the healthiest, best version of ourselves, and our dreams want to come true. Commitment, passion, and discipline are necessary companions on the journey, and this book is here to assist you in the process. It is based on the Gates of Power® Method, a path to self-transformation and self-actualization.

On the one hand, it is important to be able to experience and accept all the aspects of living as a human being and, on the other, to realize that we are beings of consciousness moving through a human life. Our journey is one of embracing our earthly existence, creatively and expressively, while at the same time coming to know our true nature as spirit, pure awareness, and ultimately one with the Absolute.

I have learned that what gives us the most fulfillment and happiness is the ability to be who we are and grow into our true power. Being who we are, as simple as it sounds, is not that easy. It takes time, awareness, self-knowledge, and courage. It is a life-long process of learning to accept and express ourselves, to give of and to ourselves, and freely and confidently open up to receive and create happiness. We have a deep yearning to feel and know everything that lives within us. Since we're made of the same intelligence and energy that the whole universe is made of, we have a natural appetite to experience infinite possibilities within ourselves—an appetite that entices us to constantly grow, change, and learn. This wonderful yearning for life is our jewel.

How is it, then, that sometimes it seems as though we are living alongside life, not really in it, as if there is a glass wall between us and life? A sense of emptiness and sadness is born out of that. I remember myself in my twenties, sitting on a bus and watching a group of people my age laughing, kidding around, and being silly. It sounded like they were miles away. There was that glass wall feeling. I was so withdrawn and joyless at that point in my life that laughter and silliness were things I observed, not things I experienced.

I think of children before they lose their spontaneity: their sense of curiosity, adventure, presence of being, playfulness, creativity, and open-heartedness. They have the ability to love. They are empowered and moved by things around them. They *are* fully. We were all children at one time, then something happened within us and we lost touch with our innocence, simplicity, and spontaneity. As adults, we do have extra responsibilities; we all do have to grow up, but the loss of our openness and spontaneity is not a necessary part of growing up. Our personal life history, as well as the cultural and societal influences, can inhibit our capacity for being fully alive and present. In varying degrees, we lose touch with our spontaneity. At times, it is buried so deep that it feels like we cannot reach it.

I hope this book inspires and encourages you to make a commitment to find a path that takes you back to an open and expressive state of being. These abilities have not disappeared—we have just lost touch with some of them. We can reclaim them when we return to our source.

A beautiful poem by the Persian poet Rumi about the journey back to ourselves struck me as I was writing this chapter, and you will find passages from it scattered throughout. I am not including the entire poem, but it is called "If A Tree Could Wander," and it is widely anthologized and available on the internet if you would like to look it up.

> *The drop that left its homeland,*
> *the sea, and then returned?*
> *It found an oyster waiting*
> *and grew into a pearl.*

When we become committed to our fulfillment, we begin to ask ourselves what really makes us happy. What brings us joy? What fulfills us? We're all unique, and our needs are different. Identifying our wants and needs and honoring them is the first step to fulfillment.

> • • • Reflection Pause • • •
>
> What are some of the things that move you and bring you joy? Is it being in nature, hiking, swimming, or sitting by the sea? Is it reading, writing, dancing, or creating artwork? Is it a deep, fun-filled conversation with loved ones?

Reading the book will offer you many reflection pauses; these are a great opportunity to take time and engage in discovery. I suggest that you have your journal available when reading the book. Linger over the questions and enjoy them. Write, rewrite, ponder, and imagine. Brainstorm and question.

When I was pondering this question myself, I was utterly surprised to discover that I had written on my joy list: "Lying down in bed, watching history and art series." Since I did not grow up watching television at home (Israel, in its formative years), most of my life I have watched as little television as possible. Surely not in bed! The television set in my childhood home was in the living room, behind closed doors; placing a flat-screen television on the wall of the bedroom was new and almost felt politically incorrect. I wondered if I was becoming a "bed potato." But I had to admit to myself that a good movie in bed is fun. So, let yourself indulge while you're writing your joy fulfillment list—it will do you a lot of good.

> • • • Reflection Pause • • •
>
> Is there a common thread that connects all of the things that make you feel fulfilled? Maybe you find that travel, discovery, and adventure are a common thread for you. Or, family, friends, connections, and heart-filled dialogue fulfill you most. List your common threads. Remember, there may be more than one.

What did you find? Does what makes you happy have to do with expressing yourself? Sharing with others? Contributing? Being in a space of creating and playing? Enjoying the world through your senses? Learning new things? Discovering and growing?

A client of mine, who is a very successful manager of several stores, told me he enjoyed being in a leadership position and was on his way to making the kind of money he had set out to make. But despite this, the joy and the fulfillment ingredients were lacking in his life.

When we made his joy list, we discovered that playing soccer (an old passion of his) and playing the guitar (another oldie!) were the first two items on the list. He was not enjoying either one of them. It took acknowledging the joy these gave him, as well as making time and space for them in his busy life, to replace the missing ingredients. He had to overcome the uncomfortable feeling that he was reverting back to adolescence. And if he was, so what? A bit of adolescence is a good thing.

We found that the common thread connecting all the elements on his joy list was physical and artistic expression. Honoring that thread changed his life. I think that if you look at what truly fulfills you, you will find it has to do with being expressive, creative, open and related—which brings us back to the idea of full aliveness and sense of inner power. Our journey is to return to what we already potentially are.

As we move into adulthood, most of us become aware of insecurities, repressions, and defensiveness, as I did. We feel that we are not as expressive or as secure as we want to be, but we don't know how to go about liberating ourselves. Some of us begin to question ourselves. When did I lose my spontaneity, my authenticity, and my ability to live joyfully? What happened in my life that took me away from myself? These are not easy questions to answer. It can take months or years to fully understand how and why we have lost certain abilities, but understanding is the basis of change.

Obviously, each one of us has a unique and personal history that influences the decisions we make and the way we view the world. I remember having one of these "aha" moments in acting school. We were doing an exercise connected to childhood memories, and I found myself sobbing uncontrollably in front of the class. It seemed like I somehow unearthed a painful memory.

I went back to the age of four. I had done something that angered my mom, who was very stressed by her life as it was, and I got severely beaten. I was terrified. Sobbing, I told Mom that I would tell Dad when he got back that she was unfair. When my dad got home, I rushed to him to tell him about the unjust punishment, but he had no patience to listen (he could hardly handle the simplest chores of life at that point in time, having just barely survived being physically wounded in the war, and three years of mental anguish). At that moment, I remember feeling like the light in the room went out.

Of course, my parents were doing the best they could to keep us going, but these years of stress took their toll on me. To the four-year-old me, this was a moment of deep fear and loneliness, a moment that would color the way I experienced life. Needless to say, I had to work it out—and I did. But at that moment, crying in front of my acting class, I suddenly realized why the world up until then had felt so cold, indifferent, and punitive to me. This feeling lingered as a result of the experiences I had had as a child, and I needed to understand it to be able to move past it. I also realized that the moment was not an isolated experience; rather it was emblematic of a period of time in my early childhood.

There are different degrees to losing one's natural spontaneity and one's inner sense of power, and there are different reasons why this happens. One of the most important reasons is fear of disconnection. Because we are human beings, we naturally identify ourselves with our body and our personality. We feel separate from others, because I am in this body and you are in that body. This sense of separation makes us feel very vulnerable and transient. We need each other, and we need a sense of connection. Experiencing ourselves as separate, we try to somehow secure the connection with other people to ensure receiving comfort, love and caring. As children, we definitely felt this way.

At a young age, we create what can be called a "protective coat"—a way of being, inside and outside, that helps us feel secure and acceptable. This protective coat is an energetic, psychological, emotional, and behavioral defensive construct. It is an organized pattern associated with our response to early stresses and survival instincts. We create it in an effort to avoid feeling vulnerable and exposed to what we experience as the dangers of life: being alone, being unloved, being an outsider, feeling isolated emotionally and physically, the possibility of being different and unaccepted—all that scares us. Living under a protective coat, our expression is compromised. When we compromise our truth for a long time, the protective coat becomes our second nature, and we don't know that we are compromising anymore. It becomes our way of life. It becomes our identity.

The following story demonstrates the process of creating a protective coat.

Nina, one of my clients, is the eldest in a family of four children. Her father battled cancer on and off for eight years, and passed away when she was 10 years old. Her mom had had to go back to a full-time job when Nina was three. As Nina grew a little older, she needed to take on more and more responsibilities around the house, and with her younger siblings, to help her mother as much as possible. She learned to be a caretaker to her younger brother and two sisters. She needed to repress her needs and desires to become helpful, ready, and able at all times. Her role as a caretaker was necessary for her survival and the survival of her family. That was the "protective coat" she had had to create.

When she started working with me, she was deeply depressed and unmotivated to care for herself. She told me that as a child, she lived with the constant fear of losing her mother, too, so she did everything she could to help her. In the work we have done together, Nina has had to discover her needs and wants, which were buried under the habit of taking care of others. She has had to face the fear of losing people's affection if she lives for herself, too. Slowly, she has begun to enjoy fulfilling her desires, a bit at a time, and releasing the fear. Taking a bubble bath, for example, was unheard of in her former way of life. So was spending time reading on a bench on a sunny day. Or saying, "Not today" to a friend when she did not really want to do something. The list has grown over time, as joy has filtered in.

It is, at times, a slow and always courageous process to let go of our survival habits. What starts out as giving to ourselves overflows and becomes a joyful giving to others.

Imagine for a minute living inside an invisible protective layer. Can you see how that would create the sensation of a glass door, a separation between you and life? It is impossible to be fully present when we are constantly and mostly unconsciously feeling anxious about our survival, and living within a layer of insulation. At the same time, deep down, our anxiety persists. We worry that we might not be able to provide ourselves with the security that we need and want.

There are different colors and shapes to our protective coats. Some people create coats of shimmering colors and beautiful shapes to charm and engage others, while others create coats to hide inside, in order to appear nonexistent and as gray as possible. (We will explore more about this in the following chapters.) Moreover, in the effort to survive, we also hide away a part of ourselves—the unacceptable part that we don't think will help us survive in our family, culture, or society.

We are constantly on the lookout, constantly navigating our lives. It is a lot of work. We have gotten so used to the effort that it feels natural, like it is a part of us, like it is us, but it is a construct: a Defensive Self. We are not present and available to the moment; we are actually missing out on our lives. Our mind is constantly in the past or in the future, assessing situations. Feelings that do not fit into this attempt to survive are not allowed to come to the surface, making it difficult to fully connect and to contribute to ourselves and to others.

Writing this takes me to the memories of my first "big love." It was the first time I dared to open myself to love and, more frightening still, to the need to be loved. It was a bottomless need, and I was falling and falling. My old fear of being abandoned was so present that I could not enjoy the nurturing affection that was embracing me. I could not relax and be in the moment. I lived in the fear, not in the love. Living in my survival anxiety, I missed out on the bounty that was available to me. I remember one instance in particular: my partner was in the shower, and I was in bed, propped up on the pillows, reading. It was a peaceful, sunny Sunday morning—a moment of grace. All of a sudden, the thought that one day I might not be with him overwhelmed me, and I started crying hysterically. Sunny Sunday morning turned into Purgatory. Even though I was young and unaware, a budding commitment was born that Sunday. I vowed to myself to do whatever it takes to learn to enjoy my moments, be present in them, and become an inspiration to myself and others. Then there was the long and winding road of getting there.

> *You lack a foot to travel?*
> *Then journey into yourself!*
> *And like a mine of rubies*
> *Receive the sunbeams [...]!*

There is a good reason why people are not eager to do the work of reclaiming full aliveness. It feels very scary to let go of protection. Our protective ways have brought us a certain sense of security, but underneath, the hidden part of the self is experiencing self-rejection, fear, pain, anger, unfulfilled expressions, and needs. These emotions are not allowed expression because they threaten our guarded way of being. At the same time, our emotional side also carries loving feelings, excitement, passion, and creativity. Those too are not allowed full expression. So, all the things that we yearn for most—deep connections with other people, spontaneity, sense of play, creativity, joy, self-expression—all these treasures are not as easily accessible to us, because it is hard to be spontaneous and defensive at the same time. The two simply don't go together.

There are varying degrees of defensiveness. Some people are more open than others, and the level of our defensiveness fluctuates at different times. Most of us find little corners in our lives where we can allow some of our inner selves to come through. Artists find it when they create art. At times, we find it with our most intimate friends, family, or lovers. We find moments to be in the truth for a little bit, but we are not living it fully.

There is no need to judge ourselves for creating a protective coat. This is what we do in order to survive. As long as we identify with our body and our defensive thoughts, we live in fear. As we learn to experience ourselves as beings beyond a body and a persona, beings of consciousness (infinite and eternal) our fear of separation and death eases, our ability to relax into living grows, and with it comes our ability to share our gifts. In fact, our lives are a journey toward the realization of our truth and our spiritual power.

The journey that I am inviting you on is one of daring: dare to shed this protective coat slowly, lovingly, consciously, layer by layer, like a snake shedding its skin. Let yourself slowly emerge as that core of the creative, expressive, giving human being that you are. The core may be shriveled like a seed in the dark, unable to burst out, but it is there. It needs permission, attention, and support; it needs the loving and compassionate support of YOU, your Expanded Self, the loving companionate witness that is the essence of you.

Out of yourself? Such a journey
Will lead you to yourself,
It leads to transformation
Of dust into pure gold!

We should honor our passion to emerge into ourselves. The journey takes great courage and commitment. It requires daily practice and attention. The beauty of it is witnessing life changing within us and for us. The Gates of Power® Method offers tools to do that and a system that can support you in the process.

Notice also how you react to this invitation. You might be asking yourself: What is going to happen if I am completely myself and out there? Am I going to be *attacked, criticized, or ostracized? Am I going to become obnoxious and insensitive to others?* These are good questions. You might experience all of these things. People who live in their defensive mode resent those who are free and expressive. It threatens them. They might judge and criticize you. The fact is that when you live grounded in the expanded and companionate witness within, you are in a place of true power and freedom—a place that allows you to be naturally respectful and generous to others.

It does not mean that the possible judgment or hostility of others won't hurt you, but the fulfillment this state offers is worth the feeling of danger about what might happen. If you feel that freedom is worth the risk, then this invitation is for you. On the road less traveled the rewards are great—the ability to fulfill your true destiny, to contribute your talents and gifts, and to become who you truly are.

Are you willing to be free, accepting, and present—to be the "you" willing to open the door to endless possibilities and to the richness of your life? This is an invitation to the greatest adventure of all, the most tremendous act of creativity.

The first step in achieving something is to know what you are up against. This is a vital step, worthy of much contemplation. How can be we free ourselves if we don't know what binds us? With that in mind, let's look at the roots of our suffering so that we can use the Gates of Power® Method to liberate ourselves.

2

On Suffering

Aside from devoted masochists, who wants to suffer? We don't wait in line, eager to purchase extra suffering; most of us try to avoid it, chasing the lighter colors of life. But if we possess a serious passion for living, we need to look at the inspiring—yes, inspiring! —experience of suffering.

As an Israeli and a Jew, I should be very comfortable with the subject—and I am. Fortunately (or unfortunately), I come from a long tradition of suffering. Jews have mastered the skill of turning suffering into a spiritual goldmine and a source of inspiration. Being born and raised in that tradition, I believe that since we cannot avoid suffering, we should make the best of it. As far as I am concerned, there is nothing wrong with suffering. It seems to be an integral part of living: it tenderizes the soul and deepens our compassion; it inspires us to create, and, most importantly, it nudges us to transform.

When our pain reaches a level we can no longer ignore, most of us begin to delve into the recesses of our souls in search of self-healing and self-awareness, and that is a good thing. Our suffering brings us to our wholeness; much beauty, art, and love springs from suffering. The image that comes to mind is one of a dark, bottomless sea of emotions pulling us under; roped by fear, we are sinking. It feels like we're drowning. But there, in the midst of that darkness, if we can open our eyes, get used to the dark, find the courage to breathe, then sheepishly and tentatively begin to explore the deep and befriend it, if we can do that, we transform into divers. We are no longer victims of the waters but explorers who begin to find treasures and enjoy the experience rather than dread and resist it.

We need to respect our suffering as much as we respect our desire for happiness. Suffering, if we move through it with compassion and awareness, is a great mentor. It is, in fact, our guide to happiness. As we listen attentively to our suffering, we discover what our soul is crying out for. Our longings and needs tell us what's most important to us. By listening closely, we can distinguish between addictive, compulsive cravings and true soul needs. Once we distinguish our needs, we can learn to nurture and guide them.

> *Only through experience of trial and suffering*
> *can the soul be strengthened, vision cleared,*
> *ambition inspired, and success achieved.*
>
> **— Helen Keller**

Sarah, one of my clients, a singer and an actress, was devastated when her best friend died of AIDS. His battle with the disease was short, and his death shocked her. She realized that she had not been spontaneous or free in communicating her feelings to him, especially when it came to expressing her love and affection. After his death, she sank into deep sadness and regret. Sarah had suffered a double loss: the loss of her best friend and the loss of an opportunity to express the love she felt. I encouraged her to move through her sadness with compassion and awareness, and to see what insights and lessons would come forth.

She began to write her friend letters, expressing thoughts and feelings she was not able to share with him when he was alive. While writing, she started to compile music he loved and began listening to it. Before she knew it, she found herself putting together a one-woman show in his memory. I had never before seen her so inspired, dedicated, and open. It was as if she had moved through a thick forest of shadows and into a bright light. The show inspired and moved the audience to laughter and tears. Her suffering was transformed into a message of great love.

> *Your pain is the breaking of the shell*
> *that encloses your understanding.*
>
> **— Kahlil Gibran**

The power to transcend suffering and turn it into a blessing comes from the willingness to consciously experience, explore, and express our feelings. The treasures we find are invaluable truths about ourselves, others, and life, and a connection to our own inner power. Suffering becomes destructive when we resist and deny our emotional experience, robbing ourselves of the precious discovery of our truths and our power. Resisting, we get caught in the net of suffering; there, we either give up or, thrashing about, we get entangled, eventually destroying ourselves and others.

> *... love your suffering. Do not resist it, do not flee from it.*
> *It is your aversion that hurts, nothing else.*
>
> — **Hermann Hesse**

Watching the news reveals plenty of destruction stories. Many times, wellmeaning people get caught in the net of their own suffering. Unable to see the way out they end up destroying themselves and their loved ones. As Scott Peck, quoting Carl Jung, wrote in his book *The Road Less Traveled*: "'Neurosis is always a substitute for legitimate suffering.' But the substitute itself ultimately becomes more painful than the legitimate suffering it was designed to avoid. The neurosis itself becomes the biggest problem."

Our suffering is a strong force; we can and should harness it to take us to our bliss. The Gates are pathways to transforming suffering into inner strength.

The Four Big Questions

All prominent religions speak of suffering as part of the great plan and the purpose of life itself. So, let's dive in to befriend the dark abyss. When we ponder our lives, four fat big questions stare us in the face:

1. Who am I? Who am I beyond the obvious facts of my life history, my resume, and my beliefs? Who am I in my essence?
2. Why am I here? What is the true meaning and purpose of my life?
3. What are the roots of my suffering? What is in my way?
4. How can I dissolve the roots of my suffering and learn to experience peace?

As long as human beings have been around, they have asked these questions. Tremendous amounts of written material, oral traditions, and different teachings ponder them. Scientists, artists, philosophers, and spiritual and religious authorities all attempt to answer these basic and profound questions. All of these questions are connected. When we know who we are spiritually, beyond the externals, we realize why we are here and move toward understanding the purpose and meaning of our life. Suffering is eased by the ability to live in alignment with a deeper truth and a sense of purpose.

It helps to get to know ourselves first on the level of mind, body, and behavior—not an easy task. Then, we can learn to experience who we are in essence, beyond our mind, body, and behavior. This is a lifelong journey.

Mindfulness and compassionate witnessing bring us to discover who we are beyond our physical and psychological makeup, and our suffering can aid us to uncover our essence. The lotus flower, a symbol of beauty grounded in the mud and nourished by it, is a powerful image. Take yourself into the mud for a minute, into the roots of suffering, which are also the roots of self-knowledge.

The Roots of Suffering

I see two kinds of suffering on the suffering "menu":

- Natural, unavoidable suffering
- Self-inflicted, self-maintained suffering

Birth, aging, illness, and loss of loved ones are some of the natural, unavoidable causes of suffering. These are offered to us, along with the joy of birth, the wisdom of aging, the lessons of illness, and the love for other—a mixed bowl of sweet cherries and bitter almonds. Resisting any of these will not prevent us from being born, aging, falling sick, losing, or dying. It only intensifies our experience of suffering. Still, we resist. Can you see the face of fear behind the resistance? Acceptance, spiritual and emotional openness, and communication are naturally the better choices. They can help to gently guide us through the necessary storms of loss and change.

The other kind of suffering, the self-inflicted one, is unnecessary, insidious, and deeply painful. When we keep daggering our own chests, mechanically and relentlessly, with destructive self-criticism, rejection, and shame, the torture, although hidden, is constant. When we exile ourselves emotionally to live on a small, lonely island, or in a cellar for the guilty and the unworthy, we slowly wither and grow bitter.

If your goal is to avoid pain and escape suffering,
I would not advise you to seek higher levels of
consciousness or spiritual evolution.

— **M. Scott Peck**

> ••• **Reflection Pause** •••
>
> Find an incident in your life when your self-doubt or self-criticism hurt you. Do you have a sense of why you turned against yourself? For comparison, find an incident in your life when being brutally, completely honest with yourself helped bring you to a new level.

Alice, who started to work with me at the age of 23, used to scratch herself violently to the point of severe bleeding; it was as if she needed to tear off her own skin to escape it. When I asked her how she felt about herself, she said, "I hate her, the one inside me. I could kill her." One time, when I asked her in a session to draw a picture of herself, she drew a small black dot and said, "I was born bad. I wish I had never been born at all." Tell me about your "badness," I said. She said, "I know I'm bad because I could never make my mother love me. No matter what I said and did, I could never make her happy."

Alice's mother drank heavily and lived a life of raging conflicts with Alice's father. Little Alice took the blame on herself for her mother's suffering. Like many children who live in unhappy environments, she came to feel that it was her fault. She concluded that her innate badness was the problem, so she turned against herself. Alice needed to realize that she was not responsible for her mother's, or anyone's, unhappiness. She had to establish two important distinctions: one between her responsibility to herself and her responsibility to others, and the other between constructive self-criticism and destructive self-annihilation.

Today, many years and much awareness later, Alice is an articulate, passionate, and powerful woman, dedicated to herself and to the environment, studying and teaching sustainability.

The Unified Field – Beyond Fear and Death

The fear and pain that come from feeling unloved can turn into unhealthy self-rejection and self-criticism. Being unloved or feeling unloved means being alone and feeling you are separate. This feeling of isolation feels like death, since it goes against our deepest need: a sense of connection. Death feels like the ultimate separation from life and living, and thus is our greatest fear.

> *Our greatest fear is that when we die we will become nothing.*
> — Thich Nhat Hanh

The notion that when we die we cease to exist is haunting. I see the fear of separation and death as the root of our suffering. Fear creates attachment, gripping, clinging, and contracting. We cling to everything that feels like it would give us a sense of safety and comfort. The action and experience of clinging creates more fear, and we find ourselves in a vicious cycle.

On the spiritual plane, the energy-consciousness plane, separation and death are illusionary perceptions from our limited human point of view.

Let's talk physics for a moment. I know it might seem a little off the path, but it all connects. Quantum physics and quantum mechanics seem to join ancient spiritual knowledge and mystical experience in the understanding of the Universe as an alive, unified, and interconnected field of possibilities, a universe that is conscious and evolving. Within that universe, we are active participants with our very thoughts and actions.

An atom is conventionally known as the smallest building block of matter. However, "matter" has been found to be 99.9 percent empty space. The subatomic particles (or the pieces that form an atom) moving at the speed of light through this space are actually vibrating waves of energy. Science is finding that there is a continuous communication, a dialogue so to speak, among all subatomic particles. Information moves across the unified field of energy instantly. Thus, the invisible Universe is imprinted and impregnated with information—it is full of unseen intelligence. In other words, the Universe is a unified field of consciousness in a flow of creative process. We are one with this unified field of intelligence. As such, we are part of the greater order. There are clearly areas of commonality among mystical experiences, different spiritual teachings, and what scientists describe as the quantum field.

It may look like we are separate forms, but we are part of the whole. In fact, each one of us is a mini-version of the unified field, and we are all connected to and one with that wholeness. We have an active part in creating and contributing to the fabric of existence. As beings of consciousness who are directly connected to universal intelligence, we are endowed with all that we need. Being one with universal consciousness provides us with endless possibilities for visions, perceptions, choices, and actions for actualizing our goals and desires. It is up to us to recognize ourselves as creative artists of the life force.

When we observe nature, we see an ongoing and perpetual renewal and transition of forms. Rain becomes rivers, rivers become oceans, and the water of the ocean evaporates and becomes rain. Every winter, we witness the leaves falling and joining the earth. Every spring, new leaves emerge. Life seems to be a constant dance of transformation, an endless cycle of renewal.

Below is one of my most favorite descriptions of the interconnection and oneness of life, from Thich Nhat Hanh, one of my favorite teachers.

> *When we practice looking deeply into this sheet of paper, we can see the forest.*
>
> **— Thich Nhat Hanh, No Death No Fear**

As beings of consciousness and energy we don't die, since consciousness does not die. We change form. We move from physical form to spirit or pure consciousness. Later, it is possible that we may assume another physical form. When I came to realize that my spirit or essence does not die, I discovered a level of inner peace I had not known before.

The feeling that we are separate—disconnected from others—is another kind of suffering that haunts us. We assume that because we have separate bodies and separate personalities we are separate, and thus vulnerable to the possibility of being disconnected from others. These two fears are intertwined and are at the root of our inner suffering. Dying feels to us like the ultimate separation from life, and from all that we are connected to and love. Since the deepest need of our soul, I believe, is to feel connected, the illusion of separateness and death creates inner torment. As a result, the fear of dying creates a fear of living.

Life's common challenges, such as wars, sickness, loss of loved ones, disappointments, and the like, all create inner suffering. However, these challenges soften when the fear of death and the illusion of separation dissolve.

I remember being six or seven years old, listening to my mother talk with her grieving friend Sophie, who had lost her son in the war. They would sit in the kitchen for hours, whispering. I couldn't figure out what they were talking about, but each time I went in to grab a cookie, I would peek at them. It always looked like my mother's friend Sophie was crying. I remember wondering if she was also crying while she was asleep or when she was taking a shower. Sophie's crying went on for months. One evening, the whispering turned into a noise of excitement. I saw them hugging each other and smiling. I found it strange, and later asked my mom if Sophie had finished crying. She explained that Yotam, the deceased son, had appeared in his mother's dream to comfort her, and to promise he would be visiting her. Sophie's crying stopped. In my child's mind, I imagined winged

Yotam flying down for a nightly visit with his mom, and I wondered if he would visit us, too. Many years later, I understood that Sophie's grief was softened by the sense of her son's presence.

The Layers of Self-Inflicted Suffering

Our fear of disconnection creates a need to protect ourselves from it. To varying degrees, we try to avoid this feeling and attempt to secure love and connection by gaining a sense of power, control and recognition. Our defensive efforts provide a false sense of security, but the underlying fear does not disappear; on the contrary, it gets reinforced and deepened by our defensive patterns. As long as we keep from realizing our nature as consciousness beings, always connected to life and related to all existence, we continue to live in a constant sense of separation and fear, consciously or unconsciously.

> *The universe has never separated itself from men;*
> *man separated himself from the universe.*
>
> **— Luhsiang Shan**

There are two forces motivating us. One is a deep longing for connection, out of which springs joy, love, creativity, and true expression. The other is the fear that keeps us feeling separate, disconnected, and despairing. Our life is a tapestry of choices guided by either passion and connection or fear.

> ••• **Reflection Pause** •••
>
> Do you recognize these fears within yourself? What is your personal experience of them?

Children who don't experience unconditional love from their parents (who might not have the ability to love unconditionally) feel pain and interpret the reason for the lack of love as a lack within themselves. Thoughts such as "I am not good enough," "I am not worthy," "I must be bad," and "There is something wrong with me" are common examples. These interpretations cause deep anguish and a haunting fear of disconnection (which feels like an emotional death to a child.) Our reaction is to create what I earlier called a "protective coat," a way of being that will secure our parents' love and approval. Some other names for the protective coat are a "strong suit," "armor," a "defensive self," a "false self," and a "mask." Our survival efforts get us the attention and approval that we need but at the cost of our authentic expression. We survive, but we don't really live. Our emotional self is buried under the protective construct. We deal with our inner pain by escaping it through addictions—work, business, food, drugs, alcohol, sex, relationships, or even spiritual or religious practices.

> • • • **Reflection Pause** • • •
>
> Can you recognize the ways that you have escaped from yourself?

In observing the roots of our self-inflicted suffering, I see layers that build, one on top of the other, and result in something like a "suffering sandwich." The first layer involves living in the illusion that we are separate from others and from life, and the fear that comes with this feeling of separation. The second layer involves feeling a lack of love and misinterpreting it as a lack within ourselves, as a result, experiencing ourselves as unlovable. This reinforces a further fear of separation. The third layer involves burying our emotions under a false self, trying to secure love, and creating a conflict between our authentic nature and our false self. The fourth layer involves cultivating addictive practices (to ease the pain and get comfort) to further inner numbness and self-alienation. And fifth, all four layers create a sense of self-betrayal and self-rejection. Now we might sink into hopelessness and helplessness—a "dark night of the soul."

> • • • **Reflection Pause** • • •
>
> After reading about these layers of suffering, take a minute to identify how they resonate within you.

I have personally experienced all these layers of suffering. I managed to create a good deal of self-inflicted suffering on top of the natural kind and, of course, then needed to unravel my own self-created knot. As I mentioned in the introduction, I was born and raised in Israel at the time that the country was forming itself. My parents survived the Holocaust in Bulgarian work camps and came to Israel in 1944 to find a safe home. Four years after they arrived in 1948, a war broke out; this was known as the "Independence War," and my father was drafted and severely wounded while taking part. He went through years of physical and mental anguish—as did my mother, who suddenly had to carry the burden alone. As with many Israeli children, my life took place in the shadow of war. At the age of 18, I too was drafted and found myself in the army in the midst of a war. Death—and fear of death—were my constant companions.

Growing up became a lonely venture; I did not feel that I mattered. My parents, who were heavily burdened by the battle with poverty, health challenges, and mental stress, were busy surviving. Like most children, I interpreted their lack of attention to mean that there was something lacking within me and that somehow I was not lovable. I carried a deep inner pain, which I buried under layers of overachieving and excelling. I achieved plenty, but that did not ease the pain. Only when I realized that I was pinching myself and causing my own pain did I begin to entertain ways of releasing this inner grip. It took years of dedicated work for my power of expression and joy to flourish and my trust in being a part of the infinite to nestle me into peace.

I believe that our most important learning experience is the realization that we are one with the universal consciousness. We have the capacity to feel this when we sit in silence and learn to witness our emotions and thoughts without identifying with them. This is the seat of our Expanded Self. The realization of unity starts with an intellectual understanding and becomes an actual experience. It starts a process of shedding the illusion of separateness and the pain and fear that come with it. It opens a door to an experience of ourselves as vibrant beings sharing the dance with all creation. There are many paths that lead to this realization; Gates of Power® is one of them.

Being one with, and part of, the wholeness means that our natural state is wholeness; each one of us is a field of energy, vibrating with unique talents, intentions, and feelings. Respecting our uniqueness and nurturing who we truly are dissolves the illusion of being wrong or bad, and as that dissolves, we begin to shed self-doubt, self-rejection, and false defensive layers. Not to worry—the process of letting go of our negative beliefs does not mean losing a healthy sense of self-evaluation. When our awareness grows, we become able to challenge ourselves in a positive and proactive way toward higher levels of self-actualization.

The return to our authenticity allows us to experience life in a deeper and more intimate way. A trust in our nature as creative and intuitive beings empowers us to actualize our soul's desires and talents and experience greater freedom and joy.

> ••• Reflection Pause •••
> How can we dissolve the layers of suffering? What is your experience?

Self-knowledge is the key to self-liberation; it is impossible to liberate what we don't know. Knowing ourselves can take a lifetime, but it is necessary if we are to reclaim inner freedom. There are many paths and numerous practices and teachings that lead to inner transformation. The Gates of Power ® Method is a practical guide to self-knowledge and self-healing. The goal is to return to a sense of connection and to a trust in ourselves as the co-creators of our destiny.

You are the content of your consciousness,
in knowing yourself you will know the universe.
— **Kris Hnamurti**

3

The Gates of Power

Conscious travel into the roots of suffering takes us into our truest yearnings, the hidden needs of the soul. Like the roots of a tree, when understood, acknowledged, and watered, our yearnings transform into soul desires. Soul desires are vibrant wants and visions that create the powerful, passionate pulse of life: our trunk. With proper care, it blossoms into branches of true expression, carrying the fruits of our lives. We can imagine the seven Gates of Power ® as seven branches of experience through which our consciousness and life energy are flowing. The branches of our soul's tree grow and expand, nurtured by inspiration and attentive awareness. It is up to us to water our inner roots. True power is never dependent on external circumstances, people, or things. Like a tree, we are grounded in the soil of existence; we are supported by life. Still, it is up to us to nurture our soul and cultivate our visions.

Twenty-six years of coaching and counseling others, working with great teachers, and making my own personal journey have provided me with a long, fruitful observation time. My observation revealed seven channels or pathways of inner power through which our psyche finds expression. I call these channels "Gates." A gate, by definition, is a portal or a doorway. Our inner being flows through these seven Gates and expresses itself. The Gates are also portals for receiving. There is an exchange between our inner self and life. All of the Gates are interconnected and complement each other. Through them, we learn, expand, and experience life.

You can think of these Gates as seven branches of a tree, or even as seven Gates leading from and to the center of town (the center being our internal core). Yet another way of envisioning the Gates is as different garments of the soul, separate and woven together into a shimmering unity. Over the years, as my inner work and my work with clients progressed, my knowledge and understanding of these Gates deepened. The seven Gates of Power® are not to be confused with the chakra system, the meridians (pathways of energy in the body), or the auric layers. All these important systems of energy are acknowledged through the work with the Gates, but they are not the Gates themselves. Each Gate is a channel of experience and expression; in the Gates of Power® Method we explore, energize, and unblock these channels.

Imagine yourself as a diamond with seven facets. Your inner light reflects itself through the seven facets, and the light from outside shines through, reaching your inner being.

The seven Gates of Power ® are:

1. **The Gate of The Body**

    This Gate explores the body, its expression, energy field, and physical wellbeing, as well as its connectedness to our emotional and spiritual experiences.

2. **The Gate of Emotions**

    This Gate explores the power of emotions and their expression, with the aim of creating inner balance and emotional integration.

3. **The Gate of Dialogue**

    This Gate explores the "inner" (within ourselves) and "outer" (with others) dialogues. The aim is to create constructive, fulfilling, and successful relationships.

4. **The Gate of Creative Expression**

    This Gate explores and expands our ability to create and express. The aim is to use and enjoy our natural creativity in all areas of life.

5. **The Gate of Life Path**

    This Gate explores personal choices, life goals, and visions, with the aim of helping us to both actualize them and be a contributing force to ourselves, life, and our communities.

6. **The Gate of Silence**

    This Gate explores the realm of silence, prayer, and meditation, with the aim of creating a peaceful mind and developing a spiritual connection.

7. **The Gate of Knowledge**

    This Gate provides a space of inquiry for life's big questions and personal insights regarding them.

This chapter is intended as a short overview of the seven Gates; the subsequent chapters will then cover each Gate in greater detail.

First, a bit of a background about my discovery of the Gates. My first professional career was in the theater. As an actress and a dancer, I have always been fascinated with the body and the way it reflects our inner being. I find the body to be a powerful channel of expression and a great teacher of truth. When I worked on a character or choreographed a dance, my favorite thing to do was to discover the character's inner rhythm and physical expression. When I discovered how the needs and feelings of the character expressed themselves in my body, I knew how to *be* the character. The ways in which a person's physical, energetic expression and their inner experience sculpt their bodies continue to intrigue me daily.

An actor must be in touch with their emotions. Acting opened up the world of feelings for me, and I gained great respect and appreciation for their power. Later, my experience and training with emotive modalities of psychotherapy, such as primal therapy and bioenergetics, increased my awareness of our emotional power. It was natural for me to choose to train in primal therapy and bioenergetics, since these modalities are feeling and body-centered. The training and my personal experimentation inspired the different processes and exercises I have created for the Gate of the Body and the Gate of Emotions.

Diagram of the seven facets of being.

The Gate of Dialogue developed out of my training in Gestalt and psychodrama. Both of these modalities heighten our awareness of the different voices and aspects within ourselves and the way they relate to each other. If we listen to the inner conversations that go on between the different aspects of ourselves, we hear an orchestra of conflicting needs and different voices. All of these aspects merge to create our inner landscape. It's hardly a secret that the way we relate to ourselves leaks into the way we relate to others. If our inner dialogue is one of criticism and rejection, our dialogue with others will be tainted by that. Conversely, if the dialogue within ourselves is peaceful and loving, it overflows into our relationships with others.

Creative expression has saved my life and my sanity. I was able to actualize my artistic visions in spite of the challenges I faced as a performing artist, and nothing brought me more joy and fulfillment. I came to understand myself through expression. Being a multimedia artist, I cultivated movement, sound, design, acting, and writing in my artistic career. The Gate of Creative Expression was developed out of these experiences.

The processes and exercises in the Gate of Life Path were inspired by the various workshops and courses I took that dealt with life vision and goal achieving. I found that when our vision and goals are grounded in our true soul needs they become easier to achieve.

The Gate of Silence and the Gate of Knowledge grew out of 35 years of personal spiritual investigation and exploration. A hunger for inner peace kept little mountains of books by my bed. I studied different spiritual traditions and meditation techniques, sat with some amazing teachers, traveled the world, and plunged into scientific findings in the quest for answers to the question: "Who am I, and why am I here?" My morning and evening meditations have become my most precious companions. They bring me insights, an appreciation for the beauty around me, and peace. The Gate of Knowledge, the portal to that mysterious, magical, infinite realm of truth, is as intriguing to me now as it was 30 years ago.

Most of us experience a blockage in one or more of these Gates of expression. The blockages are created by limiting or negative experiences, feelings, and beliefs—all of which can be transformed. Each of the Gates offers its own unique approach to freeing the inner self.

I have created the Gates of Power® Method to assist my clients in the process of self-transformation. The method weaves together ancient and modern techniques to create an effective, comprehensive, and holistic system for self-healing and self-actualization. It encompasses all of the important aspects of human experience and is dedicated to the science, art, and craft of self-inquiry and self-empowerment. Although they seem separate, all of the Gates are woven together into a unified fabric. Exploring and expressing ourselves through these seven channels creates inner freedom, power, and growth. The Gates of Power® Method facilitates the developing and harmonizing of all seven channels.

This method is experiential, expressive, and creative in nature. The book provides theoretical information, case studies, and personal stories of people who have done this work, as well as some practical exercises. Doing the exercises will help you in achieving a basic understanding of the Gates of Power® Method, and will offer you insights for creating a personal practice leading to growth and fulfillment. Hopefully you will be inspired to continue investigating the Gates on your own or in the workshops offered by White Cedar Institute, the home of the Gates of Power® Method. Each one of the Gates leads to endless information and knowledge.

What follows is a short description of each of the Gates, which are explored in greater depth in the chapters of this book. As you read about each of these Gates, think of the ways you experience them.

THE GATE OF THE BODY

Our bodies are our gardens; our wills are our gardeners.
— **William Shakespeare**

Within this Gate, we explore the body, its expression, and its energetic patterns through different processes and exercises. We gain awareness of our relationship to our bodies. We learn to understand the body as a mirror of our consciousness. We experience the body as an instrument of creativity and expression.

We are encouraged to find a way to move freely and authentically and enjoy the body's energies and physical abilities. We investigate where and how we block our energy and constrict our aliveness. We discover where chronic tensions, trauma, or unexpressed feelings are being held. We enter these places within our body and bring to the surface feelings, memories, and beliefs. Once the feelings are expressed and guided, we can release the unnecessary ones and embrace healthy feelings, needs, and desires. We explore the connections among mind, feelings, and body.

THE GATE OF EMOTIONS

Let's not forget that the little emotions are the great captains of our lives and we can obey them without realizing it.

— Vincent Van Gogh

In order to become emotionally healthy and balanced, we need to be able to experience and explore our feelings and then express them appropriately. Some of us find it difficult to stay in touch with darker feelings, such as fear, pain, anger, or need. Others find the lighter feelings of love, joy, and peace difficult to experience or express. I believe that we cannot be whole without the ability to experience the full spectrum of our emotional self, from the darkest to the brightest of our feelings. Just as a pianist needs to know how to play all the keys of the piano, we need to know how to experience all of our feelings. Emotional integration opens and frees our energy field, removes energy blockages, and allows us to be expressive, creative, and present. The exercises within this Gate encourage emotional openness, integration, and expression.

THE GATE OF DIALOGUE

In true dialogue, both sides are willing to change.

— Thich Nhat Hanh

The exercises within The Gate of Dialogue help us explore the importance of relating consciously and constructively with ourselves, others, and all living things. Science has shown us that all life is an intricate fabric of subatomic particles, or waves, continuously communicating with each other.

Being part of and one with the fabric of life, we are naturally interconnected and interrelated. Unresolved feelings block our energy flow and create a sense of separateness and stagnation. Many of us engage in a negative dialogue with ourselves. We tend to be critical, harsh, and blaming toward ourselves. It is important to transform our internal dialogue into a compassionate, creative, and constructive one. A positive inner dialogue creates clarity and confidence, which in turn allow us to relate and communicate with others authentically and effortlessly. Healthy relating leads to effective communication. Effective and expressive communication leads to strong relationships. Strong relationships mean productive and joyful partnerships, and a sense of connectedness and fulfillment.

THE GATE OF CREATIVE EXPRESSION

*Every moment of your life is infinitely creative
and the universe is endlessly bountiful.*

— **Mahatma Gandhi**

There is much joy, power, and inspiration born of our creative expression. Whether we acknowledge it or not, we are all creative and expressive. Artists are born with a heightened sense of creativity, but we can all become more available to our creative abilities. Creativity and expression strengthen and deepen our knowledge of ourselves, and free us to share our experiences with others. Creativity and expression are present in nature, in the nature of our being, and in the whole universe. Within this Gate, we develop our creative and expressive abilities. We use movement, sound, writing, drawing, and other forms of expression to explore important life themes. Most of the time, new and surprising discoveries emerge. Clarity, a sense of completion, and a deeper understanding are achieved. We can see by now how the Gates are interconnected. We use our body to experience and express emotions. We use our emotions and our body to create, and we learn more about ourselves when we feel and express.

THE GATE OF LIFE PATH

*In the part of our happiness shall we find the
learning for which we have chosen this lifetime.*

— **Richard Bach**

Our Life Path can be defined as who we are and how we choose to live our lives. How do we share our abilities and talents with others? What do we choose as our career? What is our life purpose, our innermost passionate way of contributing to and communicating with others? This Gate emphasizes the importance of defining our life path clearly, having a sense of direction and focus. Our Life Path is born out of what we are most passionate about, what really thrills and inspires us. It is not just some logical or intellectual choice. For many of us, the sense of true purpose and vocation is lost in the need for status and money, or is buried under socio-cultural pressures, or bogged down by our parents' expectations. When our Life Path is uncovered, direction and focus create our vision. Our vision informs and motivates us to make choices and take on responsibilities followed by actions.

This Gate supports the process of finding your personal life path. It guides you in creating a clear vision and then taking steps to actualize it. The exercises assist in finding the clarity and the commitment needed to fulfill your vision and your life goals.

THE GATE OF SILENCE

Silence is a source of great strength.

— **Lao Tzu**

When we can find the ability to be silent, we can enter a world of insight, understanding, and possibilities. Inner silence is not defined by sitting and doing nothing but by being able to achieve a sense of deep inner quiet or stillness of the mind and heart. Our mind is mostly obsessive and compulsive. It is constantly obsessing over the past or projecting into the future. It reflects our worries. It is busy, speculating, calculating, and trying to figure out life. Even when we sleep, our mind is working. It is rare to find the ability to just be. The Gate of Silence emphasizes the importance of learning how to truly be truly silent. It uses different kinds of meditations and silent processes to train the mind to let go. As a result, we can allow the body and the feelings to relax.

Within silence, we can experience profound clarity and peace and hear the voice of our intuition. At times, important life questions or insights reveal themselves spontaneously. A deep sense of connectedness emerges.

THE GATE OF KNOWLEDGE

Science is organized knowledge. Wisdom is organized life.

— **Immanuel Kant**

The Gate of Knowledge holds a space of inquiry for the most important questions. Who are we? Why are we here? What is life all about? What is most important to us? What is the nature of reality? What happens after we die? What is the meaning of our life? Why do things happen the way they do? Is there a higher intelligence that guides the universe? The Gate of Knowledge does not provide answers to those questions; instead, it encourages us to liberate and expand our minds so that we can find our own answers over time. Different scientific, spiritual, and psychological texts are explored within this Gate, which provide a forum for open discussion and fertile ground for the continuous pursuit of knowledge. The chosen texts are intended to stir the mind and bring forth new insights.

The Gates, true to their name, are channels of inner power. Each one contributes a different flavor of strength to your palate, a different color for your living canvas.

4

The Four Commitments

The Gates are pathways of fulfillment. The pathways create a road map, and just as there are traffic laws, there are a few guiding principles that make your journey through the Gates a safe and a fruitful one. These guiding principles work magic when they become commitments. Taking on these commitments, you transform from a mediocre, haphazard driver into an excellent one. Believe me, on this journey, you want to be well equipped; it can be a bumpy road.

THE FIRST COMMITMENT:
Knowing Yourself

> *The aim of life is self-development. To realize one's*
> *nature perfectly – that is what each of us is here for.*
>
> — Oscar Wilde

We are all diamonds in the rough—cliché, but true. And, we are our own diamond polishers. It is said that man is the "jewel of creation." In potentiality, we are all jewels. It is our responsibility to honor and realize our potential and our spiritual nature. Respect for self, respect for others, and respect for all creation springs from and leads to the realization of unity. Just like the diamond polisher needs to know the nature of the diamond to be able to refine it, we need to know ourselves in order to polish our inner diamond—and we need much polishing, indeed.

How does one get to know oneself? Just like one gets to know anything. The secret is heartfelt observation—observation accompanied by patience, compassionate witnessing, listening without judgment, becoming aware, noticing, being present. To know ourselves, we must cultivate loving mindfulness toward ourselves. In short, we must learn to become emotionally intimate with ourselves.

No one taught me to listen to myself. When I grew up, there were always things I was expected to do and be. Who *I* was and what *I* needed were not of any great importance in my childhood home; there were other priorities. I had no idea how to listen to myself; in fact, I did everything to avoid listening. Needless to say, this did not prove to be an effective life strategy. I had to teach myself the art of listening somewhat later in life.

What about you? Do you take the time on a daily basis to sit with yourself? Do you ask yourself: *What is going on with me today? How am I feeling? What do I need or want? How was my day? What moved me or inspired me? What feels most important to me today?* And so on.

This kind of deep listening helps you touch your pains and vulnerabilities with kindness, and it also helps you to cultivate your joys. Attentive listening is profoundly healing. From childhood on, we accumulate negative attitudes, interpretations, expectations, and behavioral patterns that diminish our selfesteem, our ability to actualize ourselves, and our sense of joy. Careful listening allows us to identify these negative imprints and assists us in the process of shifting, releasing, and re-patterning. Self-knowledge lets you discover your strengths and your gifts. It leads you to find gratitude and discover your playfulness. Creating a time to be with yourself, as your own best friend, is one of the most important commitments for health. Being present to yourself allows you to be present to the moment. Being intimate with yourself opens you to experiencing intimacy with life. Being present and intimate is where the real fun is, isn't it? In knowing yourself, you can begin to know all things. A doorway to the experience of oneness becomes available. So, sit with yourself any way you choose. You can do it by writing, walking, laying down, sitting on the couch, meditating, creating, dreaming. There are many ways, and they are all good.

THE SECOND COMMITMENT:
Attending to Yourself

> *Confront the dark parts of yourself, and work to banish them with illumination and forgiveness. Your willingness to wrestle with your demons will cause your angels to sing.*
>
> — **August Wilson**

The second commitment springs out of the first one. As you begin to listen and get to know yourself, you embark on the sacred, unending, and at times daunting task of attending to yourself. Taking care of yourself means being responsible for your total well-being. The food you eat, the thoughts and feelings you feed yourself with, your physical activities, your rest time, your sleep time, the kind of work you do, the way you go about doing your work, your relationships, your communications, your playtime, your pleasures and joys, your inner growth, your education, your creativity, your goals … and the list goes on.

No wonder we get overwhelmed by all of that. But who else knows better than you what is right for you? And who else is going to take care of these needs for you? I keep telling my clients, "Whoever you're waiting for, be it the wonderful knight in shining armor or the fair princess, he or she is not coming. It's you and yourself. Make it a good dance." When we do not get the care and attention we need as kids, and many of us did not, we don't know how to go about doing this. On top of that we resist it—we refuse to let go of the hope that we will be taken care of by someone, somewhere, somehow.

One of my clients used to ask me over and over again, whenever we would talk about taking responsibility, "What is the benefit of taking care of myself? It doesn't feel like fun at all. It feels lonely and sad." Of course, now, years later, we laugh about her old resistance to taking care of herself, since she would not give it up for the world. Finally, she realized the emotional/psychological loss of being dependent on others for her well-being, and caring for herself has now become her passion. If we move through the resistance, taking care of ourselves becomes a great pleasure, a great adventure, and a great discovery. Needless to say, our skills as friends, nurturers, lovers, and parents get tremendous practice. Take care of yourself, and you will naturally and effortlessly find yourself caring for others, including plants, animals, rivers, and mountains.

THE THIRD COMMITMENT:

Creating Discipline for Self-Transformation
If we don't discipline ourselves, the world will do it for us.

— William Feather

The third commitment emerges from the first two. Knowing yourself and attending to yourself both need time, focus, and awareness—in other words, discipline. When devoid of pleasure, discipline is not nurturing, so it is important to create a marriage between discipline and play. Your discipline can be a joyful self-guiding: a deliberate creation of the "you" that you want to be and the life that you want to lead. Nothing is achieved without discipline, and nothing is enjoyed without a sense of play. Learn to mix and match these two, infusing discipline with play and play with discipline.

Most of us have unresolved experiences or feelings that weigh us down. Many of us struggle with poor self-image and a negative view of others and life. These limiting programs within our conscious and subconscious mind result in restricting energetic and physical patterns. Let's explain this further. Along the way, as a reaction to stress and difficult experiences, we collect perceptions (about ourselves and life) that we internalize. Many of these perceptions and patterns are negative and constricting. To take just two examples: the belief that we are not capable of doing something limits us and becomes a self-fulfilling prophesy, while the belief that rich people are corrupt is obviously limiting—if we embrace it, we will never allow ourselves to become wealthy.

We all have sets of confining perceptions and beliefs that translate to frozen energetic emotional structures and lead to negative programming. We may not be aware of the limiting programs that are running us (unless we study ourselves), and we may get frustrated and saddened by the fact that we cannot change things we want to change, but it is the inner program that has to change before our lives can begin to change. Misplacing our anger about our inability to change is as ineffective as being frustrated with what's coming out of a printer; directing your anger at the printer will not change what's being printed. Instead, we must go to the computer and change the document itself. The printer only gives us what's in the original document.

The third commitment is a commitment to creating a discipline, a practice, dedicated to clearing out and restructuring our inner programming. This means releasing as much as possible all that does not contribute to our well-being, true sense of self, and the kind of life we want to live, and instead cultivating new beliefs and energetic and physical habits that support fulfillment. Since we are consciousness/energy beings—consciousness translated into vibrations—when our consciousness shifts, our vibrational patterns shift, and vice versa. Restructuring physical energetic patterns helps to shift our consciousness. As a result, what we experience, express, and manifest shifts. The creation of our happiness is our responsibility, and the adventure of transforming limitation into an expansion takes discipline. It's called the "hard work miracle."

Creating a discipline includes understanding the universal laws and abiding by them. Some examples of the universal laws that we will discuss later include the laws of vibration, the laws of attraction, the laws of polarity and rhythm, and the laws of cause and effect. The Gates of Power ® offers guidelines for creating this kind of discipline.

THE FOURTH COMMITMENT:
Living a Life of Contribution

Life, like a mirror, never gives back more than we put into it.

— **Anonymous**

Each one of us is a bundle of skills, talents, and gifts. Naturally, we are destined to cultivate and enjoy these treasures and contribute to ourselves and others. Our natural tendency, if unimpaired, is to be passionate about expressing and exploring our gifts. The idea of "following our bliss," in the words of philosopher Joseph Campbell, means simply following what we naturally love to do and be, or, put differently, following our need to actualize our essence and talents. As I said earlier, painful, unresolved experiences and negative beliefs act as a heavy tombstone that covers our real sense of self. Rolling away the stone to uncover our depths and riches is a must if we intend to enjoy our life. I cannot think of anything more exciting than sharing and expressing our talents.

In the Jewish tradition, the concept of *tikun olam* translates to "repairing the world"—the understanding that we are here to partner with God (or Spirit) in healing the world. We are endowed with the ability to repair, renew, beautify, and manifest goodness, and so, to establish Heaven on Earth. *Ata baelunim vaanachnu batachtonim* means "God has dominion over the heavens, and we in turn were given the earth to take care of." So, we are God's assistants. Each one of us has a unique color and light to add to the magical tapestry of life. The fourth commitment is to find what your gifts are and how to make the most out of them.

All four commitments are connected and build on each other. We must know ourselves to be able to attend to ourselves through a loving, joyful discipline so that we can contribute to life. Living your life as a contribution inspires the greatest joy. These commitments will be present throughout the rest of the book. They will be expounded upon and further developed.

5

The Inner Aspects of the Self

*If there is any recognition of the soul,
then it must be as a goal-directed unity,
whose parts can only be understood
if one has come to understand the whole.*

— **Alexander Neuer**

We are all aware of different aspects of ourselves. Sometimes, we are soft and vulnerable; other times, harsh and defensive. At times, we are playful and silly, and other times we are solemn, severe, and humorless. One moment, we can be friendly, open, and accepting. The next moment, we can be judgmental and rejecting. We seem to be a sea of contradictions, a puzzle to ourselves and others. We find ourselves wondering what within us is creating different colors and expressions.

It is natural to experience different aspects within the self. The key is to have all the aspects work together in harmony to create strength and unity. Most of us experience deep conflicts between different aspects of ourselves and, as a result, we experience a feeling of sadness and anxiety. Doing the following exercises will help you observe your inner landscapes and the different forces operating within you. The chapter will also explain the Gates of Power® process of harmonizing the self.

When I started to observe my own inner landscape, I remember being struck by the extreme difference between my "sensitive-vulnerable" aspect and my "fierce passionate" one. It almost felt like there were two different people living within me. When I was in my sensitive, vulnerable aspect, I could cry at the drop of a hat; while in my fierce aspect, I would experience a tremendous, relentless sense of determination. One aspect felt soft, the other somewhat hard, even harsh at times. I had to spend time learning to understand these seeming opposites. I had to realize the connection between them and find a way to unify them. You can think of aspects in terms of different energies, colors, attitudes, or ways of being inside yourself.

> ••• **Reflection Pause** •••
>
> What different aspects do you observe within yourself? Can you define three or four different ones? See if you can give the aspects names, for example, my "soft and loving self," or my "tough guy self." How would you describe each one of the aspects?

How are these aspects relating to each other? For example, how is the "tough guy self" relating to the "loving self," and vice versa? How are they getting along? Is there a conflict? Which one is dominating your life?

Are you content with the way these aspects express themselves or not? For example, is there too little of the "soft and loving" and too much of the "tough guy?" Or, is there too much of the "soft and loving" and too little of the "tough guy?" Is there too little of the "expressive self" and too much of the "must-look-right self"? What do you feel might be a better balance between your inner aspects?

In my own inner process and my work with clients, I have observed three clearly defined aspects of the self. The Gates of Power® Method emphasizes working with these three aspects. These aspects have been defined and recognized by different spiritual and psychological traditions, so they are probably familiar to you. However, the Gates of Power® Method establishes a unique way to strengthen and harmonize the relationship and the dialogue between these three aspects or states of being. The names I am using for the three aspects are:

- The Emotional Self
- The Defensive Self
- The Expanded Self

After the description of each aspect you will be asked to take a minute and actually experience the aspect emotionally, physically, and mentally. Try to have an experience of each aspect rather than just a mental concept. Each one of the chapters covering the Gates will further expound on the three aspects and the ways to unify and balance them.

The Emotional Self

The Emotional Self is the aspect that contains all our emotions. What are emotions? Emotions are made up of feelings that have enough intensity to organize themselves into a physical and behavioral pattern. Within the Emotional Self, we find two shades, light and dark, and, of course, some gray in between. We experience joy, playfulness, innocence, and love, as well as suffering, pain, fear, anger, shame, guilt, and a host of other feelings. Our Emotional Self is extremely powerful and deeply affects our energies, our bodies, and our lives, even when it is repressed and shut down. It is our gateway to ecstasy as well as the gateway to hellish suffering. As children, we operate mostly from this feeling self, experiencing the world through feelings and sensations. Later, we learn to hide, repress, or distrust our feelings. Or, we get stuck in the darker feelings, unable to resolve them and move on. Feelings are the nectar of life, and it is extremely important to clear negative feelings and move through and beyond them.

Experiencing the Emotional Self: I would like you to take a minute and truly experience your Emotional Self. Choose a place in the room where you can sit, close your eyes and take a few minutes to move into the world of your emotions. See if you can witness your feelings without judgment. Feel the different colors and energies of your emotions. Gently keep asking yourself, "How do I feel?" "What is present for me today?" Irritation, sadness, joy, frustration, loneliness, peace, anger, need, or affection? Which are the dominant feelings within you now? Where are you feeling them in your body, your energy field? How is your posture affected? How is your breathing affected? How do you experience the world from here? If you want, write a few sentences about your experience.

The Defensive Self

The "Defensive Self" is the aspect of the self that is concerned with emotional and physical survival. It originates out of the need to secure love and connection and out of fear of physical or emotional alienation. The defensive self is an energetic, physical, psychological "strong suit" we create in order to feel secure and accepted.

It is the expression of our survival structure—a survival mode of operation. Other names for the Defensive Self are the Ego (spiritual term), "character defense," and "false self" (psychological terms). As I said in the first chapters, there are different ways to protect ourselves. These are imprinted in our bodies and our psyches. The following are some examples of defensive behaviors. Some of us become charmers, jokesters, the life of the party, doing everything possible to attract admiration and attention. Some of us escape into isolation and hiding. Some of us push ourselves beyond a healthy balance to excel at all cost. Some of us make sure to be good, perfect, and to please everyone around us. Most of us have one central way of being defended, backed up by a few secondary nuances. For example, we might be the good, perfect pleaser, and use isolation and addiction to further protect ourselves. Or, we might be an overachiever, with nuances of a charmer and pleaser thrown into the mix.

Our Defensive Self makes sure that we stay in control and maintain a sense of safety at all cost. Here again, our Defensive Self as two faces—the face we present to the world and the critical resistance we direct toward ourselves. We focus on anything within ourselves that might threaten the success of our social image and sense of control. This critical resistance is mostly directed at our Emotional Self, whose vulnerability or suffering we feel we must hide from the world. Inherently, there is a conflict between our Emotional Self and our Defensive Self. One wants to feel and experience; the other wants to stay in control—two opposing intentions. Most of us, before we engage in transformation work, live by the law of our Defensive Self at the expense of our Emotional Self. This inner split causes us suffering since we are not feeling free to express our feelings, let alone feel them. When we don't feel, we cannot heal: cliché, but true.

Experiencing the Defensive Self: Choose a place in the room across from where you sat to experience your Emotional Self. Sit down and close your eyes, move into the world of your Defensive Self. Ask yourself, *How do I operate in the world from my Defensive Self?* We tend to be more contracted and hardened when we are in our Defensive Self, so notice how your defensiveness registers in your body, in your energy, and in your breath. Notice how you experience the world from this aspect of yourself. As you think of your Emotional Self, sitting across the room, ask yourself, *How am I feeling toward my Emotional Self?* Are you critical or annoyed by your Emotional Self? Or are you accepting of it? Write a few sentences about your experience if you wish.

> **• • • Reflection Pause • • •**
>
> Did you notice any conflict, tension, lack of acceptance, or judgment between these two aspects of yourself (the Emotional Self and the Defensive Self)? Most people experience conflict or tension between these two aspects.

The Expanded Self

I call the third aspect of the self the Expanded Self. It has different names in different traditions: the Higher Self, the Sud Guru, the Divine Spark, the Inner Christ, Neshalma Elohit, the observer, and so forth. This aspect of you is the one capable of awareness and witnessing—compassionate observation. It possesses intuitive heartfelt knowledge and wisdom. It is capable of great courage and understanding. It knows what is genuinely "right" or "wrong" for you. It is the still voice that guides you, the healer within you, the visionary, and the creative force behind your growth and your true expression. It is your individual expression of the consciousness that is behind everything.

This aspect of yourself is your true nature, beyond feelings that come and go, beyond your defensive construct, beyond your personality and your concepts of yourself. It holds your essence, your spirit, your soul. It aides you in the continual journey of creating and choosing what is most important to you.

Within this aspect, there are two faces: the witness and the healing guide. One face is only observing—it is pure awareness; the other is actively guiding our journey toward wholeness. Most of us don't experience life from our Expanded Self. We are aware of it, and are always guided by it, but we are not fully living from it. To become settled in the Expanded Self and have our life be an expression of it takes work. It is the work of healing and supporting our Emotional Self and dissolving or softening our Defensive Self.

Experiencing the Expanded Self: Choose a place in the room that forms the third corner of the triangle with where you sat to experience your Emotional Self and Defensive Self. Sit down, close your eyes, and move into the world of your Expanded Self. Find an inner place of peace and acceptance, then ask yourself, *How do I operate in the world from my Expanded Self?* We tend to feel more relaxed, peaceful, and compassionate when we are in our Expanded Self. So, notice how your expansion registers in your body, in your energy, and in your breath. Notice how you experience the world from this aspect of yourself. As you think of your Defensive Self and Emotional Self, sitting across the room, ask yourself how you are feeling toward them?

> ••• Reflection Pause •••
>
> Do you understand the roles they play in your life? Write a few sentences about your experience if you wish.

So, as you may have noticed, there is an ongoing dialogue among the different aspects within you. Most of us, before doing inner work, are stuck or bound by the conflict between the Emotional Self and the Defensive Self. Mostly, we don't

In a State of Misalignment

The three aspects of the self in a state of misalignment

know how to bring in the wisdom and compassion of our Expanded Self to help us heal and harmonize our inner space.

The greatest gift that we have is the gift of loving wisdom, the ability to know the truth and act from a place of kindness toward ourselves and all life. As conscious beings, we have the ability to be aware, to witness, and to have compassion and understanding. Awareness and compassion creates wisdom. Our consciousness is one with the Source of all consciousness. We are guided, inspired, informed, protected, and healed by this Universal Consciousness. We are in direct connection with it, since it is our very own consciousness.

The aspect of ourselves that I named The Expanded Self is the part of us that is in direct connection with Universal Consciousness. It is our source of true strength, wisdom, creativity, and insight. It is our well of loving-kindness, a fountain of all that is innovative, imaginative, and inspiring. In short, we have within us a powerful source. This power source is waiting for us to reach for bliss and fulfillment. It is there to lead us to a life of pleasure, adventure, success, and knowledge. We need to tap into it and let it heal and guide us into wholeness—our original and true state. The Gates of Power® Method offers exercises and processes

In a State of Wholeness

The three aspects of the self in a state of wholeness

that help us connect to our Expanded Self and create a healing inner dialogue among all three aspects.

The good news is that every one of us, with no exception, is born with an Expanded Self. No matter how estranged we have become from it, it is always within us.

Human experience is fraught with different experiences. Our Emotional Self gathers hurt, trauma, loss, sadness, fear, and other stressful emotions. We tend to interpret some of our hurtful experiences and losses as personal deficiencies. We create a negative sense of self and a negative outlook on life and people. We hide our pain and lack of self-esteem under our Defensive Self, and live a contracted, limited, and at times destructive life. But there is no need to keep ourselves in bondage. Each one of us has unique and meaningful gifts, talents, and capabilities that are meant to be expressed and enjoyed. We are meant to be a contribution to each other. The secret is acknowledging your Expanded Self and learning to live within its expression and guidelines.

The processes offered for balancing and healing the relationships among the aspects are intended to establish the Expanded Self as the leader and guide of the inner space. By creating a conscious connection and a feeling dialogue between the Expanded Self and the Emotional Self, we can heal our inner suffering and support our emotional ability for joy, love, and play. On the other hand, no less important is the connection between the Expanded Self and the Defensive Self. The dialogue between these two begins to slowly dissolve and soften the Defensive Self. The true power of the Expanded Self replaces the false sense of security provided by the Defensive Self.

Once we establish the Expanded Self as the witness, guide, and protector of the inner space, a process of healing and balance begins to occur. We open up to pleasure, fun, and fulfillment, and free ourselves to be spontaneous and powerful. The world transforms into a playground of possibilities, and we feel inspired to go for the highest vision. I don't mean to make it sound like an easy transition; it is not. But once we tap into our Expanded Self and start the dialogue, it becomes easier and easier.

I suggest that you take the time to notice when you are operating from your Emotional Self, when you are reacting and acting from your Defensive Self, and when you experience life from your Expanded Self. Become aware of the relationship among these three aspects and teach yourself to be guided by your

Expanded Self, since that part possesses your wisdom, insight, and compassion. The following is an example of a healing dialogue.

A client, whom I will call Debbie, discovered when we were doing her inner dialogues that her Defensive Self adopted the attitude that she must be perfect at all times. She must always know the rules and play by them, and never show any signs of vulnerability, confusion, or lack of knowledge. She had a very strict and punitive father who did not tolerate any personal expression that did not fit with his code of behavior, so she learned to be a pleaser and a "perfect good little girl," in order to survive in her household.

The dialogue between her Defensive Self and Emotional Self was a one-way conversation. Her Defensive Self was constantly ordering, criticizing, and repressing her Emotional Self, demanding compliance to all rules. Her Defensive Self took on the voice of her father. First, she needed to become aware of her negative inner dialogue. She then needed to find the loving positive voice of her Expanded Self. That was difficult since she was so used to criticizing herself.

It took us some time to be able to quiet the Defensive Self enough to begin to discover the feelings underneath the repression. When we were able to bring the feelings forth, she discovered within her Emotional Self a profound sadness and a deep sense of loneliness. Later, when she found her connection to her Expanded Self, she learned to bring that aspect into the picture. She learned to align herself with her Expanded Self, allowing healing and supportive dialogues to emerge between her Expanded Self and her Emotional Self. She began to be able to provide compassion, guidance, and an expressive space for her feelings. Gradually, her joy and playfulness, as well as her sadness and needs, found expression and balance. A sense of freedom replaced the old repression and disconnection. In our sessions, when she was able to be silly and not perfect, I knew that she was beginning to trust her expression and her experience rather than just being obedient.

It is most important that we take responsibility for our "inner space" by learning to create healthy inner dialogues and inner balance among the three aspects. Learning to nurture myself and create a healthy inner balance saved my own life from despair and hopelessness. When we take care of our "inner space," we begin to take care of all of the other elements of our life. Eventually, we feel moved to nurture all life around us. One of the Gates within the Gates of Power® Method is the Gate of Dialogue. More information and other exercises will be presented in the chapter that covers that Gate.

As we step through the Gates of Power®, we enter the field of healing and realigning possibilities. At this moment, I suggest that you choose 1–3 of the most important themes in your life. These themes are areas of difficulty to work through and transform. Here are a few examples of themes people struggle with: low self-esteem, or a feeling of inadequacy; feelings of hopelessness; fear of intimacy; lack of focus and consistency at work; obsessive-compulsive patterns; inner rage turned against the self or others; a feeling of being unsafe in the world; addiction; inability to express or create; and so on.

After you choose your themes, see if you can find a connection among them, and possibly explore which one of the themes is the "root theme." For example, low self-esteem might be connected to fear of intimacy, lack of focus and commitment, and addictions. In fact, in this example, the theme of low self-esteem is the "root" out of which the other themes grow. From now on, while reading the book, keep your personal themes in mind, especially the root theme. If you're not sure yet which one is the root theme, don't worry: it will become clear to you as you go along. Work with your personal themes creatively and consistently while reading this book to allow new possibilities and shifts of consciousness. By doing so, you are taking steps toward realizing your real power. Each one of the Gates will shed new light on the theme you have chosen, and will provide a different layer of understanding and experience.

Our spiritual, emotional, and energetic evolution is our most important task on Earth. Insight, wed with passion for growth and discipline, bears the fruit of self-transformation. Be willing to work using all Four Principles/Commitments; taking on only one or two will not accomplish the job. I will be referring to these again and again as I introduce new layers with each Gate. Each one of the Gates of Power ® presents a different perspective through which we get to know our limiting patterns, our lessons, and, most importantly, our potential power.

The Four Commitments

1. **Knowing Yourself.** By this I mean a nonjudgmental understanding of yourself and a compassionate witnessing of self and others. We use our awareness to observe and comprehend our truths as well as our difficulties. I think this step is the most important one, since knowledge is power, as the saying goes.

2. **Attending to Yourself.** Cultivate a passion, and a commitment to create a shift that would dissolve or realign your difficulties. Consistently create and maintain wholeness.

3. **Creating a Discipline for Self-Transformation.** Engaging in a loving and responsible practice of self-knowledge and self-empowerment. The Expanded Self within each one of us is by nature compassionate and wise. It provides unending possibilities and creative outlets.

4. **Living a Life of Contribution.** Use your talents, your gifts and abilities to enrich your life and the lives of others.

6

The Gate of the Body

*Create your body to be an instrument expressing
the highest and the best in you.*

We know how critical the Gate of the Body is; this is why it is the first and the most basic of the seven Gates. Our existence as humans depends on having a body, and the body is a great teacher. If we listen to it carefully, it will reveal secrets, whisper instructions to help us transform, and show us what we need to let go of. The body offers a world of experience and creativity. It is an instrument for the soul's music. The beauty of our being radiates through our body and its expression, and with the same accuracy, our body reveals suffering, contraction, and numbness. Finally, the body offers us perhaps the greatest lesson: our mortality. Each one of us will eventually shed our body. It is important to cherish the body while we have it, and be ready to let it go when the time comes.

As an actor and a dancer, I am fascinated by the expressive power of the body. I find it amazing to watch a great actor using his or her body to express a character and that character's journey, or a strong dancer or athlete whose power, agility, and grace leave me breathless.

In my teens, before enrolling in the Academy for the Performing Arts, I was the most unathletic person I knew. A stranger to my body, I hated gym classes. I did my best to avoid them, as well as any movement activity outside of the most necessary ones. Needless to say, I felt awkward and, at times, tortured by the array of out-of-the-box movement classes taught at the academy. For the next three years, as I learned to move expressively, I went through an excruciating journey of unearthing deeply buried feelings. I discovered that my feelings are woven into every cell of my body, and my way of avoiding them had been to move as little as possible. Since I couldn't maintain my old formula of no movement and at the same time train to be an actor, the old structure had to go. And so, it did. It started shifting and collapsing, revealing some pretty painful inner layers.

These years in the academy (and later, acting) started my transformation. I became extremely passionate about movement and the healing expression that is possible through the body. The Gate of the Body is dedicated to understanding our body as an emotional, spiritual map—an exquisite guide to our personal history and life lessons. Within the Gate of the Body, we explore ways of regaining aliveness, spontaneous flow, and truer expression.

The Way We Shape Our Experience

The whole universe pulsates: expansion and contraction are the rhythm of life, and pulsation is the way the life force sings. Ideally, in order for pulsation to travel through the body in free waves from head to foot, the energetic, physical pathways must be clear. Continuous, repetitive patterns of emotional-energetic distress cause distortions in the inner pathways of our life force. Distress can be caused by external stresses like the cultural and emotional environment around us, or by inner stress. Once the energetic pathways are distorted, they give rise to certain experiences and feelings, adding to the distress. Children who live in a state of terror because of an obsessive parent or violence in the home will contract to protect themselves; the contraction creates compromised energetic-physical patterns. These patterns reinforce the underlying feeling and lead to an experience of weakness and lack of expression in the body. Or, the cycle can start with an internal stress, like an unexpressed feeling of rage, sadness, or fear that quickly grows into a pattern that creates more stress.

Chinese medicine recognizes the connection between consciousness and *qi* (pronounced "chee"), which is the energy field. The qi travels in the body through electromagnetic routes called meridians and vessels. The ancient system of bodily humors, emphasized by the ancient Greek Hippocrates as well as the medieval physician Galen, recognized the same connection. Last but not least, the principle of soul-energy unity was greatly emphasized by the Western psychologist Wilhelm Reich, who established that you cannot effect lasting psychological change without also changing the body—specifically, its chronic tensions, or what he refers to as "character defense." All these points of view recognize the absolute connection and unity between consciousness and energy, or mind and body.

We are essentially self-made creations. We have been shaped by our experiences; they are embedded in our bodies and psyches, and we are continuously shaping and reshaping ourselves. The way we organize our experiences creates our being. Psychology meets biology in our body. Our emotional-spiritual evolution is ongoing, unstoppable—we are meant to evolve, and we are provided with intuitive guidance, events, people, and experiences to assist our growth. Any life experience is there as a potential lesson of empowerment. We can be strengthened by our experiences if we choose to embrace them and go through them with awareness. We are here to discover, liberate, and create ourselves.

> **• • • Reflection Pause • • •**
>
> Bring to your mind the most difficult of your themes, and ask yourself where in your body it expresses itself. Usually, an emotional stress manifests in the body as tension, contraction, numbness, or discomfort. What parts of your body feel tight, tense, or uncomfortable on a daily basis? If you are aware of any physical, energetic discomfort connected to the theme you chose, you might want to note it down. These insights are an important part of the first principle: awareness.

One of my clients, whom I will call Joan, grew up in an overly strict religious household. As a young child, she experienced nightmares. She was told continuously that being afraid of anything meant she didn't trust God, and if she didn't change her ways, she would be condemned. Little Joan could not figure out how to stop her fear and become trusting of God, so she concluded that she must be a "bad seed." She lived in continual terror of herself and others. Her chest and her solar plexus had a frozen look, and the muscles were severely contracted, restricting anger and fear. These feelings expressed themselves through harsh defensive criticism of herself and others. She admitted to me that she was cruelly critical of others in her mind, and that the very presence of her criticalness caused her to feel panic since it must be further proof of her "badness."

As we studied her defensive structure, she learned to differentiate between her feelings of anger and fear and her criticism, which was a defensive way of keeping people away and making them "bad," too. At that point, we were able to explore her feelings of fear and anger. She learned to accept and understand them. Joan began to embrace her personal history as a part of her journey. We worked to soften the chest muscles through movement, breath, and sound, and at the same time encouraged the feelings to surface. As she got more comfortable with her feelings, her chest softened and her breath deepened. She realized that one of her most important lessons was to know her own heart from within rather than blindly accept her parents' views and opinions. Her childhood, as difficult as it was, served as a lesson that helped her discover her truth. It is a pleasure to watch her now be expressive, funny, and comfortable with who she is. This is an example of how experiences can provide insight, knowledge, and power.

The energetic expression of emotions in the body follows the states of water. When we brace ourselves for shock or a blow, or when we harden to restrict pain, our state solidifies like ice. We can melt with love, dissolve into tears, erupt like a geyser, dry out, cascade like a waterfall, stream, or storm. Our consciousness creates energetic shapes that crystallize and liquefy. I love Stanley Keleman's wonderful book, *Emotional Anatomy*.[1] In this book, he speaks about the startle reflex, which is an instinctual response designed to deal with danger and threat. This mechanism is intended for emergencies or short periods of alarm. We stop, pause, brace, tighten, hold our breath, and respond. If a threat is severe or persistent, like living in an unsafe emotional or physical environment, the startle pattern deepens and gets frozen, keeping us in a state of perpetual tightness. Our development from child to adult involves external and internal stresses. Continuous stress interferes with the natural waves of pulsation by freezing, agitating, or slowing them down. As a result, our flexibility and responsiveness are lost. All tissues, muscles, and organs are affected, as are our thoughts and feelings.

> ••• **Reflection Pause** •••
>
> Meditate on and write some notes about the events and experiences that might have created the theme you are working with. For example, if your "root" theme is a feeling of inadequacy, travel back in your mind to your early years and ask yourself: "What were the experiences that affected my sense of self, and possibly created the feeling of being inadequate?" Take a moment to write down the things that come to your mind spontaneously and intuitively. If you have done some personal inner work, you will find this assignment familiar. If you haven't, this is a good moment to start.

Every time you pause and allow yourself to experience and explore your memories and your feelings, you connect to needs and longings that live within you. A heartfelt commitment to nurture yourself springs out of that connection. I would like to mention again what I call the four magic E's: Experience, Explore, Express, and Empower. Here is how the magic works. When we let ourselves *experience* what lives within us, and we're brave enough to *explore* it, we can find what our needs are and how to *express* them, and expressing ourselves creatively and authentically is *empowering*. I will say more about this in the Gate of Emotions chapter.

Healthy emotional patterns follow the expansion/contraction cycles. When the flow of emotional expression remains flexible, we go from anger to sadness, from swelling to contraction, yet always return to balance. Unresolved and continual stress distorts somatic shape; the full range of emotional expression is lost. We get fixated in a chronic and limited emotional-energetic structure. The fixed pattern becomes our experience of ourselves and the narrow window through which we see the world. Physical structure influences emotional expression, and emotional expression affects physical structure. To regain our fluidity and our full range of experience, new patterns and new pathways have to be created. Old structures need to shift. The process of letting go of a rigid defensive structure is a slow one. It has been our safety belt and we are very reluctant to let it go. Our resistance is strong, and so our motivation must be equally strong. We must face difficult feelings and envision new possibilities. The "Expanded Self"—the aspect of spiritual and emotional growth within our psyche—is there forever, providing intuitive guidance. It challenges, nudges, and draws us to the "right" people, events, and experiences in order to take us forward.

Here is another example of a defensive structure and its effect.

Another client of mine, Lisa, grew up with an extremely charming and narcissistic mother and a withdrawn father. Being her mother's daughter, Lisa had become very successful professionally as a communications scholar and a multimedia producer; she was charming but overextended, always juggling six to seven projects at the same time. Lisa was very invested in her social image and in her need to be engaging and seductive at all times. She came to me because her marriage was in trouble: intimate sexual and emotional communication was lacking. Her body structure showed a very prominent chest and shoulder area, a narrow pelvis, and very thin legs. Her shoulders were pulled up and back. I noticed that her energy was overcharged on top and depleted in terms of sexual power and grounding—the bottom part. When I asked her about her emotional connection with herself, she admitted that she never makes time to sit with herself. Further exploration revealed to us that under the grandiose, overextended defensive structure, there was a sad, lonely little girl, lost and despondent. Her defensive structure, which expressed itself in the chest and shoulders, was covering her vulnerability, expressed in the pelvis and legs.

Lisa's personal work was to let go of her tendency to constantly impress others in order to receive outside reinforcement. She needed to spend some time nurturing and supporting her lonely inner girl. It was necessary to allow the feelings of loneliness to emerge. Physically, we worked on encouraging a sense of relaxation in the shoulders and the upper chest through movement, breath, and sounds. The experience of soft shoulders and chest felt extremely foreign and scary to Lisa, but she admitted "This is how I feel inside: scared and soft." Since her shoulders were rigidly held back and up, the sensation of letting go was a crucial part of the process. By introducing the physical softening of the chest, we facilitated the feelings of sadness and despair and allowed them to emerge and release. Once these were expressed and acknowledged, Lisa was able to accept the feelings and not feel threatened by them. She was able to begin nurturing that part of herself.

By studying her body and her energetic patterns, Lisa realized her defensive structure and the ways it maintained her loneliness and disconnection from herself and her husband. The realization inspired her to embrace the responsibility for her inner well-being and her spiritual growth.

Our defensive structures are not good or bad. They are there for a reason. They have helped us survive as children and young adults. As we mature and gain awareness, we can find new and better ways to experience a sense of safety and strength. It isn't necessary to pay the heavy price of being stuck in a chronic and limiting defensive structure to feel protected. Our experiences are there to inspire and strengthen us, should we choose to learn from them.

••• Reflection Pause •••

Ask yourself what you know about your defensive patterns and their expression in your body. This is a complex question; you might not know the answer right now. Take some intuitive guesses. The next exercises will help you get clearer.

Learning from the Body

The following pages will present three different "body scans," which will help you tune in to the different forms of expression in your body. Each scan offers a way to understand the psyche through the body, and all three scans are connected. The first—the Preliminary Body Scan—is based on physical observation. The second—the Meditative Body Scan—leads to emotional understanding. And the third—the Energy System Scan—reveals spiritual lessons. Keep your main theme in mind as you move through each scan. You can actually do all these scans, or you can do one or two. Even just reading about them will be educational and inspiring. The process of recovering our wholeness happens in stages. Each of the coming Gates will add a new layer of understanding and practice. This chapter unravels the first one.

The first exercise, the Preliminary Body Scan, is a basic study of your body. We're using physical, energetic sensations to learn about the connection between our psyches and our bodies. Hopefully by now, you are asking yourself, *How is my body reflecting my emotional map? What might be constricting my energy, and how can I find out about it?* This exercise, along with the ones that follow, will provide an opportunity to find some answers.

FIRST SCAN: The Preliminary Body Scan - Part I

Have you ever passed by a mirror, caught a glimpse of yourself, and for a minute seen yourself with the clarity of a stranger looking at you? We are used to looking at ourselves with blinders on, mechanically and through a veil of judgments and preconceived notions. That is why it is a bit shocking and refreshing to see ourselves even for a moment with fresh eyes.

The exercise is an invitation to discover and experience your body as if you notice it for the first time. I suggest that you stand in front of a long mirror with minimal clothes (make sure you are alone so nobody suspects you went insane!). You might feel immediately a need to fix your posture, maybe drop your shoulders or pull your belly in, lift your chin, and so on. You will also probably be flooded by an army of judgments, negative feelings, and beliefs about your body. A whole lot of "I wish this or that were different" will come up. If you can keep looking and slowly and intentionally drop the judgments and wishes, you might relax into your most natural stance and just see what you see (not an easy task!).

Don't be surprised if you need to do this a few times before you can look at yourself halfway objectively or with "fresh eyes." While struggling, you can gain insight into your present relationship with your body. Most of us are at war with our body, always wishing we had a different one or at least some of the parts changed. To know ourselves we need to let go of judging who we are. Our bodies, when we learn to understand and listen to them, tell us a tremendous amount about ourselves.

The art of reading the body and the face has been studied for centuries. There are many excellent books that cover it; one of my favorites is *The Betrayal of the Body* by Alexander Lowen.[2] Chinese medicine has always studied the body, its energy, and its expression in depth. Of course, the inner system of energy, the chakras, offer us deep insights.

FIRST SCAN: The Preliminary Body Scan - Part II

Before we proceed with Part II of the basic body scan, I must comment about categories of people who need to pay extra attention while doing this scan, because the appearance of their bodies might not visually reveal obvious insights about their energetic emotional map. I am referring to people whose bodies are affected by extreme conditions, such as extreme athleticism (athletes, acrobats, dancers) or people whose bodies are affected by physical disabilities, chronic illness, or old age. These individuals would need to work a little harder in order to penetrate the very dominant shape of the body and glean insights beyond it. Remember that your body houses your state of mind, and reflects it back to you in subtle ways.

As you are doing this scan, look at your body with the eyes of your intuition. It's not just about shapes and forms. It is about seeing through the external form. There are young people and old people. People have different body shapes and sizes. The trick is to listen to stresses, energies, and feelings within the body, and to begin to intuit how they manifest themselves in the body's appearance. This exercise is not about how aesthetically pleasing the body is (or isn't) but rather, its energetic quality. If you think about good actors and the way they work on creating a character, one of the most important things they work with is the energetic quality and form of the character's body. They understand that the inner life of a character is shaped in the body, and when they find that connection and express it, they truly bring the character to life. In a way, by doing this exercise you're discovering some deep truth about your "character" and how it reflects in your body.

You already know a lot about your body: its strengths and stress points. Use that knowledge when doing the exercise. Each step of the body scan provides a list of insights and suggestions. We are uncovering the first layer. Things that may seem confusing now will gradually become clearer. Using your notebook to organize your insights for this chapter would be tremendously useful.

Now, let's go back to you and the mirror. I hope you are successful in relaxing the chatter about your body and that you are now beginning to "see" it more clearly. To help you do this body scan, use all of your senses:

- Visual – What do you see? (For example: "I see that one of my shoulders is higher than the other.")
- Physical – What do you sense? (For example: "I sense tightness in that shoulder.")
- Energetic sensations – How is your energy? Is it flowing or does it feel stuck? (For example: "I feel like the energy is not moving much in that shoulder.")
- Feelings – What feelings can you identify in any one of the parts of your body? (For example: "I think I identify anxiousness in that shoulder.")

The First Stop

Look at your feet. We start from the bottom up. The feet are our grounding points, our metaphorical roots into the earth. How are you standing on your feet, physically and symbolically? Are your arches collapsed? Are your feet coiled meaning not the whole foot is spread comfortably? Are you tending to lean forward or backward? Are your toes crammed together? Use all your senses to feel into the quality of your grounding. Your ankles, shins, and calves are a part of your grounding. Feel into your knees. Are they locked? Overextended? Backwards? Tense? Weak? Hurt? How is the flow of energy in your legs? Taking into consideration all the levels (physical, energetic, emotional) mentioned before, what can you observe about the way you are grounded or not grounded?

Insights and Suggestions for First Stop

First Stop: Feet and legs, grounding. (Connected to the Root Chakra)

Principle 1: Awareness and Understanding.
Themes connected to weak grounding:
1. Shaky sense of safety in the world.
2. Anxiety about the sense of belonging.
3. Difficulty in standing your ground or standing up for your rights.
4. A lack of assurance about your path, which means your direction, goals, or focus in life.
5. A pattern of self-doubt and second-guessing.

Self - Analysis: If you identify with one of these themes, ask yourself, "What are the emotional and psychological sources for my difficulty?" This can be at times a hard question to answer. These are big questions that can take years to unravel. As a starting point, write down what immediately and intuitively comes to your mind.

_____

_____

Principle 2: Commitment to transformation.
Ask yourself, "What is the level of my commitment to growth? What am I willing to do, feel, or be in order to shift the patterns within this area? Am I attached to the safety of the known? Do I resist change? (Limiting patterns are familiar and provide a sense of safety. They prevent us from taking risks or responsibility.) How can I generate a deeper commitment to my transformation?"

Principle 3: Suggestions for loving, disciplined, daily practice.
NOTE: A sense of inner safety and self-assuredness is cultivated by recognizing and honoring our true self, and by expressing ourselves authentically and creatively. Claiming our personal power can be scary. We have to be willing to grapple with resistance and fear. Keep your heart and sight on the potential feeling of freedom and strength that follows self-respect. The following suggestions will help you begin the process of creating a new experience:

1. Make a list of your talents, gifts, abilities, and strong points, then share the list with a good friend—acknowledging your gifts helps you express them. Take a moment daily to feel gratitude for them. Use each day as an opportunity to cultivate, enjoy, and share your gifts.

2. Make a list of situations and relationships in which you want to speak your heart and mind clearly and directly. Cultivate the ability to do so on a daily basis.

3. Physically ground yourself by mastering standing and balancing asanas (postures) in yoga, jogging, fast walking, tai chi, martial arts, African dance, and so on.

The Second Stop

The second stop is your pelvis. Your pelvis is the center of your physical, sexual, and creative power. There is a relationship between your legs—your grounding—and the expression of power. It makes sense that if you are not well grounded, it affects your pelvic region. And vice versa: if your pelvis is rigid, pulled back, or tucked under, it will affect your grounding. Check with yourself: Does your pelvis feel free or immobilized? Maybe it feels freer on one side and more frozen on the other. Many of us shy away from our creative and sexual power. As a result, we tense the pelvis. What do you notice about the way you inhabit your pelvis?

Insights and Suggestions for Second Stop

Second Stop: Pelvic area, sexuality and creativity. (Connected to the Abdominal Chakra)

Principle 1: Awareness and Understanding.
Themes connected to tightness and weakness in the pelvic area:

1. Feelings of guilt and/or shame connected to sexuality.
2. Sexual performance anxiety.
3. Fear of sexual intimacy.
4. Inhibitions, self-doubt, and insecurities relating to the expression of personal and creative power.

Self - Analysis: If you identify with one of these themes, ask yourself, "What are the emotional and psychological sources for my difficulty?" Remember, these are big questions. To start with, write down what immediately and intuitively comes to your mind.

_____

_____

Principle 2: Commitment to transformation.
Examine your willingness to shift, change, and grow in this area and, at the same time, your fear, resistance, and attachment to safety.

Principle 3: Suggestions for loving, disciplined, daily practice.
NOTE: Being sensual and creative can be scary. Keep your heart and sight on the pleasure, sense of freedom, and joy that come with it. Notice your resistance and fear, and keep working through them. The following suggestions will help you begin the process of liberating your sexual and creative power.

1. Without intellectualizing or censoring yourself, write down your opinions, beliefs, gut reactions, and feelings about: a) sexuality, in general, (b) your sexual feelings and their expression, and (c) your creative self-expression. Next, look at the lists and identify fears, negative beliefs, and difficult feelings that are interfering with the experience and expression of your sexuality and/or creativity. Acknowledging what is in the way is the beginning of a change.

2. To embrace your sexuality and creativity, make two lists: a) sensual and sexual pleasures that give you joy, and (b) creative outlets that contribute to your sense of well-being. Practice doing some things that are on your lists daily, even if it is tiny steps taken in the right direction.

3. By committing to your sexual and creative nature, you learn to experience and enjoy the sensual, creative nature of life. It is all around you. Physically move your pelvis—put on music and experiment. If you have a sense of play, pretend that you are Elvis. It is a silly and fun exercise that will keep you laughing while freeing your pelvis. Go dancing and if you can, take a beginner jazz, belly dance, or African dance class. You can stay a beginner forever—it doesn't matter. If you belong to a gym, check classes that activate the pelvis: Pilates, for example, works with the core and will help you discover strength and mobility in your pelvis. Most yoga asanas engage your core—the plank position and the boat are especially good. Any movement that is done correctly originates in the core; that is why it is considered the center of power.

The Third Stop

The third stop is your spine—your backbone, literally and symbolically. How flexible is it? Or how rigid? The spine symbolizes our support system, both inner (that is, emotional and spiritual) and outer (structurally). What can you observe about yourself from the way you hold your spine? What part of it feels tense, frozen, or rigid? Is it the lower back, the neck, the middle back? Are you slouched? Are you swayed to one side? Here, again, the way you hold your spine is directly connected to the way you hold your pelvis, and vice versa. If your pelvis is tucked under or swayed back, it affects your lower back. Think back to the beginning of the exercise: in a way, you are looking at your spiritual, emotional, energetic map—not just a physical body.

Insights and Suggestions for Third Stop

Third Stop: Spine, support. (Different Chakras according to the section of the spine.)

Principle 1: Awareness and Understanding.

Themes connected to tightness and weakness in the spine: The spine represents support, both inner and outer. Different parts of the spine represent different areas of support. (For example, the lower spine is connected to survival and a sense of belonging, mid-spine is connected to a sense of self and trust in oneself, and the upper spine is connected to emotional openness and expression.) Themes connected to lack of support are:

1. Feelings of loneliness, or a sense of having no support system.
2. Lack of attentiveness and support toward oneself.
3. Difficulty in reaching out to receive and give support from and to others.
4. Lack of trust in life's sustaining nature—for example, the power of the body to heal itself, or the natural process of emotional and spiritual maturation.

Self - Analysis: If you identify with one of these themes, ask yourself, "What are the emotional and psychological sources for my difficulty?" Remember, these are big questions. To start with write down what immediately and intuitively comes to your mind.

_____

_____

Principle 2: A commitment to transformation.
Examine your willingness to shift, change, and grow in this area and, at the same time, your fear, resistance, and attachment to safety.

Principle 3: Suggestions for loving, disciplined, daily practice.
NOTE: I define seven areas of life that I call the Seven Gates. I suggest that you make a short list of specific ways to support each one of the following Gates:

1. Gate of the Body: Your physical environment – this includes your body, your apartment or house, your car, your office, your clothes, your finances, and so on.
2. Gate of Emotions: Your inner world (feelings, needs, desires, and so on).
3. Gate of Dialogue: Your relationships.
4. Gate of Creative Expression: Your fun, adventurous, playful pleasures.
5. Gate of Life Path: Your work and creative projects.
6. Gate of Silence: Your spiritual practice.
7. Gate of Knowledge: Your education and new learning.

The following suggestions will help you begin the process of creating stronger inner and outer support systems:

1. Choose 1–3 areas that you feel need attention, and dedicate a week to each one. Create a specific list of supportive choices, commitments, and actions to enhance that area of life. For example, if you choose the area of your physical being and environment, you might want to take steps toward decluttering your home, shifting your diet, creating a clearer budget, or getting some new clothes. As you keep rotating the areas, you will sharpen your choices and commitments and deepen your ability to support your well-being.
2. Yoga is excellent for strengthening and aligning your spine, especially the backward and forward bends and spinal twists, as well as the simple cobra position. Walking, weight-bearing exercises, and working with weights all strengthen your spine.

The Fourth Stop

The fourth stop is your stomach region, center of "gut feelings" and survival intuition and a major storehouse of all kinds of feelings and memories. Ask yourself how it feels deep inside your stomach. Does it feel like your stomach is pulled in tight? Squeezed, knotted? Does it feel hollow, weak? Or bloated, droopy, numb? Here, you really need to feel and sense into the energetic patterns in your stomach. Look for consistent and familiar sensations, not just a digestive reaction to a big meal or lack of food.

Insights and Suggestions for Fourth Stop

Fourth Stop: Stomach, gut feelings. (Connected to the Solar Plexus Chakra.)

Principle 1: Awareness and Understanding.
Themes connected to tension and weakness in the stomach area:

1. Lack of trust in oneself.
2. Low self-esteem.
3. Fear of rejection, criticism, or abandonment.
4. Anxiety about one's ability to protect or "fend for" oneself.

Self - Analysis: If you identify with one of these themes, ask yourself, "What are the emotional and psychological sources for my difficulty?"

_____
_____

Principle 2: A commitment to transformation.
Examine your willingness to shift, change, and grow in this area and, at the same time, your fear, resistance, and attachment to safety.

Principle 3: Suggestions for loving, disciplined, daily practice.
NOTE: To create a strong sense of self and a trust in one's abilities takes self-respect and self-love. Your Expanded Self is the source of love within you. You can tap into that source, even if it feels foreign in the beginning, and practice an attitude of caring toward yourself. Use the suggestions offered in the first stop; grounding and sense of self are closely related.

1. In addition, you would need to learn the art of loving inner dialogue; the Gate of Emotions and the Gate of Dialogue will help you with that. For now, notice the quality of your inner dialogue. Are you loving toward yourself, or are you neglecting, shaming, critical, or even abusive? Note down your observations.
2. (If you are unkind to yourself, your inner dialogue needs to change.) List all that you would want to hear or receive from a loved one or a best friend in

terms of appreciation, acknowledgment, care, understanding, compassion, and so forth. Realize that *you* are that friend. Commit to a daily practice of emotional self-care.

3. Physically, lay on your back on a bioenergetics roller, gym ball, three pillows, or yoga bolsters. Then stretch your arms above your head and take deep breaths. This will open up and stretch the areas of the stomach and chest. Meditate or rest with your hands on your stomach. Practice sending loving messages to yourself through your hands. Your hands can transfer healing energy to your stomach; gentle self-massage can be very healing, too. Some yoga postures that are good for relaxing and opening the stomach area are the Bridge, the Camel, the Wheel, and the Fish. Pilates tones the gut, and these postures open it up.

The Fifth Stop

The fifth stop is your chest. Your chest is another part of your body that you need to listen to deeply because many times, there is nothing obvious that you can see. Does your chest feel contracted, collapsed, or rigid? Inflated? Or does it feel open, wide, and free, flowing? Is one side different from the other? Your chest is a center of "heart feelings." Our vulnerability, longing, and ability to connect to others all reside in the chest, as do hurts and emotional traumas, all mingled with expanded loving, joyful feelings.

Insights and Suggestions for Fifth Stop

Fifth Stop: Chest, heart feelings. (Connected to the Heart Chakra.)

Principle 1: Awareness and Understanding.
Themes connected to constricted or collapsed chest area: Experiences of abandonment, neglect, rejection, control, abuse, or loss can lead to:

1. Fear of emotional vulnerability.
2. Feelings of deep loneliness, despair, hopelessness, or helplessness.
3. Emotional distrust/fear of hurt, disappointment, betrayal, abandonment, or abuse.

Self - Analysis: If you identify with one of these themes, ask yourself, "What are the emotional and psychological sources for my difficulty?" Remember, these are big questions. To start with write down what immediately and intuitively comes to your mind.

_____

_____

Principle 2: A commitment to transformation.
Examine your willingness to shift, change, and grow in this area and, at the same time, your fear, resistance, and attachment to safety.

Principle 3: Suggestions for loving, disciplined, daily practice.
NOTE: The pain of the heart takes much loving and attention to heal. The Gate of Emotion and the Gate of Dialogue will address the art of mending the heart. Be aware that working through very traumatic experiences alone is not easy. If you feel you need help, do yourself a favor and work with a counselor. For right now:

1. Make a list of the difficult emotions you're struggling with—fears, pain, anger, and so on—and notice the way you treat these emotions. Do you allow yourself to feel them? If you do not, you will need to learn to do so. Practice acknowledging feelings, and gently open yourself up to them (by journaling, sharing with a loved one, allowing emotional expression). Learn to express and share your emotions privately and within your close relationships as much as possible, without apologizing for them, masking, or pretending. This is not an easy task. It takes much practice to be direct, simple, and honest.

2. Make a list of some wonderful, joyful, pleasant feelings, and do the same as above: acknowledge, experience, and express them. Many times, happy feelings are as hard to feel and acknowledge as the difficult ones. To physically open the chest, use the bioenergetics roll, gym ball, pillows and yoga asanas that open the chest, like the Backward Bend, the Fish, the Camel, the Bridge, the Wheel, and so on. Even a simple stretch on the back of a chair with the arms up or backward will help you open the chest.

The Sixth Stop

The sixth stop is the shoulders and the arms. The shoulders represent the way we "shoulder" life and its responsibilities. The arms express the way we reach out to give and receive. What is the feeling in your shoulders? Is there a difference between the right and the left? When you look at your shoulders, are they pulled up? Is one shoulder higher than the other? Are the shoulders pulled back or hunched forward? Tense? Loose? Knotted? Any disturbance in the shoulder girdle affects the mobility of the chest and respiration functions. Tensions in the shoulders also affect our arms. The arms are an important means of communicating our feelings, and the way we hold our arms can tell us how we reach out to the world.

Are your arms moving in unity with the rest of your body, or not? If the scapula is chronically contracted, we develop weakness in the muscles of the arms. Or, if muscles are bound in the chest and shoulders, they will create tense arms. In their relaxed position, how are your hands? Are they open, free? Grasping? Tense?

Insights and Suggestions for Sixth Stop

Sixth Stop: Shoulders, arms; the way we "shoulder" responsibility and reach out to others. (Connected to the Heart and Throat Chakras)

Principle 1: Awareness and Understanding.
Themes connected to tense or weak shoulders and arms:

1. A feeling of burden, shouldering too much responsibility, or the opposite: a feeling of not being able to take on one's responsibility.
2. A sense of inability to reach out and ask for help.
3. Difficulty in expressing love, needs, talents, and abilities.
4. Difficulty in asserting boundaries, saying no, expressing healthy anger, or pushing away violations.

Self - Analysis: If you identify with one of these themes, ask yourself, "What are the emotional and psychological sources for my difficulty?"

_____

_____

Principle 2: A commitment to transformation.
Examine your willingness to shift, change, and grow in this area and, at the same time, your fear, resistance, and attachment to safety.

Principle 3: Suggestions for loving, disciplined, daily practice.

1. Make a list of all the elements in your life that you feel are your direct responsibility, and notice whether you are caretaking or enabling other people by taking on their responsibilities. On the other hand, notice if you are actually taking on your own responsibilities. We are 100 percent responsible for ourselves, the young children we have or choose to help, and disabled or elderly family members. We're not responsible for capable adults, and we should not take over their responsibilities. It doesn't serve them or us. Supporting or helping others does not mean taking on their personal responsibilities. Cultivate a daily practice of making clear choices and decisions about your responsibilities for that day or in general. Take care of the ones that belong to you, and make sure to let go of responsibilities that belong to others.

2. The arms are important channels of expression. Notice how you use and move your arms. Find new ways to express through them. Reach out to touch your loved ones or reach out to ask for a hug. When you express your thoughts or feelings, integrate your arms and hands into your expression. When you are moving or dancing freestyle, find new ways to move your arms.

3. Physically, take a few minutes a day to move your shoulders—up and down, forward and back, in a circular motion backward and forward. Our shoulders tend to stiffen, and it's good to loosen and strengthen them on a daily basis. Simple arm and hand motions should similarly be done on a regular basis. Dance, yoga, tai chi, and martial arts all exercise the shoulders and the arms extensively. Pushups, if done right, strength en the shoulders and arms; many resistance training machines cultivate a range of arm and shoulder motion. Swimming is particularly good for the shoulders and arms.

The Seventh Stop

The seventh stop is the neck, the center of expression and will. Many of us have painful and stiff necks. Is your chin pulled forward, pulling your neck out? Is it pulled back, held up, or tucked down? All these will affect your neck, or will be affected by the way you hold your neck.

Insights and Suggestions for Seventh Stop

Seven Stop: Neck; personal will, and voice. (Connected to the Throat Chakra)

Principle 1: Awareness and Understanding.

Themes connected to stress and blockage in the neck area:

1. Difficulty in exercising one's will and expressing one's voice. This means a diminished ability to choose, speak, or act in accordance with one's true needs and interests.
2. Distrust in one's ability to have dominion over one's affairs.
3. Feeling controlled and repressed.
4. Unexpressed feelings of anger, sadness, or grief.
5. Fear of taking in breath/life fully.
6. Defensive stubbornness and lack of flexibility.

Self - Analysis: If you identify with one of these themes, ask yourself, "What are the emotional and psychological sources for my difficulty?"

Principle 2: A commitment to transformation.

Examine your willingness to shift, change, and grow in this area and, at the same time, your fear, resistance, and attachment to safety.

Principle 3: Suggestions for loving, disciplined, daily practice.

NOTE: You have dominion over your life. Notice when you give your power, responsibility, or rights away. Practice reclaiming ownership over your inner and outer environment. In order to know and choose what is right for you, be able to voice your choices and commit to them, you need to understand your nature and your true desires.

1. Make a list of important desires and needs you're aware of at this point in your life. Commit to honoring and supporting these on a daily basis. Notice your choices, and practice aligning them with your needs and desires. Remember that your highest good will benefit everybody around you.
2. Take daily risks, voicing feelings, needs, or thoughts. Aim for clarity, honesty, and emotional integrity in your communication. At the same time, cultivate empathic listening skills and the ability to accept others' personal perspective and emotional truth.

3. Practice making sounds: sing, cry out loud when you cry (if you do), find the sounds of joy, fear, or anger and express them—not necessarily always with others; I am suggesting a private study of sounding. Most of us are intimidated by natural sounds; we're brought up to think that raw sounds are only for kids, actors, or the mentally challenged. It is not so. Sounds are very healing and fun. Try them out. It will liberate your expression. Physically: Gently move your neck every day for a minute or two by doing neck rolls or neck stretches.

The Eighth Stop

The eighth—and last—stop is your head and face, the center of understanding and knowledge. Does your head tend to tilt to one side? Drop down or pull up? Look at your face. Do you notice a dominant expression? How do you hold your jaw? Is it tight? What do you see inside your eyes? It is true: the eyes *are* the windows of the soul. The face can also be a mask, the way we want to be perceived. But the truth is within our eyes. It is important to become aware of unconscious expressions that are frozen, and to learn to tap the feelings they hold so that these feelings can be released and integrated.

Insights and Suggestions for Eighth Stop Eighth Stop

Head and face; perception, knowledge, understanding, and personal expression. (Connected to the Third Eye and Crown Chakras)

Principle 1 : Awareness and Understanding.
Themes connected to stress, blockage or numbness in the head and face area:

1. Trying to keep a "good face," we are not allowing feelings into the head area.
2. Tendency to overanalyze things,
3. Blocking the sensory world and living "in the head."
4. Blocking openness and intuition.

NOTE: Our head houses four major sensory organs: the eyes, the ears, the nose, and the mouth. In addition to that, our head houses our brain (which we are not directly addressing in this stop). It is one of the main perception and understanding centers. Our face is also a main expression conduit. Stress in the head or face can cause diminished ability to clearly perceive the world around us and/or be present. If parts of the face are tight, frozen, or lifeless, our personal expression is compromised.

Self - Analysis: If you identify with one of these themes, ask yourself, "What are the emotional and psychological sources for my difficulty?"

Principle 2: A commitment to transformation.
Examine your willingness to shift, change, and grow in this area and, at the same time, your fear, resistance, and attachment to safety.

Principle 3: Suggestions for loving, disciplined, daily practice.
NOTE: A blockage in the head or the face area can happen when heart or gut feelings are not allowed to travel freely and express through the face (the eyes, the mouth, the voice, and so on). The need to present an attractive and acceptable "face" to the world, no matter what, creates an emotional and perceptual shutdown.

- Become aware of the "face" you present to the world. Do you feel that your expression is authentic, or are you hiding behind a mask—"happy," "serious," "cool," and so on? If you are, make a conscious decision to loosen up the mask. It would mean relearning to show your emotions and true temperament (not an easy task!).
- If you are someone who is trying to analyze life in an effort to be safe and sure at all time, you will create stress all over, but your head might express it most. Life is to be experienced, not necessarily figured out only intellectually. Notice feelings or experiences that you are repressing or disregarding. One of the ways to avoid feelings and experiences is to intellectualize them. This kind of avoidance creates internal stress and energy blockages. To shift this defensive tendency, practice letting go and letting be. Moving/sound/feeling meditations are wonderful for loosening up tension in the head. In these types of meditations, we allow spontaneous expression and learn to drop judgment and self-consciousness. The Gate of Creative Expression and the Gate of Silence will further explain this type of meditation.
- Train yourself to use your five senses fully, moment to moment. Notice details of shapes, colors, and lights. Differentiate smells and tastes; listen to nuances in voices and sounds. Become aware of the world through your senses. Using your senses opens up your ability to be present, aware, alive, and out of your head.

- Physically, here are some suggestions to loosen up the face and the head. Facial exercises are fun and very helpful in enlivening the muscles of the face and releasing the fixed expression of a mask. One exercise that I recommend is squeezing the whole face tight toward your nose and then following that by opening the face: opening your mouth, sticking your tongue out, and opening your eyes very wide. One action contracts; the other opens. If you repeat these two back to back several times, holding each one for a few seconds, you will sense how enlivened your facial muscles are. The other ex ercise is moving your face around, simply making faces and exploring moving it in different directions. Yoga eye exercises are also excellent; research that if you want to strengthen and relax your eye muscles. For the ones who practice yoga: Headstand, Shoulder Stand, Handstand, and Downward Facing Dog are some of the asanas that bring blood to the head and help loosen up energetic blockages. If you've never practiced yoga or are a beginner, teach yourself the asana called Downward Facing Dog and incorporate it into your usual stretches. Simply folding forward and letting your head hang heavy is also good, as are the neck stretches I explained in the previous stop.

Each one of us is a unique tapestry of psychological, spiritual, energetic patterns reflecting our soul's history. It's our loving obligation toward ourselves to investigate our inner world and our outer structure in order to facilitate healing and balancing shifts. The map of chronic tensions and blocked energy is the map of defensive compensations. We can, if we choose to, liberate ourselves gently and creatively from our defensiveness and reclaim our life force and our spiritual-emotional power.

SECOND SCAN: The Meditative Six-Layer Body Scan

This exercise uses the body to delve into emotions and conscious as well as sub conscious information. While doing this exercise, keep your focus on the root theme you have chosen.

When the mind is quiet and the body relaxed, we can receive further informa tion and insights. The Gates of Power® Method offers a deeper version of the body scan—one that is more intricate and possibly more revealing. This scan is done by lying down with the eyes closed. The process is guided by a Gates of Power®

coach; it is called the "Meditative Six-Layer Body Scan." After reading about it, try experimenting with it, on your own, if you feel comfortable.

The First Part

The Meditative Six-Layer Body Scan is a form of meditative relaxation, much like the one practiced at the end of a yoga class or in meditation. It is done to prepare the mind to become calmer and the body relaxed. Lie down comfortably with your legs and arms spread. Close your eyes, and let the body release and sink into the floor. Relax your mind, and center your thoughts and feelings in your breath.

The Second Part

Using six levels of investigation, scan all parts of the body, starting at the feet and moving on to the pelvis, and so on. Ask the following six questions: What are the physical energetic sensations that I feel in this part of the body? What colors do I see? What images do I associate with it? What feelings? What memories? What insight? The information that we receive through asking these questions is intuitive. We are using our senses and intuition to delve into the body and allowing spontaneous answers to emerge.

The Third Part:

Choose a specific part of the body, such as the chest or the pelvis, to explore further. I suggest that you choose the part that you associate with your main theme. Envision yourself entering that part of the body, the way someone would enter anenvironment or a landscape. The process continues as you move through an experiential journey, much like a waking dream with a storyline, people, and things. Don't consciously conjure the journey; let it happen, and let it move you to its natural conclusion. When done right, this process helps with the release, integration, and alignment of body, mind, and spirit.

> • • • **Reflection Pause** • • •
> What did you discover about your theme by doing this exercise?

Here is an example of the kind of insights we can receive by doing the Meditative Six-Layer Body Scan.

Ted, a young man of 28 years of age, came to see me because he had, in his words, a difficult time maintaining intimate relationships with women. He was eager to have a steady girlfriend, and spoke about his desire to have a family. One day, after a period of working through some emotional themes in which Ted reexperienced his childhood, he realized that he had never mourned the death of his father. His father had died when he was four years old, and his mother had been so stressed and devastated that she could barely function. Ted remembered the feeling of having to be strong for his mother. In his child's mind, he had to make sure nothing bad happened to Mom; the loss of his father was bad enough. Little Ted could not let himself break down emotionally. Feeling helpless and lost, he tried his best to be courageous and helpful.

As grownup Ted was talking about that, his eyes began to tear up, but his crying was choked. A few sessions after this one, he told me he was experiencing a strong pain in his chest—he described it saying that the muscles on the left side of the chest were severely contracted. He also told me that three days before the session, he had met a girl he really liked and felt anxious about his ability to maintain a connection with her.

I suggested we do the Meditative Six-Layer Body Scan centered around the chest. We did the first part—lying down in relaxation—and then the second part, scanning the chest on all six levels:

1. Physical – energetic sensations
2. Colors
3. Images
4. Emotions
5. Memories
6. Insights.

Then, I asked him to enter his chest, with his mind's eyes, the way he would enter an environment or a landscape. When he did that, I asked him where he saw himself. He said he imagined himself sitting in a domelike, empty room so wide he couldn't see the walls, but he knew they were there. I asked about the light in the room, and he said the room was red; the light in it was red, and the color of the floor was red.

"Are you sitting or standing?" I asked.

He said he was sitting on a big pile of thick, knotted blue ropes.

"How do you feel?" I asked.

He said, "I feel the urge to loosen and untie the ropes, but I don't know how."

Then, I asked why the ropes were so heavily knotted, to which he replied, "I feel that these ropes are intense feelings and energies squished together and stuck like a big pileup of cars."

"How can you untie them?" I asked.

"The only way is to liquefy them," he answered.

At that point he started crying, first softly and then sobbing. After a few minutes, he told me that the big piles of knots were feelings of sadness blocked in his chest, and that he realized the need to release the sadness. He felt much better after the process; his chest felt softer and more open. I recommended journaling for the next few weeks and encouraged him to allow crying, if tears come up, as a way of keeping his chest open and his feelings available. After the scan, Ted was able to maintain a connection with the new girlfriend, and, for the first time in his life, he was able to share his sadness with an intimate partner.

THIRD SCAN: The Energy Center Body Scan

This scan reveals the spiritual lessons that our themes can teach us. The physical body is a microcosm of the universe, revealing its order and balance. It is also a map that charts personal evolution. Another way to scan the body for information and insight is the system of the energy centers in the body, which in the Vedic tradition is called the chakra system. The chakra system is a wonderful example of how the body organizes and expresses the soul's journey. Each one of the chakras is a database of experiences recorded in the body, and it reflects a level of consciousness. We can use the chakra system as a tool for transformation—as we master the lessons in each level, we move up the ladder of our personal evolution. The Vedic tradition defines seven energy centers that are directly linked to the physical body; the Kabbalistic tradition defines 10 layers of existence, called the Seffirot. The Christian tradition speaks about the seven sacraments. In her wonderful lecture series "Energy Anatomy," Caroline Myss shows that all three systems talk about a similar concept: the various levels of spiritual, emotional, and energetic evolution available to us.[3] We create our reality according to the content of our consciousness; each one of the seven energy centers holds an aspect of our consciousness, both negative and positive. Our job is to master the lesson and the personal power available to us within each center.

Lessons of Empowerment

The energy centers can be thought of as gradations of consciousness, or states of consciousness; ideally, all the centers should be balanced and vibrate in unity. Energetic imbalance within the centers or between them creates a continuous feeling of unease and dissatisfaction. As a result, we look outside of ourselves for fulfillment. True fulfillment is an internal state of being; it cannot be achieved without the connection to our inner life.

Spiritual and emotional lessons are reflected in the sevenmain energy centers (called chakras). The question is how to use our knowledge to reclaim true power and fulfillment. I will briefly review each chakra and its spiritual message. An ocean of information regarding the energy system is available, and a short mention of it here is not intended to simplify or short-change it. Readers who are interested will investigate further or have already done so. Please also bear in mind that each one of the lessons mentioned is life-altering and can take sometimes a whole life to be learned; knowing what these are, initiates the process of learning.

There is a reflection pause after each center; take the time to sense and reflect so that your understanding is experiential and not just intellectual. If there is a blockage that you can sense in any one of the centers, don't get discouraged. Identifying a blockage is always the first step and maybe the most important one. It might provoke you to inquire deeper into why the blockage is there. As you compassionately keep inquiring with awareness and open-mindedness, you're actually starting the process of releasing the blockage.

FIRST CENTER: The Root Chakra

The Root Chakra is located at the base of the spine in the area of the tailbone not for from the anus. This chakra reflects security, trust, connection with the physical body, the earth, and the immediate community—all these are grouped together under the theme of Survival. On the level of physical survival, we are social animals. We need and depend on each other. We also depend on our bodies and the earth to survive. If any one of these elements is threatened, our physical survival is in question. The theme of survival can hold us captive in fear and tension. How can we loosen the grip and transform the fear?

What is the lesson of this energy center? It is to realize and learn to trust our oneness with nature and all things—a oneness that is forever there—and to find a sense of security within that knowledge. This inner sense of trust frees us to enjoy life and allows us to cultivate our individuality away from an insecure and blind loyalty to our social "tribe." It spells spiritual and personal freedom. I think of my own example: as my experience of being connected to all things deepened, I felt freer to choose my own beliefs and my own way of living. Leaving Israel (the "tribe"), and with it the belief that I had to be or live a certain way, liberated me to explore a much wider terrain. I have become a "citizen of the world." I still of course have a very strong, loving bond with Israel, but it is of love, not a guilt-driven obligation—which in my case needed to drop away.

> ••• **Reflection Pause** •••
>
> Contemplate the way you are handling the theme of Survival in your life.

SECOND CENTER: The Abdominal Chakra

This chakra is located 3 inches below the navel—physically, in the lumbar area, the reproductive system, and the abdomen. This chakra reflects our need for sexual expression, desire to reproduce, create, and express. The themes of Sexuality and Creativity are potentially explosive: they are powerful urges that can be a source of joy or a source of destruction. Of course, we also witness every shade in between. A blockage in this chakra is common—fear and oppression of our sexuality and creativity keep our vitality and expression repressed.

The lesson of this energy center is to cultivate our ability to make love with life and experience it sensually and creatively. Furthermore, it is to enjoy individual expression while honoring others and their individual expression and to be nourished by the creative exchange among all living things.

A client of mine whom I'll call Samantha came to me complaining of severe nightmares. Many of them presented a repetitious theme: in her sessions, she would describe pulling out of the lower part of the body—stomach, vagina, or anus—long cords or animal-like creatures. In the nightmares, she would feel frantic, almost desperate, to get rid of these elements. In her words, these were "things that did not belong there." Over time, we uncovered repressed memories of sexual abuse by her father. The lower part of her body, specifically the root chakra and the abdominal chakra, were heavily blocked. Every time we did a body scan, she would complain of heaviness, gripping, and pain in these parts of the body. Her relationship to her sexuality was ambivalent; she was both addicted to it and afraid of it. Her need to appease others so that she can feel loved and protected crippled her authentic expression.

Her lessons were twofold. The first was to create a sense of personal safety by learning to be assertive, exercising healthy boundaries, speaking up, and acknowledging and taking responsibility for her true needs (root chakra themes). The second lesson was connected to the second chakra: to harness her sexual and creative power to nurture her well-being and fulfillment, to make love with life without allowing invasion and abuse. She is learning to take charge of her energy and her life.

••• Reflection Pause •••
Contemplate the themes of Sexuality and Creativity in your life.

THIRD CENTER: The Solar Plexus Chakra

This chakra is located 4 inches above the navel on the body's midline. It deals with digestion, assimilation, and body temperature. The themes of this chakra are Ease of Being, Sense of Self, Self-Esteem, and Self-Image—in short, comfort with who we are. Many of us struggle with these themes. This chakra also contains so-called "gut feelings" or "gut intuitions," which can be very useful for emotional and spiritual growth. Blockage in this center originates in the fear of rejection, criticism, and abandonment. These fears prevent us from honoring who we are and from following our intuitive inner guidance.

What we can learn from this chakra is to honor ourselves and to let go of the tendency to be defined by outside sources—to listen within and uncover who we are and what inspires and moves us. Honoring ourselves teaches us to honor others and respect all living things. Each one of us is a unique expression of the Source; it is our privilege and responsibility to honor and express that uniqueness.

As you can see, all the lessons mentioned are major ones. They build on each other, because if we can learn to relax and feel one with life (first chakra), then we can enjoy our sexuality and creativity constructively (second chakra), which then supports our respect for ourselves (third chakra). These are lifelong lessons of empowerment, to be mastered step by step, breath by breath, with loving patience.

Tamar grew up in a kibbutz in Israel. She came to me plagued by a food disorder and a painfully distorted self-image. Her story revealed an extremely sensitive, unusual child who was taunted by the group of kids she grew up with. In a kibbutz, your group is your family: you literally live with them. Being "the strange one" means feeling like an outcast. Tamar carried a tremendous inner pain, and a lot of it registered in her stomach: the third chakra. It manifested in digestive discomfort, a sensitive stomach, and frequent physical pain. Tamar needed to learn to honor her sensitivity and uniqueness, to trust her intuition (her "gut feeling") and gain a real appreciation for who she is. This meant accepting her vulnerabilities as well as her strengths. She's still learning; it's a bumpy road, but she is holding her own in a very competitive field, being a fashion and art director, where appearance is constantly scrutinized and peer pressure is enormous.

• • • Reflection Pause • • •

Contemplate the themes of Self-Esteem and Self-Image in your life.

FOURTH CENTER: The Heart Chakra

This chakra is located 6 inches above the navel and is associated with heart and lungs. The themes of this chakra are Love, Connection, and Compassion. Actually, the fourth chakra is the center of emotions. Old, unresolved hurts block this chakra and compromise our ability to feel deeply. Pain, joy, and everything in between are necessary to keep an open heart. Most of us know the feeling of a heartbreak—it literally feels like the heart is shattered. Or the feeling of falling in love when the heart gets so wide and open that the whole universe can pass through. Most of us also know how overprotected we keep our hearts.

The lesson of this center—corny but true—involves opening up to all our emotions and learning to receive and give love, compassion, and joy. Allowing a wide-open, vulnerable heart space is an extremely difficult lesson to learn. It takes trust in life and its divine order—an order and justice that we might not understand fully with our human logic, and that puzzle us constantly. Still, can we trust life? Can we feel the oneness? Can we continuously open ourselves to love? Can we feel deeply without acting on the fear of being overwhelmed or devastated by our feelings?

Living with an open heart takes tremendous courage. It demands a great deal of emotional honesty, self-awareness, and communication skills. This kind of openness is a powerful way of being. It can take a lifetime to get there, but making the commitment to live from the heart inspires great learning, and the experiences we go through on the journey are as important as reaching our destination. When the heart center opens wide, we are able to channel unconditional love and compassion. The Expanded Self is able to work through the heart chakra, experiencing and expressing love, and, in doing so, becomes a strong vessel of creativity and healing.

Emma, a woman in her forties, came to see me after years of what she described as "torment." She suffered from frequent anxiety attacks and an inability to sleep deeply. She was living in a constant fear of a heart attack. Emma is the mother of two grown-up boys, and an extremely intelligent and accomplished woman. I was amazed at what she was able to achieve in spite of sleepless nights and constant visits to the emergency room. She complained of a chronic pressure around her heart, and a gnawing pain in the left shoulder and arm. Every few months, Emma would take herself to the emergency room, thinking she was having a heart attack; she would be checked thoroughly and sent home with the report that all was well. She was told over and over again that her heart was totally normal.

When we started examining the anxiety that kept her up at night and gripped her heart center, we discovered that, being a sickly child (Emma had had rheumatic fever), she spent many months in the hospital between the ages of four and five. She remembered days of profound loneliness in the hospital. Her parents both worked and had two other small children, so they couldn't always make the visiting hours. Emma recalled feeling abandoned. She remembered that she was afraid to fall asleep at night—falling asleep meant losing connection with other people. "It felt like death," she told me, "like dropping into a dark abyss." So, she would keep herself awake and wait for the dawn.

The same fear of abandonment and deep longing for love was still there in the grown-up woman: Emma simply could not relax into life. She compensated by trying to be the perfect wife, mother, and homemaker, always finding fault in herself (most kids who feel abandoned blame themselves for it, assuming that there is something missing within them that caused the abandonment), never feeling good enough. In the work we did together, we needed to revisit the child within her and unearth the early feelings. Then, by way of inner dialogues between her Expanded Self and her Emotional Self, we reorganized the old experience in order to release the pain, and reassure the inner child.

Emma realized that the abandonment was not her fault and that she was not alone any longer. She learned to let her Expanded Self—the aspect of the self that is wisdom and compassion—take on the role of the loving parent of her inner child (a part of the Emotional Self) and provide a sense of security and love. By doing so, she was able to calm herself down when the anxiety would overwhelm her in the middle of the night. There are no more trips to the emergency room; although she's not "out of the woods" yet, she's learning to take care of herself. Her heart is slowly opening up to life and love.

> ••• **Reflection Pause** •••
>
> Contemplate the themes of Love in your life.

FIFTH CENTER: The Throat Chakra

The fifth center is located at the base of the throat. This center reflects themes of Self-Expression, "having a voice," and Personal Will and Choice, of making choices and voicing them, so to speak. Developing a sense of will that is guided by healthy personal choices is extremely important in terms of actualizing our true life purpose. We are social creatures, always part of a group; at the same time, it is important for each one of us to realize our individual expression within the group. We best serve the whole when we cultivate our own individual potential.

In order to grow, wise choices that support our well-being are needed: the sixth center is the mind, the fourth is the heart. The throat center is the connection between the mind and the heart. All three—mind, heart, and will—must come together to serve our highest purpose. All three need to be constructively expressed through the throat center. The process of working with our will and voice is constant. At every stage of life, every fork in the road, and on a daily basis, we need to stop and ask ourselves, "What are the right choices for me at this point in 7 time?

Am I investing my energy and attention in choices that support my growth, or am I not?"

Much of our attention, focus, and energy is attached to self-depleting thoughts, behaviors, and feelings; the process of identifying these and releasing them is guided by our will and our commitment to inner power and inner freedom. The first step is becoming clear about the right choices for us. The next step is exercising our will and following through in both voice and action. At times, we are dangerously out of touch with our deepest needs. We get distracted by the nagging chores of daily maintenance and end up focusing on the inessential rather than the essential. So, we throw ourselves out of balance. That is why healthy choices, commitments, and actions are a must in the struggle of maintaining balance.

Sharon, an opera singer, came to me in a state of great distress: she had been going through a hard time with her singing. She described chest pains and a constant lump in her throat, and told me that the symptoms she experienced had been gradually worsening in the past several months. Sharon had done her best to find out what was going on. She had gone to several doctors and undergone tests of all kinds, but nothing physical was found, and she was told that she needed to seek counseling.

Her story and history are quite complex, as I found out; it would be difficult and unnecessary to go into all the details. Still, I would like to bring out a few points that relate to the throat center. First, we discovered that Sharon was angry and disappointed by her career—not by her singing, which she loved, but by the political environment within the opera as an institution. Second, she realized that she was pushing herself beyond her own healthy boundaries to succeed in a very tough field. Third, she admitted to me that she didn't know how to say no and was constantly pleasing, appeasing, and taking care of those around her. It seemed to me that she was "swallowing many frogs," so to speak, and they were sticking in her throat. There was resentment, disappointment, tiredness, and lack of personal expression—all stuck in the throat. Sharon was getting sicker and felt like she wanted to just stop and take a break. But she feared that if she stopped, she would lose the professional momentum she had worked so hard to achieve. She felt paralyzed. On the one hand, she wasn't able to sing well; on the other, she couldn't make a choice that would support her well-being. Her conflict was all in the throat: the center of Choice, Will, and Expression. At this time, we are still working to find a way to unravel the knot and release the attachment to depleting patterns. Sharon is considering letting go of a contract and possibly taking a break to rest and heal.

> • • • **Reflection Pause** • • •
>
> Contemplate the themes of Will, Choice, and Expression in your life.

SIXTH CENTER: The Third Eye Chakra

The sixth center is located between the eyebrows, near the pituitary gland. This center is connected with Psychic Awareness, Perceptions of the World, and Knowledge. The sixth center is a portal to the "global mind" and the "collective unconsciousness." It is the center of learning and understanding the truth—it can be called the place of wisdom. The lesson of this center involves cultivating the ability to see the truth beyond the physical reality that is perceived by our senses. Mystics of all spiritual paths refer to the physical world of things as an illusion; they speak of spirit, God, or Divine Mind as the substance of reality. The startling discoveries of quantum physics and quantum mechanics invite us to entertain reality as a unified field of information/consciousness and energy, collapsing into different forms as we observe it. These principles of physics are tough for even experts to explain. The subject can sound overwhelming or confusing. However, it seems like spiritual teachings and science are finally speaking in a similar way about the nature of reality. The two perspectives complement each other and can help us to grasp the nature of existence.

The sixth center, when open, allows us to understand and experience the nature of reality. People whose sixth chakra is very open can see patterns of energy, colors, and lights; if they are gifted and trained, they can interpret the patterns and receive important insights about themselves or others. For example, energy healers may receive important information and guidance through images that tell them how and where to direct the healing energy. As we learn the lessons that the energy centers make available to us, we evolve; usually the sixth center opens up after the other centers have been opened first. But there are people who are born with psychic abilities, and sometimes they start their learning from top to bottom (from the sixth center down), rather than from bottom to top (first center up).

One of my clients, Tom, started working with me at the age of 26. He was extremely frightened and closed off. He hated the physical, energetic exercises that were offered under the Gate of the Body and, unable for the longest time to experience or express any feelings, would refuse any creative expression exercises. It was tough working with Tom. I noticed, though, that his sixth center was very open. He would sense energies and see auras, and these abilities were natural to him. He also had an easy time working through images and dreams. We found a way to work through the sixth center using dream interpretation and meditative processes. Working this way, we slowly moved down to the other centers and opened them up. It was a tedious process, but Tom became more comfortable with his emotional truth and expression. Now, a few years later, Tom is open to move his body and willing to be in his feelings; it is as though he needed to learn to feel safe and comfortable in the world of matter while he was totally at ease in the world of spirit. For most of us, it is the opposite.

> ••• Reflection Pause •••
> How do you perceive the nature of reality?

SEVENTH CENTER: The Crown Chakra

The crown chakra is located on top of the head, along the midline of the cranium, also known as the vertex, and is related to the pineal gland. This center reflects themes of Unity and the Realization of the Interconnectedness of Life. It is the storehouse of grace and spiritual guidance. When this center is open, we experience being one with life and with the Source. We live trusting in the Divine Order, and we feel the infinite and eternal nature of life.

The lesson of this center is to know the oneness of all things, not just intellectually but experientially, and to know ourselves as infinite and eternal beings of consciousness. Once we achieve this, we can rest within the peace that this knowledge provides. Obviously, this state of mind—as desirable as it is—is not a common experience. It is described as the state of enlightenment, nirvana, satori. The halo around saints' heads in paintings is the artistic expression of an open crown chakra. It is a state of utter bliss.

I cannot offer a story about an enlightened client of mine, but I myself was blessed to have the guidance of some wonderful teachers. The experience of being around someone whose crown chakra is open and literally pouring out light is inspirational. One of my teachers was Shri Brahmananda Sarasvati,4 who was the founder of Ananda Ashram in 1964. Shri Bhrahmananda was also a prolific author on a broad range of topics, including the science and philosophy of Yoga-Vedanta. His expertise ranged from Ayurveda to modern psychiatry and neurosurgery, and he was a master of the Sanskrit language. Shri Brahmananda Sarasvati's life was committed to integrating Eastern and Western sciences, culture, and philosophy.

Shri Brahmananda, or Guruji, as we called him affectionately, was an extremely charismatic and eloquent teacher. He exuded a bright intellect mingled with a fun-loving sense of humor and an extremely compassionate heart. He was a joy to be around. In 1983, Guruji suffered a stroke and became paralyzed on the right side. His speech was affected, and he had to have his words, which sounded more like sounds, translated into clear sentences by his assisting disciples. His body was in constant pain and discomfort. In spite of all that, we all noticed that the light radiating from his joyful, playful eyes was getting stronger: his face and especially the crown of his head were glowing.

Guruji used to comment on the powerful transformation he experienced as a result of his illness. One particular moment comes to my mind as I'm writing this. I was sitting in the meditation room looking at him as he was telling us a funny story. His eyes were sparkling, and it looked like streams of light were pouring out of his head, illuminating the whole room. I remember being struck by a blissful emotion that took over my whole body. I felt his spirit dancing around the room—free, powerful, and joyful. At that moment, I realized the truth of his teaching: "We are consciousness, beyond the body, mind, illusion." It was a moment of great beauty and peace, and one that I cherish.

• • • **Reflection Pause** • • •

Reflect on the theme of Enlightenment and your personal experience with it.

Consciousness, Energy, and Disease

Science (quantum physics and quantum mechanics), ancient traditions, faith, and mysticism all inform us that we are a part of and one with the universal consciousness/energy field—the Great Oneness. This life-filled matrix manifests highly intelligent order; I refer to it as Divine Order. The question that haunted me for years was this: If we are one with the Divine Order, why is it that we are plagued with so much disease? I'm not talking about some aches and pains of old age, but the prevalent array of illnesses manifested in people of all ages. Since we are on theGate of the Body, it seems appropriate to touch upon the subject. There are different schools of thought addressing the question of what creates illness, and literally thousands of books have been written in an attempt to shed light on the topic. Here is my humble understanding.

I will begin by saying that I believe that our bodies (the energy field) and our consciousness (the spirit and soul) are constantly and forever in the process of creating and re-creating balance and harmony. Divine Order is the law of the universe. All is governed by it, and the whole is constantly realigning itself. Disease is an action of balancing—an attempt to return to a harmonious state. In other words, the balancing tendency is using disease to shape, alarm, and awaken us. It cajoles us to examine how, why, and when we have allowed or created imbalance and, by doing so, caused ourselves suffering. Some diseases are considered "silent killers"; they have no obvious observable symptoms until they reach critical proportions. Even these diseases present an opportunity to return to balance. Here, too, we are called to understand how we might have created them and what changes we need to make in the way we think, feel, and act. Only then can we put ourselves back on the path to wholeness and health. A disease can be the voice of suffering within the soul calling for healing. It acts like a compass that can—if we pay attention to it—orient us back onto the path toward wholeness. We can look at illness as a creation we participated in, and at the same time as a beacon of illumination. This way of looking at illness might not seem to apply to all forms of it. Nevertheless, I feel that it's a powerful point of view that encourages us to take responsibility and actively participate in our own healing.

Let's develop the idea of seeing illness as a creation a little further. The idea that our consciousness is a creative force is not new: we are all on a continual journey of creativity in terms of our life. I believe it all starts before we get here. The soul reincarnates with the intention to evolve. Without being in a body, and in the world, there can be no experience, and thus no learning. So, the soul makes some important choices before it reincarnates. These choices are informed by the lessons it needs to learn and the accomplishments it needs to experience on the way to its realization. Each soul manifests its choices in a different manner. These include (among others) what family it will be born into, where, and when; I believe that the soul chooses familial genes, social circles, and life circumstances that will challenge it to grow. Once reincarnated, the soul is presented with possibilities and opportunities. At any given moment, the aware and growing soul can change its choices, or the way it utilizes a specific choice, in order to experience a greater spiritual wholeness.

Life can be seen as a creative journey of choices. We all know people who were born with either disabilities or unusual abilities. Some create a life of achievement that is awe-inspiring, while others destroy or self-destruct. We come into the world with physical tendencies, emotional abilities, talents, gifts, and attributes—I call these the "soul potential learning bag." We also bring with us our soul's history. Our job is to pay attention to what we create physically, emotionally, and spiritually, and to learn from it. As we take on the responsibility for our creations, we gather inner power and wisdom. We fine-tune our process by letting go of what does not serve our growth and cultivating what does.

The soul's journey is difficult. It is manifested into a body and into a chosen (yet at times challenging) condition. Fortunately, it is endowed with the ability to witness and be aware, the power of creative thought, the freedom of choice, and inner guidance. All of these are helpful companions on the bumpy road.

How is all this connected to illness? Choices, actions, experiences, expressions, thoughts, and feelings all weave the fabric of our being. We are the weavers; we choose the colors and the shapes of our life's tapestry. Illness is a creation, just like a beautiful family, an artwork, or a fulfilling friendship. Luckily, like all important creations, illness offers a powerful healing and learning opportunity. Some of the ways we can create illness are: by ignoring our bodies, feelings, dreams, or desires and by repressing our true expression; by disrespecting ourselves; by living in fear, shame, or guilt; and by failing to recognize our oneness with all things. Each illness is a unique creation, and in order to understand it fully, we need to examine the details of our lives and the way we're living them. Ultimately, we are here to experience and trust the amazing power, love, and creativity that are our true nature.

It's important to nourish ourselves on all four layers of being: the physical, the emotional, the mental, and the spiritual. Each layer needs to be fulfilled, and every one of us is responsible for fulfilling these layers within ourselves. When we do this, our being nourishes others.

I'd like to share with you a personal story about disease and its potential to be a lifesaving guide. At the age of 34, I went through a very traumatic separation from a man I loved deeply. After the separation, I slipped into a severe depression that stretched for a couple of years. All my buried and not-so-buried demons burst out of the box, and I was overwhelmed by my feelings of abandonment, hopelessness, and helplessness. Old feelings—I would say ancient (lifetimes-ancient) feelings—poured out of me. In hindsight, I can see that this breakdown was necessary for my growth, but while it was happening, it felt like a very long dark night of the body, mind, and soul. I experienced profound loneliness and vulnerability—a feeling of not being safe in the world that was haunting. When I had been in the relationship, I had felt protected and cared for; being out of it was as if I was stripped of all clothes in the middle of a harsh winter.

Slowly but surely, my immune system (our first protection against threats to the body) began to reflect my feelings: it started to break down. I became allergic to certain foods, and eventually to almost all foods; the pounds were dropping away uncontrollably, and I looked like skin and bones. Of course, I went to see many doctors, regular and alternative, nutritionists and homeopaths, but nothing helped. I feared for my life. A good friend recommended that I meet Lillian Schwabe, a Christian Science practitioner. I remember saying to my friend, "What am I going to do with a Christian Science practitioner? You must be kidding!" She insisted, and so I went.

I sat with Lillian every week for the next five years, and enjoyed every moment. With her guidance, I learned to confront my sense of separation, my distrust in life, in God, and in love. I understood that I was looking for a sense of safety in a relationship with a man rather than in my connection to the Source. Of course, feeling safe and cared for in a relationship is wonderful, but it does not replace our sense of connection with the greater whole (God, Spirit, Divine Mind, and so on). As my feelings shifted, my body started to realign itself. My illness was a creation of my state of mind. It was a torment and a lesson, and I am grateful for both. Sometimes we're able to shift a pattern of an illness, and sometimes we're not. What we learn while we go through the experience is to me the important factor.

The Ten Commandments for Cultivating Power Through The Body

1. **Keep a Loving, Attentive Dialogue With Your Body:** Your body is your best friend, and your life depends on it. It is important that you cultivate an attitude of gratitude and respect toward it. Many of us treat our bodies as servants that we overwork, or strangers that we barely tolerate, or storefronts that uphold our image in the world. None of these attitudes is appropriate when it comes to the way you treat your body. Pay attention to your body on a daily basis; it talks to you about your stresses, your pleasures, your feelings, and your choices. It shows you what it needs and what you need, and it is guiding you constantly. Learn to listen to it on every level, from the most basic (muscle stress, pain, hunger, thirst, need for rest, and so on) to the most sophisticated (the energy field and the connection between your body and your psyche). Realize that these listening skills get better with practice and commitment. As you cultivate a loving intimate relationship with your body, you will learn its language and fine-tune your observation skills.

2. **Take Care of Your Inner Life:** The healthier you become emotionally, mentally, and spiritually, the easier it might be for your body to cope. When you commit to taking care of your inner life, you naturally begin to attend to your outer life—your body, your environment, your finances, and so on. The distinction between inner and outer life is some what arbitrary; all of it is your life. Make a commitment to your well-being, your fulfillment, and your growth. A soul that is well taken care of brings happiness to its energetic temple. As we get farther into the Gates, you will find additional insights and exercises to support the inner growth process.

3. **Breathe:** The breath is God's music playing through you. Treat it as you would a most precious gift. Become grateful for and mindful of your breath; learn to deepen, calm, and enjoy it. Most of us are not breathing fully. Tensions, stress, rushing, and overload of activity cause the breath to be shallow and irregular. I suggest that you investigate the world of breathing exercises and practice a few minutes a day as part of your meditation practice, or when you walk, jog, or exercise. Treat the breath as an integrated part of the process. To start your investigation, I recommend *The Breathing Book* by Donna Farhi 5 (Holt, 1996). The cultivation of mindfulness and the ability to be present in the moment will help you release the breath when you catch yourself freezing it, and the habit of enjoying your breath will in turn ground you in the present moment.

4. **Take in Good Nutrition:** If you are like me, you read tons of books about nutrition; if you're not like me, you've still heard plenty about it. There are people who swear by the macrobiotic diet, and others who are devotees of Peter D'Adamo's *Eat Right for Your Type*. Still others are vegan, vegetarian, or raw food believers. There is the Mediterranean diet, the Ayurvedic diet... and the list goes on. It can get confusing. New research appears every day, and with it different supplements that are promising to de-age, detoxify, or rejuvenate us. My simple advice is: eat as naturally as you can, as close to Mother Nature as possible. Eat real food, if possible organic, unprocessed, clean of chemicals and additives (read labels), and lots of fresh vegetables and fruit. If you eat dairy, goat cheese and yogurt are easier to digest and are lower in lactose. Stay away from refined flours and sugars and heavily deep-fried or greasy foods. Eat three balanced meals a day, even if they're small meals. Combining foods correctly helps with digestion. It is important to enjoy your food. Prepare it with love, eat mindfully, chew well, and remember to be grateful for it.

It is paramount to drink lots of clean water. Taking some vitamins and supplements could be very helpful. I recommend that you see a good nutritionist once in a while to make sure you're on the right path, especially if you have specific dietary needs. Each food has its own energetic vibration, and certain foods are healing for certain conditions. By paying attention to what you eat and how it relates to your body, you can learn what foods are healing and strengthening for you.

5. **Move, Dance, Exercise:** It is the nature of the body to enjoy movement. I suggest that you always explore different ways of moving. Put on music while you're cleaning or doing something around the house, and experiment with some freestyle movement in between the chores. Take different yoga classes; try new exercise classes. If you like to play sports, keep up with it. Jog, speed walk, stretch, or swim. The key is variety, fun, and new discoveries. Even if you are limited in your ability to exercise, keep exploring on a small scale. Move different parts of your body gently and mindfully; make it playful and interesting. Moving meditations are wonderful. Close your eyes, put some music on, drop your thoughts, settle into your breath, and begin to move the body however it feels like moving. Let your body lead. Think of it as cultivating the body's expression through movement. Remember that your body loves to express itself—if you let it.

6. **Rest and Relax:** As much as the body loves to move, it also loves to rest and relax. The balance between exertion and rest needs to be maintained at all times. Many of us have forgotten how to rest and relax. We keep ourselves so busy that the art of relaxation has become foreign to us. I have to remind myself frequently to take time out. Lazy moments can be wonderfully energizing. If you are a meditator, you know how helpful it is to completely relax the body as a preparation for a meditation.

I highly recommend meditating once or twice a day, but if you're not there yet, at least give yourself time for total relaxation. When you do, consciously say to yourself: *This is my time to just rest. I'm letting go of everything: my worries, my to-do list, my obligation list, and even my want-to-do list.* I'm taking time out. Lie down on the sofa, on the rug, on the grass, or sit in your favorite big chair with your legs up, on a bench in the park, or a rocking chair. Close your eyes and let it all go. You can put on beautiful music or just let the sounds of life around you be your soundtrack. Rest and breathe. As the different lists and thoughts come up, notice them and consciously let them go, reminding yourself, *I'm resting; this can wait for later.* Keep taking yourself back to your blissful lazy moment. Enjoying 15–20 minutes of blissful laziness every day is great medicine.

7. **Groom, Clean and Beautify:** We have to admit that it feels wonderful to clean, groom, and beautify the body. Our bodies so deserve it. They carry us around so loyally and bring us so much pleasure that our loving attention is very appropriate. When cleaning your body, I would recommend soaps and lotions that are simple and pure (just like the foods you feed your body). Beautifying and grooming mean different things to different people, so do whatever feels good to you. A wonderful bath, a beard trim, a good shave, a great haircut, nails, feet, a facial— whatever it is, enjoy it. Grooming is an opportunity to say thank you to your body. It can also be a relaxing and fun way to receive nurturance from another person. Remember the wonderful lazy moments I mentioned before? Here is your opportunity to create one of those for yourself. Grooming is also an opportunity to experience and appreciate the sensuous nature of the body. It is all around delicious.

8. **Touch and Be Touched:** We all need touch; it is a must for healthy living. Find ways that are appropriate to experience loving expressions through touch. Hug the people you're close with, and do so often. Be receptive to their loving touch. If you have a lover or a mate, explore different ways of touching each other— sensuous, affectionate, or both. Get a massage once in a while, or experiment with your intimate partner to find ways to massage each other. Massage your own shoulders, feet, hands, or back as much as possible. Exchange back and shoulder massages with a good friend. I recommend exploring different forms of healing modalities that focus on the body, such as acupuncture, shiatsu, Reiki, polarity, Rolfing, craniosacral therapy, and so on. If you're a parent, simply be tactile and affectionate with your kids. As much as possible, create a place for touch in your life.

9. **Enjoy Sensuous Sexual Pleasure:** I'm a great believer in the power of good, healthy, sensuous pleasure. Sensual pleasure means different things to different people, so I will not bother with the details. The idea is to discover, experiment, and enjoy. I would say, though, that it is important to engage in pleasure that is safe, emotionally fulfilling, and nonaddictive in nature. Addictive sexual activity is a way to cover up emotions or run away from them. If possible, make that distinction and orient yourself toward pleasure that is healing rather than addictive.

10. **Keep Adventure as Part of Your Life:** Body, mind, and soul thrive on new experiences and new adventures. Find ways to introduce new learning, new places to travel, new people, and new ways to experience familiar things. Try new foods, listen to new types of music, do something you have never done before. Keep your life interesting. Look for and create adventure—it keeps your spirit on its toes. The brain needs to learn new things constantly in order to stay healthy, the soul loves the growth that adventure brings, and the body is energized by it.

7

The Gate of Emotions

*Use your emotions as an instrument to express
the highest and the best in you.*

Can you imagine your life without the presence of feelings? All the magical and painful moments that infuse life with depth and richness would not exist. The fire and the passion, the stillness of awe, the sweetness of prayer, the inspiration of beauty, the depth of love, and the fleeting fragrance of bliss would all be gone. Feelings are life's elixir, the most precious gift we have.

Feelings and Emotions

Let's take a minute to distinguish between feelings and emotions. When a feeling becomes intense and its energy creates an obvious expression in the physical body and in one's behavior it has become an emotion, energy in motion. Some of our feelings pass through us fleetingly and leave a slight trace, like the smell of flowers or firewood burning that is carried by the wind. Other feelings stir us deeper and energize reactions, both psychological and physical. I call these emotions.

Let me give you an example. A man sees a cute baby fashionably and colorfully dressed, sitting solemnly in a stroller. Something about this image makes him smile. It's certainly possible that this little flicker of happiness will have some ripple effect on the man's day, but essentially this seems to be an isolated moment. Another man sees this same baby but feels something very different. The prettiness of this picture touches him in a painful way. Maybe this scene reminds him (consciously or unconsciously) that his own mother had to work weekdays and couldn't spend her afternoons with him in the park—or that he himself doesn't get to spend much time with his own son. Maybe the fact that this child seems so privileged and protected makes him angry at how unfair the world is. Maybe the child brings to mind a love that he lost and the children he never had. These are the kinds of emotions that the Gate of Emotion helps us deconstruct. Rather than censoring these difficult emotions (and feeling guilty about them), we can learn to look at them in an accepting manner, as expressions of our deepest needs. Feelings are energy, creative vibrations, forces that create action, connection, visions and manifestations. Feelings create reality. In this chapter, I will use the words "feelings" and "emotions" interchangeably.

The heart, home to our emotions, is innocent and direct. When it is open, it is a source of love and joy, a generator of playful bliss and creative impulses. When the heart is closed, caged, or repressed, our life force is blocked. In other words, when we are not emotionally open, speaking, and breathing, we are not fully alive; we are simply existing. The heart is also the master of our physical reality—it conducts the music, which is the energy of our being. All physical manifestations are informed and affected by our feelings. If we are committed to being emotionally alive and physically healthy, we must recover and release the heart so it can return to its open and magical nature.

We need to accept all of our feelings, including the ones that are difficult and painful. Accepting and understanding our feelings helps us release or restructure them. Feelings help us survive, express, and transform. Each feeling contributes to our understanding of ourselves, others, and life. For example, sadness can inform us of unfulfilled needs and longings, and it can move us to find fulfillment for them. Anger might inform us about our boundaries and a possible violation of them. Fear can alarm us or teach us to find courage. And so on. The poetic, ecstatic, and inspiring moments of our lives are born out of our ability to feel.

Since all feelings and emotions spring from the same source, our emotional center, the fact is that when you shut down the difficult ones like pain, fear or anger, you will shut down the blissful ones as well. There is no way around this fact; no cheating will help. Each one of us needs to choose which we commit to—an open or closed heart. By committing to the process of opening the heart, we begin to step slowly into a greater state of openness and vulnerability. Feelings and emotions are energies. Energy is indestructible; it does not die; it only changes form. We can bury our feelings, repress or deny them, but we can never kill them. They will keep haunting us and will manifest themselves in our body, behavior, and everyday life. The good news is that since energy transforms, we can shift the energy of feelings from negative to positive.

To create a receptive heart, all feelings must be accepted, experienced, and allowed to move through and be released. That is how feelings integrate feelings in a healthy way. The Four Magic "E's"—Experience, Explore, Express, and Empower—which I alluded to at the beginning of the book, offer guidelines to emotional receptivity. I will briefly define all four, and will elaborate on them as the chapter unfolds.

The Four Magic "E's" unfold in the following order:

1. EXPERIENCE

Learn to fully experience your feelings and emotions. Experience means the kind of surrender that involves your body, mind, and soul. Some feelings can be too scary or overwhelming to fully experience without guidance. Deeply painful emotions that might be connected to severe trauma or intense rage need to be allowed into experience slowly, peeled away carefully, layer by layer. Use your judgment and awareness to discern whether you need emotional counseling. If you do, give yourself the gift of professional help—it can save you years of suffering.

The loving compassion of your Expanded Self and its ability to witness can help you in the process of experiencing, understanding, and releasing your feelings. When emotions arise, whether you are in counseling or working by yourself, teach yourself to experience them in the purest form. Remember feelings are not necessarily logical or fair; they just are. Much like the world of dreams, the world of feelings has its own logic. It is a magical, wild, and tender world. We are taught to be suspicious, condescending, and even dismissive of our feelings. Most cultures promote the repression of feelings, and Western society encourages shallow façades over emotional authenticity. It is extremely important tolearn to attend to the unpleasant feelings that we tend to resist. Wouldn't it be wonderful if we could feel purely the way children do, without self-judgment or self-consciousness?

Experiencing feelings does not mean reacting, exploding, acting out, or even sharing them. It is a private event that happens within you. You might find yourself crying, shaking, screaming into a pillow or at God. Whatever occurs, it is between you and your soul, or you and your counselor. Hopefully, throughout the experience your Expanded Self is witnessing your Emotional Self with nonjudgmental kindness, thus helping the emotions move through, flow, and be released.

2. EXPLORE

After you have experienced a feeling, it is time to explore it. Begin by asking the following questions: "Why I am feeling this way?" "When do I feel this way?" "Since when do I remember myself feeling this way?" What is the need, the desire, or the longing that is expressed in this feeling? When you understand the need behind an emotion you can find a healthy way to fulfill it. Allow yourself to free-associate or go down memory lane. The purpose is to find out the source of the emotion you have experienced. Allow for a deeper understanding of the emotion to emerge, insights, and "aha!" moments.

3. EXPRESS

A true expression of an emotion would never take the form of blaming, dumping, attacking, or victimizing yourself or others. All the above are actually ways of avoiding true expression. Some people confuse anger and blame. Anger is different from blame. If someone has truly wronged you, the natural feeling is anger, and assertion of personal boundaries is appropriate. For example, if your business partner betrayed your trust by making a deal behind your back that you should have been a part of, it is natural and appropriate for you to express your feelings and assert your rights. On the other hand, if you make it all about blaming your partner, you are actually not expressing your feelings. I will address this distinction further in the Gate of Dialogue.

Use writing, drawing, moving, sounds, or sharing to find an authentic and effective form of expression. When communicating an emotion to another person, make sure that you state your feelings as clearly as possible, acknowledging to him or to her that this is your subjective experience. Speak using the Four Magic "I's": I Feel, I Think, I Need, and I Want. This will keep the communication personal and authentic and avoid putting the focus or blame on the other. More on the Four Magic "I's" later.

Expressing your feelings to another person must be followed by listening to them and taking in their feelings and/or their reaction to your expression. Communication is a two-way street. Both our listening and expressing must be developed. As we summon the courage to confront the things that scar us, it becomes easier to empathize with the feelings and needs of others.

4. EMPOWER

Your Expanded Self is the eternally loving, wise witness. Your emotions come and go. Your defensiveness is a construct. Your true wisdom lives in Your Expanded Self. Listen to your emotions with the ears of your Expanded Self. Your emotions tell you, if you listen carefully, what you truly need and desire. Use the insights you reached in the exploring stage to acknowledge your needs and take responsibility for them in a constructive, creative way. Your Expanded Self is your inner parent, best friend, truest lover, and most effective healer. It is the bridge between your Emotional Self and Universal Consciousness. Learn to use the love and the guidance of your Expanded Self to reclaim wholeness and happiness. It helps you fulfill your needs, release emotions, express creatively, and create. Later, the Gate of Dialogue will further explore the relationship between your Expanded Self and your Emotional Self and will provide tips and tools to help nurture and guide yourself.

The heart's fulfillment is our most passionate quest and our sacred right. Someone asked me once to explain the difference between happiness and fulfillment. The way I see it, fulfillment is the state of being that is the result of following our deepest dreams, desires, and needs in a dedicated manner. Happiness is a feeling of joy that can be inspired by any simple daily experience or by just being. Most of us long for emotional freedom, the ability to feel freely and express creatively. If we commit to it and practice daily, we can regain personal authenticity and a free flow of feelings. To feel deeply and honestly is to be fulfilled. Recovering an open heart is called the "hard work miracle," and indeed it is.

We can think of feelings as colors or musical notes. They merge into each other to create emotional landscapes, some dark and oppressive, others passionate and exuberant, yet others tender and peaceful. These inner emotional landscapes move, shift, and dissolve into each other constantly. If we are free emotionally, the flow of our feelings occurs effortlessly. On the other hand, if our emotional fluidity is blocked or repressed, we might experience being stuck in the same landscape with the same colors.

We have primary colors—red, blue, and yellow—with which we create many secondary colors. On the emotional scale, I define seven primary emotions out of which all of the secondary emotions spring. The first three, I call the Dark Emotions: Fear, Pain, and Anger. The fourth, I call the Bridge Emotion: Need, or Longing. And the final three are the Light Emotions: Joy, Love, and Peace. Out of these seven primary emotions, endless combinations are born. For example, pain combined with anger can give us Frustration. Fear combined with pain can create a feeling of Hopelessness. Fear combined with anger can create Rage. Of course, the Dark and Light Emotions can intertwine and create interesting combinations. Imagine a combination of pain and joy, or the anger and love combination we are all familiar with. The list goes on.

I call Need (longing, heart desire) the Bridge Emotion, because it acts as an intermediary between the Dark Emotions and the Light Emotions. If you can experience the need that hides in the belly of fear, pain, or anger, and you can work with it through the Four Magic "E's" discussed above, then a Dark Emotion will transform into a Light Emotion. For example, let's say that you are intensely angry with your spouse. I suggest that you take yourself through the process of the Four Magic "E's". You might find that underneath the anger there is hurt or disappointment—maybe an old hurt that was triggered by a present incident. Looking even deeper, you may find that underneath the old hurt, there is an unfulfilled need, let's say to be listened to. Once you find the need, accept it, acknowledge it, and let it be. Some needs are fulfilled just by us feeling and acknowledging them.

Some are fulfilled by expression or actions. This becomes clear to you when you allow a need to be. You, your Expanded Self, can empower your Emotional Self in processing needs and feelings.

Here are four simple steps to use as a guideline while you navigate emotional situations concerning others:

- Learn to listen to your own need with love (feel, breathe, let it be).
- Ponder ways to fulfill it; most of the time it is simply in need of the loving attention that you, your Expanded Self, can give to yourself.
- If you need to express your need to another person, engage in a dialogue with your partner and explain your need, asking for his or her heartfelt attention.
- Listen to your partner's reactions and feelings.
- Find a mutually fulfilling way to address both partners' needs.

By the end of the process, your anger will be transformed, and you will feel empowered. Even if you are not able to address a need fully by yourself or with your partner, the act of taking responsibility for it is empowering. Keep moving forward to discover more of what is possible.

EXERCISE: Using the Four Magic "E's"

I have asked you to choose a theme to work through while you are reading the book. Hopefully you read the Gate of the Body chapter with your theme in mind and were able to uncover something new about it. Let's get back to your theme. Choose one feeling that is obviously present within your theme. For example, if your theme is Self-Doubt (feeling like you are not good enough), ask yourself what is the most obvious and dominant feeling that you experience within this theme. It might be fear of failure, hopelessness, pain, shame, or self-hate. It could be a combination of a few feelings. Choose one of them, and take it through the process of the Four Magic "E's."

During the first stage, **experience** the feeling as fully as possible (this might not be a pleasant moment, but it is necessary). Notice how it feels in your body, energy, and in your emotional center. What do you feel like doing when you are in this feeling? How do you experience yourself, other people, and your environment? What images come to your mind? What are the thoughts and beliefs that are connected to this feeling? In this stage, try not to rationalize or analyze your feelings, just stay on a gut level.

In the next stage, **explore**, ask yourself questions about the origin of the feeling. Intuitively sense the answers, free-associate, allow memories and insights to come up, and write down some notes.

Then continue to the third stage, **express**. By the way, you don't have to go through the whole process in one sitting unless you want to. You can work through stages one and two in one day and move to three and four the next. When you are expressing the feeling, keep it totally private at first. You can write, draw, move, make sound, or release the feeling through crying or pounding—anything that allows you to express the emotion and experience a release. While expressing the feeling, sense the need that hides at the heart of it. If we go back to our example of self-doubt, the need is obviously to trust one's worth and one's expression.

Once you realize the need, move into the fourth stage: **empower**. Let's say that you are the person in the example, you would ask yourself, "What would empower me to begin to trust my worth?" Your Expanded Self is your true healer and coach. It is the one that knows your worth and can relax your self-doubts. Sit in that place always in order to free your Emotional Self, and from that place inside yourself:

- Write a list of empowering ideas.
- Engage in a positive internal dialogue.
- Do an inner dialogue between you and another person, one who seems to be directly connected to the need that you have discovered. Tell them how you feel. Many times, this kind of inner expression helps release and defuse the feelings.
- If after doing that you still feel it is important to share your need with another person, then discuss it with them as authentically and honestly as possible.

The art and the craft of inner and outer dialogue will be covered fully in the next chapter, The Gate of Dialogue.

> ••• Reflection Pause •••
>
> What do you notice about the feeling you worked with after you have completed the Four Magic "E's" process?

The Biology of Feelings

Everything exists within the unified field of consciousness and energy. All is connected to all. Thus, feelings are a whole-body experience. Every cell feels, and every feeling registers in each cell.

When we have a thought or feeling, our brain makes a set of chemicals known as neuropeptides— "neuro" because they were first found in the brain, "peptides" because they are protein like molecules. Brain cells speak to one another through these chemical messengers. They are sending and receiving communications, in a similar manner to how we dialogue with one another. There are receptors for these messengers on the surface of brain cells. When a cell wants to speak to another cell, it sends a neuropeptide that is received by the other cell's receptor, and communication is achieved.

At first, scientist believed that this communication was unique to brain cells. Later they discovered that these "receptors" exist on cells throughout the body. They also discovered that other cells generate the same chemical messengers as the brain. As it turns out, our whole body is thinking, feeling, and talking to itself constantly. We have a body that is a master communicator. Feeling and thinking is not only in the brain; every cell in our body participates. Every event is a communal one. When we say, "I have a gut feeling," we are not speaking metaphorically; our gut makes the same chemicals that our brain makes when it thinks. Our gut is talking to us. It is communicating its messages to the whole body, and we know how accurate "gut" feelings are.

Another example is our immune system. Its cells have receptors that respond to chemical messengers when we are joyful, anxious, or peaceful; our immune cells are receiving the messages and are thinking and feeling with us. They are also producing chemical messengers to communicate to our whole body/mind. As we can see, immune cells are moving around in the body as a circulating nervous system. They are listening to every move within and without, ready to send, receive, and respond immediately. Immune cells are like a mother who is attuned to her young child; she knows its need even before it does.

Two additional communication systems in the body that carry feelings are the nervous system, with its neurotransmitters moving at the speed of electricity, and the endocrine system with its hormonal messengers. This symphony of communication is totally orchestrated, and all systems work together in absolute coordination. Our emotions affect our biology, and when biological, energetic patterns are established, they maintain the emotions that originated them. These two, emotions and biology, feed into each other. If a pattern is a negative one—for example, repressed anger that creates an ulcer—it calls for a shift.

We can think of the brain as the CEO of the mind/body system: the chief organizer. It has two distinct, vertically divided hemispheres: right brain and left brain. These are connected with a cross wire located at the center of the brain. The brain is also partitioned into three horizontally divided segments. The "low-brain" is referred to as the "reptilian-brain," and deals with unconscious body functions. The "mid-brain," also known as the "mammalian-brain," contains the limbic system—a sophisticated electronic network that provides the emotional charge to our experience. This part of the brain processes our emotional responses. It contains within it, the hypothalamus, which controls the pituitary gland, the director of hormonal equilibrium. Biology, emotions, and hormones meet here.

The "upper-brain," also called the neocortex, guides functions of thought and rationality. It projects meaning onto our experiences. This part of the brain acquires its material from the sensory low-brain and the feeling mid-brain and out of this material, it forges stories and meaning. It appears as if the mid-brain's center of emotions is the connector between meaning (upper-brain) and body (low-brain). So, we can say that feelings are the link between mind and body.

As previously mentioned, every experience generates neuropeptides, which receive information from each of the three sections of the brain. The brain operates as a whole, and its responses keep all information bits united. It is important to understand that memory lives throughout the body. Our cells maintain the memory of all our experiences and store it. The information carrying neuropeptides are the mind-body link. If we understand that, we realize that change must work as a whole-body experience. It must involve awareness, emotions, energy, expression, and creativity to fully register.

When balanced, our body thinks, feels, communicates, and maintains all functions. It creates the precise antibody for each invader that threatens it and it's all done with absolute precision—right dose, right time, right organ, with no side effects. When the communication breaks down or is imbalanced, we are in a state of disease. A balanced mind/body is quite amazing! What we are witnessing is consciousness in motion, or spirit in action. Our body is a microcosm of the in telligence permeating the entire universe. I feel tremendous gratitude and awe whenever I take a minute to experience the miracle that is life.

The Wounded Heart

Being alive and human is quite risky. The possibilities of being hurt, disappointed, and devastated wait at every corner, and the probability of growing up bent out of shape is undeniable. Our hearts will not escape the wounds caused by living. To assist us in navigating the stormy waters of life, we are endowed with the capability for awareness, the built-in urge for growth, and the innate blueprint of wholeness. These attributes are there to help us transform our experiences, no matter how difficult they are, into lessons learned and inner power. Our mind-body system has a blueprint, which guides it toward balance and harmony when it functions correctly, hence the tendency to maintain wholeness. Our system also exhibits a strong orientation toward survival, which means that any intense feeling that threatens our emotional and physical survival will be repressed, split, and encapsulated automatically in order to keep it out of consciousness.

> ••• Reflection Pause •••
>
> How are your emotions affecting your body? Choose an emotion connected to your theme. Meditate on its effects on your body. Write down specific symptoms, manifestations, and reactions within your body that are connected to this emotion.

The two tendencies complement each other: survival and wholeness. We need to respect both of these aspects if we are to grow and thrive. The twist is this: emotions that were buried mostly in the early stages of life for the sake of survival later become the very threat to our survival. This is where survival and wholeness clash. Repressed emotions generate a tremendous amount of stress and anxiety in our system. They short-circuit our energy field, creating pockets of disconnected tissue. They cause psychological fragmentation within us and separation between ourselves and the world. All of this creates a fertile ground for physical and mental disease.

So, what are we to do? We must survive first, but then we shouldn't get stuck in the old survival mode. We should use the guidelines of our Expanded Self and move forward to integrate ourselves back into wholeness—our innate state. Within the state of wholeness we still, naturally and instinctively, guard our survival and keep growing. These two begin to complement each other rather than clash.

Where Does It All Start?

As children, we are innocent beings, completely dependent on our parents or caretakers. They are the gods of our lives. When they, out of their own woundedness, hurt us (neglect, reject, abuse, control, shame, or manipulate) we are devastated. At a very young age, it is difficult to see our parents' shortcomings. They are our role models, perfect and just, and their behavior toward us reflects our worth. As children, we learn to know ourselves through their eyes and their relationship with us. Yes, there are grandparents, siblings, cousins, neighbors, friends, classmates, teachers, and so forth—even dogs and cats—that can help define us. Nevertheless, our parents are major influences. When they are unloving, we assume we are not lovable and are defective in some way.

The effect of our parents on our feelings starts before we are born. From the sixth month on, and perhaps earlier, the unborn child leads an emotionally active life. We are affected by the mental stresses, strong emotions, and attitudes of the parents. Then we are born. It is a known fact that the process of birth is a traumatic event. It takes about two and half months for the infant to slowly come out of the birth shock. Most of us carry unresolved fragments from birth trauma repressed in our system. Now, as young beings at the start of our life's journey, we are vulnerable to the effects of our physical and energetic surroundings, our parents, and the society and culture into which we are born. Most of all, we are at the mercy of the people we love most. Even if you believe, as I do, that the soul chooses its conditions (specific culture and society and specific childhood environment) in order to leverage its evolution, the woundedness of the heart is real and difficult, and it takes much effort to heal.

We are motivated by the need to avoid pain. Painful experiences are tagged for self-protection and stored away from consciousness. As mentioned before, our system has the ability to split off and disassociate from painful feelings. It is a survival tactic. The energetic imprint and the memory of a painful experience are split into fragments in order to neutralize its impact. Then the fragments or the bits of emotional information are repressed and tucked away. They stay within our system but away from our consciousness. Once that is accomplished, we will not feel the pain. However, the fragments are still floating within our nervous system, generating anxiety and tension and locking certain bodily responses into the tissues. Emotions are energy, and the energy when repressed does not die. Although we are not feeling the pain or remembering the experience, all the fragments of the emotional experience are alive, active, and become a part in the creation of ourselves and our world view.

Based on our experience, repressed or not, we form interpretations, beliefs, patterns of behavior, and expectations. Thus, we ultimately create our view of the past, our experiences of the present, and our future. We can call the internal canvas of our assumed reality the "inner map." By that, I mean the total mind-body way of experiencing and interacting with self and life. Our inner map affects the way we see, feel, and interact with reality. Our interpretation of reality generates, as we know, all kinds of biochemical reactions. These, in turn, reinforce our interpretation. And the cycle goes on, as shown below:

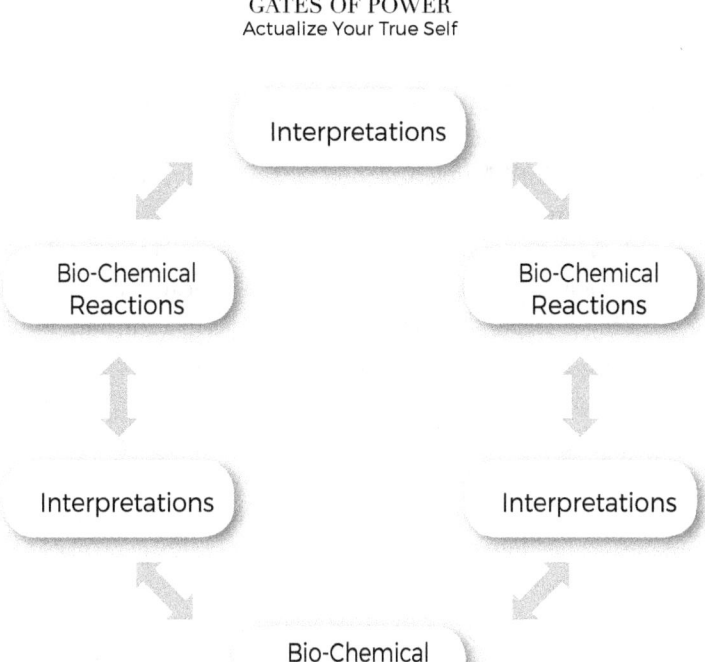

The cycle of interpretations and biochemical reactions

Our self-created inner map is driving us to re-create situations in our lives that reflect it. For example, if you felt betrayed or abandoned as a child, you probably will interpret the experience as a bitter fact of life: "People who I care about betray and abandon me." The full emotional impact of the experience might have been repressed; still, the interpretation has created a set of beliefs and a pattern of defensive behavior. You might be closed off to intimate connections out of fear of betrayal, and/or you might be working hard to keep your loved ones happy at any cost in order to avoid abandonment. Every aspect of your life is affected by the inner map that this experience generated. You will eventually re-create situations that reflect betrayal and abandonment because you are navigating your life by this inner map. All new input will be experienced through this existing "prism," and as a result you will not be able to experience reality freshly.

Another example: A physically abused child placed in a foster home might have a hard time accepting the genuine loving touch of an adoptive mother. She might stay locked into an abusive inner reality. The past becomes our present and our future.

We come into the world with a relatively wide open nervous system, and we absorb and internalize myriad negative and limiting impressions and experiences. These occupy our being, impacting our mind, body, and spirit. Unresolved traumatic events or unmet needs are continuously re-created and repeated long after the traumatic circumstances have changed. The repetition of difficult or unsatisfying experiences reinforces the pain. The repeated experiences build on each other, creating a deeper devastation. This puts us in a constant state of conflict between our desire to validate our beliefs and the frustration we experience in situations that we consciously or unconsciously create. It is a "lose-lose" situation.

Fortunately, the discomfort drives us to search for answers. Many of us seek help when we realize that we are trapped in our repetitious, self-created hell. That is when we begin to move forward toward change. We (our Expanded Self) possess tremendous healing capacities, and change is always available to us.

> ••• **Reflection Pause** •••
>
> Are you re-creating painful or unsatisfying experiences? If you are, choose one specific experience connected to the theme you are working through, and write it down. Can you make a connection between the repeated pattern and a difficult experience that might have originated it? Write down your experiences.

One of my clients, who I will call Sam, grew up in a physically and emotionally violent home. He came to me because of severe anxiety attacks. Sam described himself as a lonely and isolated child, emotionally homeless, living in a war zone bound by fear and a total sense of helplessness. He grew up to see the world as unsafe and to experience people as hurtful and untrustworthy.

Being painfully shy and extremely vulnerable, he found it difficult to express himself. He shared with me that the few intimate partners he had had were men who were neglectful or abusive. It was clear to me, and later to him, that he was repeating his childhood relationship with his father, a drug addict who had violent fits of anger. Sam saw his mom being beaten on a regular basis. He and his two sisters were terrified of him. They would be beaten over any behavior that was interpreted as disobedience. Most of the abuse seemed to come out of nowhere. and the children lived in constant fear, unable to predict their father's next attack. Ted shared with me a memory of hiding in the closet for a whole night, fearing for his life because his father had threatened to kill him. He then snuck out and ran away from home to his uncle's house, seeking shelter for a few days.

Sam admitted to me that over the years, he'd become increasingly more desperate and hopeless about finding a love partner. It took a little while to help him see that he was living in the world of his childhood and re-creating it, imprisoned by fear and lack of self-worth. He needed to discover that his current view of life was not the only possible one. At some point, he made the important distinction between his current perspective and other possibilities available to him. He no longer identified his experience as the "truth about life," and he was willing to shift his perspective.

We explored his childhood experiences and the interpretation, beliefs, and behaviors that had sprung out of these experiences. The exploration was cognitive and then experiential, physical and expressive. All the Gates were involved in his process of re-experiencing and realigning. Feelings, memories, and belief are energetic experiences. In order to reshape them, we need to go beyond just understanding them intellectually. We need to move into the center of the heart, unlock the door, be moved, express, release, and confront, thereby shifting the energy patterns. We need to discover and re-create. When we uncover our emotions, we unlock a powerful force that helps us break the hold of the old inner maps and loosen the grip of their negative beliefs and behaviors.

Sam resisted the process in the beginning. He was understandably afraid to relive the pain of his childhood. Slowly, one step at a time, with the help of his Expanded Self, he found the courage to dive deeper. Every time he allowed himself to experience a part of his past, he was able to release some of the grief and feel freer and more forgiving toward himself and his father. He learned to acknowledge and respect his emotional needs and gained skills of self-parenting. His inner dialogue shifted to being constructive and loving. At present, he is enjoying the company of some new friends and is enjoying a loyal and fulfilling relationship with a life partner. In the process of Sam's healing, as in all realigning processes, the soul seeks to recognize its essence and source. We long to know who we truly are, beyond the obvious manifestation of our body and mind. We are cut from the same cloth as Universal Consciousness. We are one with it. Our Expanded Self has the ability to directly experience this oneness.

Mending the Heart

How do we return to the original simplicity and authenticity of our Emotional Self? What took us away from it was our defense against pain and the belief that we need to be different from what we truly are in order to receive love and survive. But what will bring us back to our emotional core is to pass through the Gate of our repressed pain and in doing so, liberate ourselves from the fear it engenders in us.

We all have experienced the feeling of dreading someone or something so much so that we are paralyzed by fear. Then, for whatever reason, we decide to confront the person or the thing we dread most. We muster the courage and go through with it. A sense of relief and freedom follows—a total shift in the mind/body state. It is the same when it comes to liberating the heart. It takes courage to confront old painful experiences. When we relive them with awareness, compassion, and creative intuition, we can glean lessons of strength and wisdom. we pass through and beyond our pains and fears, we come to experience our unboundedness and ultimately our eternal and infinite nature. You might note that even when things don't work out as we'd like after a big confrontation, they're rarely as bad as our worst-case scenarios; and even when they are, we feel better for having expressed ourselves and listened to the other.

What Helps Our Emotional Self Find The Courage To Feel?

The aspect of our being that I refer to as the Expanded Self is our helper. Imagine a loving hand, a reassuring voice, a cheerleader, and a mentor who is there to take you through fears, pains, and uncertainty. There is no need to imagine; we have all that and more available to us within our Expanded Self. The Expanded Self is the compassionate witness within. It is the connector between our individual consciousness and the Universal Mind. We can think of it as the place within our consciousness where universal wisdom and knowledge lives, the One-Self reflected and expressed within our human self. This is our ultimate healer. Your Emotional Self needs the loving guidance of your Expanded Self in order to release its pain and negativity. Most of us get glimpses of the power and beauty of our Expanded Self, but we don't know how to utilize its healing wisdom to liberate our Emotional Self.

The chapter about the Gate of Dialogue will further explain how to consciously create a bond, a channel of communication between the Expanded

Self and the Emotional Self. For now, draw on your experience of the guiding intuitive voice within you. We all have experienced it. It feels like a good inner parent or a kind friend. When you say to yourself, *Breathe. Calm down, and count to 10,* it is your Expanded Self coaching your Emotional Self. When you find yourself giving a friend a surprisingly wise council and are able to see straight to the root of the problem, you are speaking from your Expanded Self. When you are able to go beyond your comfort and your personal desires to help someone in need, it is your Expanded Self that takes you there. And the list goes on. While reading the next few pages, connect to that part of yourself, as well as to your emotions. Your Expanded Self will assist you in understanding your emotions and attending to them.

Freeing the Emotional Self

All the stages of our evolution are living within our Emotional Self: the baby, the child, the adolescent, and the adult. Nurturing, parental love is necessary through out our emotional development, especially in the early stages. When any one of these stages is disrupted, our needs are not met and our feelings become fragmented. As a result, our natural development is compromised, and the smooth transition from stage to stage is interrupted. It makes sense that it is beneficial to access the earliest stage that was disrupted. By re-experiencing the emotional reality of it, including unmet needs, pain, and fear, we release repressed emotions and give ourselves the nurturance needed to heal and complete that stage successfully.

At a young age, when our needs are not met, we get angry. This anger is a natural reaction. It is a cry for help and a protest against being ignored. Most of us were trained to repress pain and anger. When these feelings are repressed, excess neurotransmitters and other neurochemicals flood the brain and the whole system. Our receptors get clogged. As a result, a state of toxicity develops, which is a source of future emotional and physical disease.

The excess of neurotransmitters overexcites the nervous system, causing symptoms that range from mild anxiety to mania or violent feelings. These symptoms are healing events, and it's best if they are not suppressed. If handled properly, these symptoms will escalate to actual violence. When pain and anger are trying to surface and release, it is important to redirect these emotions toward our memories of the original abusers or wrongdoers. I stress this should be done as part of a therapeutic process and not any other way. Only when the anger and pain are expressed within a therapeutic process toward whoever feels like the real source can these feelings be released effectively.

At times, it takes some soul-searching and peeling of layers to truly discover why we are angry. Misdirected anger is very common. We get triggered by our spouse, a neighbor, or the news. Instead of looking for the origin of our anger, we explode or attack the trigger. These explosions can be called vicarious detoxification crises. Misdirected explosions don't clear repressed emotions; they only serve to continue the cycle of toxicity and our inner suffering.

We need to train ourselves to recognize the origins of our anger. When we realize that we are overreacting, we need to stop and look within, identify our emotions, and in a private, expressive, and creative way, address the source of our disgruntled feelings. It takes discipline to refrain from reacting to the present moment's trigger. Whatever triggered it, it is only a reminder of an unresolved relationship or event in the past.

Addressing the source of your anger is a private process that you do as part of your inner work. I am *not* suggesting that you rage against your real parent in person, even if they are the original abuser. The emotions are directed toward the parent *in your memories*. It helps to keep in mind that your parents did what they were able to do at the time. They have probably changed and transformed since then. The present-time parent might be very different from the parents you have experienced in your childhood. By redirecting your angry emotions, you are allowing yourself to become the child that could not express themselves in the past, and are encouraging the very expression of feelings and needs that are still within you, waiting to be released and acknowledged. All of this happens as a result of your private or counseling inner work.

Two important elements are achieved by this process. First, you get in touch with an important part of yourself that was repressed and have the opportunity to heal and integrate it; second, you relieve the body from an overloaded pressure created by repressed emotions. Over time, this process dissipates the overload from the past and grounds us in the present. We are digging up the buried heart and teaching ourselves to feel. The process can be painful, but the loving guidance and awareness of our Expanded Self helps us release blocked emotions and reintegrate ourselves.

EXERCISE

Here are four steps to effectively clear emotional overload. These are done in the privacy of inner work or with a counselor and are not always easy to accomplish, but with practice, you can master them, and you will be happy that you did.

1. Recognize when you are overreacting. Overreacting means that your emotional reaction to a situation, a person, an event, or a fact is far more intense than the moment calls for.
2. Refrain from actively reacting to the present trigger. It is only an echo, a reminder of an unresolved relationship or event from the past.
3. Take time to actually feel your feelings and look within for the origin of your anger. See if you can trace it to an early experience. (I suggest that you use the first two of the Magic "E's"—Experience and Explore—to accomplish this.) Many times, it can be difficult to trace the origin of an intense feeling and the best most of us could hope for (at least without professional help and years of psychoanalysis) is to identify a parallel experience from the past that stirred a similar emotion.
4. Do the internal work of redirecting your emotions in an expressive way to address the original upset. (Again, here, I suggest you use the third and fourth Magic "E"—Express and Empower.)

The action of accessing an early stage of development is called regression. We consciously regress to an early stage in order to heal and complete it. I am referring to emotional and physical regression, not just cognitive understanding. When we integrate on an emotional level the issues dissolve, because our emotions are able to gather their fragments and find expression. Traumatic experiences are fragmented by our psyche as a way of protecting us from them. The process of regression allows us to slowly gather the fragments of a traumatic event and process them properly. Contained within the loving space of our Expanded Self, our emotions are honored, understood, and accepted. Our needs are acknowledged and met, and our inner sense of security and trust grows. We begin to feel comfortable with who we are.

One of the methods I trained in was Primal Therapy. This method uses regression to facilitate healing. Having used the process of regression with clients for many years, I am still amazed by its effectiveness. I have witnessed clients shake, sweat, scream, and sob, as memories of early pain invade their consciousness. I find that it is tremendously beneficial to use a gentle and directed process of regression to work through an early stage of development that had trauma.

The power of regression lies in the fact that when you regress to an early stage, you naturally drop your masks, façades, and most of your defensive behavior. You experience a physical, energetic, and emotional shift; there is a certain nakedness and rawness that is characteristic of this experience. The release of pain or anger can be quite thorough. Following an experience of regression, I have found that my clients are much more relaxed and present. Their breathing becomes deeper, as if a heavy load has lifted from the soul. The adult mindset alone can compensate for trauma but not truly release it; it takes an emotional and physical regression to fully accomplish the process.

One should not attempt to regress without professional help. Regression can feel scary and overwhelming. The process should be conducted after appropriate preparation with a trained counselor. The good news is, after you have done this kind of work under guidance, you can move into intense emotional states alone, without fear, because you have been there and "survived." You learn to handle intense feelings and are less afraid of them. I train clients to use their Expanded Self as their facilitator when they need to do emotional work by themselves.

Our emotional journey involves leaving the comfortable and known realms to cross over the barrier of fear and, at times, to descend into the valley of what feels like death and despair. Ultimately, we return renewed. The journey takes us to the place we're most afraid of, which is the experience of being alone or unloved. To a young child, and even to an adult, this experience equals emotional death. If you have struggled for love, care, or acceptance all your life, you have probably been doing everything possible to get it. Your effort involves avoiding the black hole within your soul. The regression work will take you to that black hole, and maybe, for the first time ever, you will feel it. Confronting it, you begin to let go of the struggle for love and realize, slowly but surely, that love lives within you, flows to you, from you, and all around you. The end of the struggle for love feels like a form of death. We let go of a life-long struggle and die to our old self to give birth to our next self. Death is a necessary part of the renewal of life. Freedom is contingent on our ability to let go daily of the old and rediscover the new. The courage to feel develops with practice, and the ability to practice comes from our desire and commitment to this process.

> **••• Reflection Pause •••**
>
> How do you treat your emotions when they surface? Choose a specific emotion that came up for you recently, and note the way you have handled it. Did you brush it off, avoid it, repress it, or did you take a minute to sit and feel it?

Getting to Know Our Emotional Self

One of the ways to find out about your emotions is to visit them regularly, pay attention to them when they surface, listen carefully, and write down a few lines about certain emotions that moved you. Taking time to acknowledge emotions is a way of respecting them. Respect leads to understanding and acceptance. Emotions that are understood and accepted move more freely, and are more easilyreleased and transformed.

A guided visualization I often use with clients helps to uncover the secrets of our Emotional Self. It is called "Visiting the Home of Your Feelings," the place within your Emotional Self where all your experiences and emotions live. This "home" contains many "rooms," and each one reveals landscapes, images, colors, people and objects—bits of memories, smells, sounds, and words. Each room is never quite the same when you visit it again; it continues to reveal itself, taking you to new and familiar realms. There is the Room of Fear, the Room of Pain, the Room of Need, the Room of Peace, the Room of Sexuality, the Room of Loneliness, the Room of Adventure, and so on. As you can see, it is a vast home.

When I use this visualization, I always suggest to clients to visit one specific room at a time, and choose the one they feel they need to visit most at the time of the exercise. They are always surprised by what is revealed to them when they enter the room they choose. Below are the guidelines for this exercise if you wish to do it at home by yourself.

EXERCISE: Visiting The Home of Your Feelings

1. Lie down on your back in a comfortable position. Make sure that you will not be interrupted for the next 30–45 minutes.

2. Start with general relaxation. First, work to relax your body and all of its parts, then, relax your mind by suggesting to yourself that it is time to drop thoughts and create stillness. Then center in on your breath and begin to follow your breath up and down.

3. Once you feel you are relaxed, imagine walking on a wide, tree-lined country road. It is a sunny day, and you are walking to the home of your feelings. After a minute or two of imaginary walking, notice the home of your feelings from afar, at the end of the road. These images should come to you easily, directly, and spontaneously. Trust whatever comes up first!

4. As you approach the home of your feelings, notice what it is it made of, where it is located, and what is around it. Allow yourself to see as many details as possible: the colors of the walls, the surroundings, the path leading to it, the front door, and any objects around the home.

5. See yourself coming down the path to the front door and opening it. Notice if the door is locked or not. If it is locked, do you have the key? Once inside the home, notice the general feeling in it. Is it a pleasant, open, and lit environment? Or is it dark, brooding, dusty, or mysterious? Are there windows? Is there a basement or attic? Are there staircases leading anywhere?

6. As you are walking around the house, pick a room that you want to visit that is particularly connected to the theme you have been working with. Search the house to find this room. It may be in the basement, on the top floor, or down the hallway. For example, you may choose the Room of Self-doubt, the Room of Shame, or maybe the Room of Love and Intimacy.

7. When you have found this room—the room that would deepen your understanding about the feeling that you have chosen—open the door to the room, and step in. Take a minute to discover what is in the room. Do you see people? Who are they? What objects are there? Is the room completely empty? What's the feeling that you have when you stand in this room? The next few moments are especially important: If you allow yourself to experience whatever happens in this room, you will discover something new and important about this emotional space. Sometimes emotions that are repressed come to the surface. Memories can come up, imaginary figures may show their faces, and the voices and sounds of

your emotional past and future might come to you. Your subconscious is bringing forth images, symbols, and feelings, much like being in the state of a dream, so do not try to control it. Allow the experience to flow as it may. Most of the time, the journey has a natural beginning, middle and end. A sense of clarity and relief should follow.

8. Once you have completed the process, it is time to say good-bye to the room. Bear in mind that you may want to visit the room a few more times; saying good-bye really means "see you later." Come out of the room, walk to the front door, step out of the house, and begin to walk back to the country road that has taken you here—back into your actual reality.

This is a self-guided visualization—it can be done without any outside guidance. Feel free to experiment with it as a meditation on emotions, and follow the steps in the guidelines. Let go of rationalizations, expectations about the content and result of the exercise, and pre-conceived notions. Allow yourself to be surprised, and at the end of the exercise, take a minute to write down your thoughts about the exercise. I asked a client to record one of his visits to the "Home of the Feelings," and this is what he wrote:

■ ■ ■

I was walking along a country road on my way to the Home of My Feelings; trees lined the dirt road, and it was a beautiful sunny day. The closer I got to the house, the younger I became. By the time arrived I was a child again, probably around the age of 6 or 7. I recognized the white shingle house with the black-painted porch floor. As I entered the house, it was completely dark, cold, and drafty. I could tell no one had been there in a very long time, and there was no sign of life. On this particular journey to the house, I would be visiting the Room of My Fears. Even though the house was dark, I knew exactly where this Room of My Fears was located, and I walked through the dark to the door of this room.

I opened the door and sensed the stairs that led down to the cellar. I could not see anything, but I felt my childlike hand on the metal railing. I could feel the dampness coming up from the cellar. I momentarily froze before beginning my descent. I held on to the railing and walked down the steps. It was still dark, and I could not see anything at all. As I arrived at the bottom of the steps, I stepped into cold water. I could feel it around my feet, ankles, and calves. I stood there still gripping the railing. My vision began to adjust to the darkness, and a bit of light began to seep in. I could see some silhouettes a few feet in front of me, but could not recognize what they were. Slowly, the water at my feet began to withdraw, and more light infused the room. I could now see what was in front of me. There were four chairs lined in a row, and I could see that my stepmother, father, maternal grandfather, and grandmother sat in the chairs, respectively from my right to left.

I approached my stepmother first. She looked me in the eyes, held my hands, and began to tell me that she had come to this earth as a soul to cause me pain in order to make me stronger (I later learned in another meditation that she also wanted me to learn to have compassion for others and myself). As she looked at me, I felt and knew in every cell of my body that she really did love me and that she was speaking the truth.

Next, I stepped over to my dad, and he placed me on his lap and cradled me. I felt comforted and safe, as I always did as a child when he held me. I felt my stepmother's hand caressing the back of my head, and though I was not facing her, I could somehow see the look of love in her eyes. At this point, it was time for me to begin my return back. I stood in front of my grandfather and grandmother to say goodbye. I already knew what they represented for me. My grandfather was the one who ignited my imagination as a child. He was responsible for making me a dreamer. My grandmother represented safety, stability, and nurturance. My most vivid memory is of her in the kitchen on their farm with a bunch of women cooking for all the family when we would visit in the summertime.

I said my goodbyes and began my ascent up the stairs. As I opened the door at the top of the stairs, I was pleasantly startled to see that the house was now full of life, there was light everywhere, music, flowers, warmth, and color. I walked to the front door, went outside, and started to skip back up the dirt road—I felt happy! As I returned to the room where I began my meditation, I knew a healing had taken place. To this day, whenever I think of my stepmother, I don't see myself as her victim or see her as a villain. I know deep in my cells that as a soul she really did love me and came to teach me to be strong.

My client and I were both surprised and pleased with the peacefulness of the ending. A deep pain of an unresolved relationship was lifted.

The Ten Commandments for Attending to Your Emotions

1. **Practice Awareness:** Sit in the big armchair of your Expanded Self and witness. Feelings are the cause; conditions are the effect. The order of manifestation, which will be covered in detail in the Gate of Life Path chapter, is as follows: 1) Experience, 2) Emotions, 3) Interpretations of Experience, 4) Beliefs, 5) Behavior, 6) Actions, and 7) Reality. The best way to create something different or new is to shift the pattern at its source, which means we need to tap into the first two—Experience and Emotions. Without awareness, we cannot bring about shifts in consciousness.

    Notice what triggers your emotions. Begin to investigate the root of your responses. Notice your words. What is it that you say to yourself or to others? What is it that you think and feel about yourself, others, or life in general? What inner conversations shape your life, thoughts, beliefs, and assumptions, and reinforce your emotions? Identify your feeling and thinking patterns—which ones are expanded and joyful, and which are contracting and constricting? What is it that you enjoy? What makes you happy? What causes you to suffer? Choose to be the master of your inner map, rather than the victim of it. Awareness will help you shed what is unreal and unfulfilling. When you are aware, you are able to look at the reality that you have created, are creating, and want to create. Become accountable and responsible for your state of mind and body. Mastering your state of mind is like playing an instrument or learning a new skill: at first it takes a concerted effort, but over time it becomes

2. **Connect to the Source:** Your Expanded Self is your internal compass. By connecting to it, you can begin to find your way back to authentic self. Work with prayer, meditations, visualizations, dreams, and insights to connect to the Source of life.

Whatever and however you experience it, the Source is within you and all around you. The "Master Program" in your DNA is a memory of perfection and wholeness. It is never lost; it is only covered by distorted perceptions. Your Expanded Self will help you clear the clutter in your Master Program.

3. **Self-Acceptance and Self-Nurturing;** Your Expanded Self is a source of loving acceptance. Draw upon it to nourish yourself. Lack of self-acceptance is established early in life. The self-image that we internalize can be distorted. The need for outside approval dominates the world of a child or a young adult. When approval is not forthcoming, it compounds our self-criticism and disapproval, and the negative cycle feeds on itself. You must, therefore, a) Accept your life the way you have created it up until now. Take responsibility for it. This might not be an easy task. Regrets, a sense of self-betrayal, and self-blame can emerge when we face what we have created. Begin to forgive yourself. You have done the best you could. Take the pearls, learn the lessons, and use them to generate growth and strength. Be okay with being wrong. Embrace your mistakes. b) Allow yourself to make mistakes in the future. You will make them. You are a work in progress, and your journey is creative learning in action. Can you see the perfection in the now? Can you see that it all happened for the sake of your learning? Can you embrace your past and use it as a springboard to create your future? c) Relinquish blaming yourself and others. You are responsible for yourself. Make a commitment to get the tools you need to become the master of your inner and outer reality. d) Commit to self-love and care. Open your heart to yourself. Do this daily, as it takes practice to love oneself completely.

4. **Do the Emotional Work:** Commit to exploring and doing deep emotional work. It takes courage, discipline, and passion to achieve emotional freedom. Go beyond your comfort zone. Visit the roots of your emotions. Dive into playful or disturbing realms within you. Confront the demons, and

discover the joyful child, the hero, and the poet. Take the ultimate adventure into the inner realms. Make it a habit to forever be a "discoverer of the inner world." All things are waiting for you there. The deeper you understand your feelings, the better you understand others.

5. **Practice Self-Affirmation:** You are a child of the universe and a sanctuary for its expression. Inner beauty, grace, and power live in you and are expressed through you. Open your heart to this truth. You have the right to express, protect, choose, and create what is meaningful and important to you. You are worthy of manifesting your needs, desires, and dreams. It is your responsibility to establish healthy boundaries and to decide what is and is not acceptable in your life. You have the obligation to yourself to stand up for what you believe. Use your beliefs and talents to be a positive force in the world. You are not a puppet; you are the master! Pull your own strings and make up your own dance. This is what it's all about!

6. **Work Toward Self-Integration:** Self-integration means unifying the different aspects of ourselves so that they all work together as a team. Our three inner aspects—the Emotional Self, the Defensive Self, and the Expanded Self—are mostly out of sync before we do the integration work. Our Defensive Self is very concerned with survival; therefore, it represses parts of our Emotional Self that might threaten its agenda. Most of us are not really using our Expanded Self to negotiate and create harmony between the Emotional Self and the Defensive Self. Ideally, our Defensive Self is softened and nurtured. In the next chapter, The Gate of Dialogue, I will provide specific techniques for harmonizing the relationships among the three and creating a better integration.

7. **Develop Your Communication and Expression Skills:** We all know how important communication and expression are. Communication and expression skills are cultivated

throughout life. It's a daily learning. When you communicate your feelings, learn to use the Four Magic I's: I Feel, I Need, I Want, I Think. Avoid talking in "you" terms. When you are describing your experience using the Magic I's, you are taking responsibility for it, and you can be honest and authentic as you speak directly from your personal experience. Avoid blaming, dumping, judging, or attacking in your communication. As far as expression is concerned, you must differentiate between expression and reaction. When we are reacting emotionally, we are not expressing. We are mostly attacking, blaming, or dumping on others. The Four Magic E's covered in this chapter help you discern what you feel, why, and the best way to express yourself. The term that comes to mind is "grounded vulnerability." Stick to expressing and listening from the heart.

8. **Practice New Behaviors:** Part of the process of making changes and shifts in our life is creating and maintaining new patterns of behavior consistent with the changes we want to make. Our awareness and our emotional work inform us of what behavior works for us and what does not. Use the information that you collect from your inner work to further the practice of altering your behavior. When your behavior supports your growth and happiness, you inspire others to do the same.

9. **Learn Nonattachment:** "Desireless desire" describes the state of nonattachment. The state of nonattachment hap- be right, to prove, or to avoid pain. When we enjoy being, doing, planning, creating, and dreaming without getting attached to fame, acclaim, power, and status, we are free. These will enslave you, if allowed to determine who you are.

10. **Live for the Sake of Living:** When you are working on a project, it is natural to want results. You do need to accomplish, but do not tie your self-worth to anything you do. Do it for the sake of discovery, creativity, and fulfillment. These sources of enjoyment nurture the soul. You can passionately go after the results you desire, but be open and allow for the possibility of a different or better outcome. Things must happen organically. Be creative with the results that arise. There must always be an element of spontaneity and release in your existence.

11. **Use Your Emotions to Contribute:** Become emotionally generous to yourself and others. Open your heart to love and be loved. Enjoy and bring joy. Share and encourage others to share. Acknowledge yourself and others. Accept yourself and others. See yourself in others. Cultivate compassion, support, and understanding for yourself and others. The beauty of emotional generosity is that it creates a joy deeper than any other. Your feelings are your most precious gift! Enjoy them!

8

The Gate of Dialogue

Use your relationships as an instrument to express the highest and the best in you. ife is a canvas of dialogue. Within this canvas of energy and consciousness, we are in a constant flow of exchange. We are sustained by an ocean of intelligence and love, nurtured by it and connected through it. Human beings have created a sense of separation. We imagine ourselves to be separate from this nurturing fabric of Being. Of course, we're not, and by maintaining this sense of separation we are creating unnecessary suffering for ourselves. The root of this separation is our disconnection from ourselves. The tendency toward being separate, consciously or unconsciously, is disempowering and harmful. Unfortunately, it has become socially acceptable and is considered normal. We have developed automatic patterns that perpetuate our sense of separateness.

On Separation

Many of us live without an intimate relationship with the Universal Source within us. Our violent and destructive history as a race has been a painful learning process of growing and evolving. One of the most important lessons—maybe, *the* most important one—is to realize our union with the infinite consciousness that lives within our hearts. It has many names: the "I Am," the Eternal Self, the Superior Soul, the One Mind, God, the Creator, the Absolute, and so on. When we don't take time to cultivate an intimate relationship with the Source within our being, life becomes confusing and frustrating. We tend to seek a sense of gratification and validation from external sources in an effort to receive a sense of strength and connection. Doing so, we separate ourselves even farther from our own essential identity and, as a result, farther from our true inner power, love, and wisdom.

Let's take the example of a movie projector. The Source within us is the light in the projector that makes the movie of our life possible. We tend to identify strongly with the images and the events that are projected onto the screen of our lives and forget that the light Source within us is actually the cause of all these manifestations. Here is another example. Imagine that you're trying to wipe off a dirty mark on your face while looking in the mirror, and instead of wiping your face you try to wipe the mark on the mirror, not realizing that you are the source of the real image. The people and things we become so dependent on have within them the exact same light that is within us. What we're looking for exists already lives within us. We are what we are seeking. Fulfillment is already available within every cell of our being. All we need to do is experience a union with ourselves. The love we're looking for is conveniently located within our hearts. We can live the greatest love affair by celebrating the union between our human self and the Universal Self, both residing within.

Since we don't always experience this union, we feel lonely and needy. We seek to depend on people and things outside of ourselves to feel secure. We cultivate attachments to them, we fear losing them, we hold on, and we try to control and manipulate them, only to further our isolation and suffering. We are designed to be sustained by our wholeness; and a natural element of wholeness is the ability to connect (which is totally different from dependency for the sake of security). We yearn to share and know one another. Nothing makes us more joyful than giving and receiving love. The desire to connect is a powerful force; it can move us beyond our tendency to separate.

> ••• **Reflection Pause** •••
>
> Do you find yourself desperately wanting to receive a sense of validation from other things or people in your life? Are you noticing a need to compensate for a lack of connection with yourself? Write some notes about your thought process.

Why Do We Feel Separate From Ourselves?

One important cause of inner separation is self-rejection. Self-judgment, self-criticism, self-doubt, self-hate, shame, and guilt all can be included in the action of self-rejection. It is obvious that when we reject ourselves, we feel deeply lonely and isolated from others and life. Another cause for feeling separate from others and life is being caught in an illusion of separate physical manifestation.

We imagine that we are separate from others because we have separate bodies. In reality we are all connected by the same energy. It is hard to fully experience the reality of being one unified field of energy, even when we know it intellectually. Living this knowledge takes a deep spiritual shift.

How Did We Get to Be So Rejecting of Ourselves?

One reason for self-rejection is internalizing rejection, criticism, or ridicule directed toward us by those close to us; another reason is going against our inner moral code, causing harm to ourselves or others, and disrupting the harmonic flow of life. Each of us needs to define what is right or wrong for us. At the same time, there are definitely some basic "golden rules." For example, physical, emotional, or mental violence (as opposed to true self-protection) is an obvious distortion of the harmonious life flow, as are the even subtler manipulations, control, or overpowering of other beings. (There is a distinction between some use of force that is absolutely necessary for self-protection and the protection of others and other kinds of violence.)

When we have violated our moral code, we can either disassociate from our actions or admit to and amend them. Nevertheless, this violation evokes in us an uneasy feeling. This feeling can be called "pangs of consciousness"—our inner moral compass tells us that we went off the path. We might feel shame, regret, or guilt, but this time it is because we ourselves went against the natural law of harmony. If we don't recognize the feeling and the action of being harmful, and we don't attend to it with an attempt to dissolve its effects, our unconscious or conscious guilt will cause us to separate from ourselves.

To summarize, the three causes of separation are: 1) internalizing and maintaining self-rejection that was directed toward us, 2) perceiving a physical illusion of separateness, and 3) experiencing moral uneasiness that results from harmful actions toward self and others. All three causes have to be addressed and dissolved for us to feel a sense of union with ourselves and others.

> ••• **Reflection Pause** •••
>
> Take a moment to think about the different causes of separation. Which cause do you struggle with in your life? How can this cause be addressed? Be compassionate with yourself as you meditate on this.

The Aspects of the Self

I have mentioned before the three aspects of the self: The Emotional Self, The Defensive Self, and The Expanded Self. These aspects are the emotional, energetic, and mental sides of our inner self that lead to physical and behavioral patterns. It is as if there are three different people living within each of us. When all three work together as a team they are unified as a cohesive self. When the aspects are in conflict with one another, the self is divided and weak. Since good relationships with others start with oneself, I have made a choice to first address the inner dialogue. A positive inner dialogue enhances our ability to relate with others.

The Gate of Dialogue provides processes and exercises to enhance the inner dialogue between all three aspects so they can become unified. It also lays out guidelines for authentic and effective dialogue with others. The goal is to return to union with oneself and others. Union does not mean the obliteration of individual uniqueness; it means different aspects or people working together, rather than against each other.

The Emotional Self

The Emotional Self is the aspect where all of our emotions, emotional imprints, and experiences reside. It is an intense and at times wild realm. Most of us have a tendency to suppress difficult emotions and experiences for the sake of psychological and physical survival. However, when we do this longer than is necessary, it becomes a habit.

The Gate of Emotions chapter emphasizes the importance of emotional freedom and emotional integration. Our emotions are extremely valuable and are necessary for creating a life of fulfillment and happiness. Unfortunately, the Emotional Self is usually burdened by unresolved or unreleased difficult experiences—from small seemingly insignificant hurts to severe trauma. Resentments, unexpressed fears, shame, or guilt, regrets, broken dreams, unrequited love, unspoken truths, and little-known longings might be stored within the Emotional Self. On the other hand, the Emotional Self is the birthplace of great joy, humor, playfulness, love, silliness, creative imagination, compassion, appreciation of beauty, and sweet nothings. You can think of this side of yourself as the inner child, the ado lescent, or the beating heart of your being. The Emotional Self is a source of great joy and happiness when it is healed, supported, and accepted; otherwise, it can be filled with sadness, anger, and fear.

> ••• **Reflection Pause** •••
>
> Think about familiar emotions you experience on a regular basis. Write them down and expand on how they feel in your body, how they affect your outlook, and why you experience them.

I am not suggesting that when we heal, our Emotional Self no longer feels pain, fear, or anger. We do. But we are able to accept these feelings better and move through and beyond them faster without getting stuck. Accepting and understanding our Emotional Self brings us closer to others and dissolves the sense of inner and outer separation.

The Defensive Self

The Defensive Self is the aspect of the self that is created to ensure our survival. It is the tightening of muscles, breath, and inner organs designed to protect us from inner and outer hurt. It is the mask we present to the world to gain acceptance and recognition. It is patterns of behavior we adopt to ensure that we will be loved, validated, and appreciated. It is our "strong suit," "protective coat," and "armor," shielding us from the possibility of loss or emotional devastation.

Unfortunately, this protective structure can become a jail, a fortress that separates us from our Emotional Self and our Expanded Self. The cost of the protection is high. We need it to survive, when we are young and fragile, but we should not stay prisoners of our creation at the cost of true expression and connection. The Defensive Self is there to protect The Emotional Self. Ironically, if we were shamed, criticized, or abused, our defensive self will take on the same attitude to make sure that we don't get out of line, for doing so means possibly being hurt. The Defensive Self rules The Emotional Self with a whip and tries to keep it repressed, much like an overbearing, critical parent does. The relationship between these two is full of tension and conflicts. Our Defensive Self keeps us separate from our true feelings. When it is transformed, softened, and relaxed, the Defensive Self can be a friendly protector and not a harsh warden. This is achieved through the inner dialogue exercises. A constructive and friendly relationship between The Emotional Self and The Defensive Self creates a sense of inner safety and at the same time, allows freedom of expression.

> • • • **Reflection Pause** • • •
>
> Identify your Defensive Self. Meditate on the type of Defensive Self you have created and how it expresses itself in your life.

The Expanded Self

The Expanded Self is the aspect that reflects the Universal Consciousness within our human psyche. It is the witness, the wise healer, and the compassionate guide, the Eternal living within and expressing through us. We are all born endowed with an Expanded Self. We need to learn to connect to it and consciously establish it as the guide and the leader of the two other aspects. The Expanded Self can heal and support the Emotional Self and soften and relax the Defensive Self. You can think of it as a wise and loving parent who can harmonize and balance the energies of the "inner home." We all have experienced moments where an inner voice clearly guided us in times of turmoil or moments when deep peace washed over us without any apparent reason—moments that are blessed with a sudden calm and deep knowing. These and many more are the gifts bestowed on us by our Expanded Self. By consciously connecting to it, we can immerse our lives in the truth and wisdom available to us.

> • • • **Reflection Pause** • • •
>
> Recall a specific moment when you have experienced the Expanded Self. Meditate on how the Expanded Self can be a source of peace and comfort to you in your life.

Using Inner Dialogue to Create Inner Balance

As a young woman in my late twenties, I was emotionally dependent on my partner. His love and appreciation were my source of validation. Since I didn't know then how to validate myself, I ended up burdening him with overflowing needs, expectations, and demands. Needless to say, it created major conflicts between us, as well as a good amount of inner torment for me. It was at that point that I realized I needed to learn to give myself the love and acknowledgment I longed for. I started that chapter of my transformation by going to counseling and making a promise to myself to find a loving voice within that would be a source of comfort to me as opposed to handing that responsibility to my partner.

As I turned my eyes within, I began to tap into my Expanded Self. I did not have a name for it then, but I felt a powerful love source guiding and comforting. It was a faint connection in the beginning, which grew stronger and stronger over time. Slowly, I allowed myself to feel the deep pain and terror residing in my Emotional Self. I felt safer because I was not alone; there was that presence that was me, yet so much more than me. It felt like it was holding and guiding me, emotionally speaking. Out of that loving exchange/dialogue, a healing took place. I found my inner home… Inner strength and peace slowly tiptoed into my soul.

My Defensive Self, which was used to protecting me by presenting an "I don't need anybody or anything" façade, was fighting the transformation and resisting it every step of the way. Becoming vulnerable, emotional, and expressive was very threatening to the Defensive part of me. My Expanded Self needed to work hard to soften this resistance. It needed to address my Defensive Self with compassion and gentle guidance—the kind of tough love that is needed with a frightened, rebellious kid. The more I allowed myself to feel, and the more I trusted the loving guidance of my Expanded Self, the softer my Defensive Self became, slowly releasing the hard grip on my emotions and energy.

EXERCISE: Writing

Learn to identify the inner voice for each one of the three aspects. Choose a recent incident from your life that provoked intense feelings. Sit down and prepare three separate pieces of paper; on top of each one write the name of one of the aspects. On the first page, write "My Emotional Self." On the second page, write "My Defensive Self." And on the third page, write "My Expanded Self."

STEP ONE - The Emotional Self

Bring the incident that you chose to the forefront of your mind/heart. Start with the first page, The Emotional Self. Write down your emotional reaction to the incident. Go with just pure emotions—no excuses, intellectualizations, analysis, judgment, logic, or interpretation. This can be hard to do in the beginning, since most of us are not used to experiencing pure emotions without commentary attached to them. Do your best.

For example, let's say that the upsetting incident was a discussion with a friend or a lover that went sour. In such a situation, your feelings might be ones of sadness, anger, disappointment, and frustration. I suggest that you write them down in the order that they appear. They might all be mixed together. If so, choose the first one—let's say, sadness—and write down: "I feel sad that I was not able to explain myself." Then proceed to the next emotion: "I am disappointed at myself for becoming defensive and short," and then to the third, "I love him or her so much." Write a few sentences about each one of the feelings. And stick to the Four Magic "I's": "I feel," "I need," "I want," "I think."

Our feelings are always ours, and we need to own them. Once you're done, sit quietly for a minute and acknowledge these feelings, preferably without judgment. Feelings are just what they are—feelings. When you are ready, move to the next page.

STEP TWO - The Defensive Self

You will now need to shift your perspective, as your "Defensive Self" has a totally different response to the incident. If we use the example I mentioned before, your reactions to the upsetting argument might be: "I'm sick of trying to communicate with her/him," "She/he never gets what I mean," "She/he never listens," or "She/he is a hard head; I don't want to talk to him ever again," and so on. If you write honestly from your Defensive Self, you will find that your reactions, feelings, and statements are about how "wrong" the other person is. Or how "wrong" you are and how you should have done it differently. Making yourself wrong, or making another person wrong, can be a typical reaction of the Defensive Self. If you notice that your body is tense, then your stance is true to the nature of this aspect: defensive. Try not to judge yourself. Acknowledge this part of yourself, and remember that you cannot transform what you don't first accept and admit. After you've finished writing, sit for a minute and take in this part of yourself and the way it is expressing right now.

STEP THREE - The Expanded Self

Your Expanded Self has yet another perspective on the situation in question. This aspect of yourself is able to view things from a place of compassion and wisdom.

It has a bird's eye view, capable of witnessing the situation in a much more neutral way. It can see the big picture—the needs, feelings, and reactions of all involved.

Write down your thoughts and feelings about the incident from this perspective. You might find yourself thinking: "He/she has been such a loving friend for so long," "He/she must be under a lot of stress trying to find a new job," or "We both get short with each other. I was reactive. I want to tell him/her how much I value our friendship."

You might find out that you understand yourself and the other person in a different way. Your feelings of hurt or anger (if these were present for you) might soften as your ability to be calm and compassionate increases. Once you have experienced the incident through the three perspectives, you can begin a dialogue between your Expanded Self and your Emotional Self or between your Expanded Self and your Defensive Self. Your Expanded Self can comfort and guide your Emotional Self, and it can soften the harshness of your Defensive Self. I suggest that you train yourself to become aware of and to feel which one of the three aspects is dominating a situation and use the tool of inner dialogue to steer clear of ineffective or destructive responses.

In my counseling room, beside the sofa and my chair, I have three sitting places. Each client assigns for themselves a place for each one of their aspects. When we work on inner dialogue, clients actually sit in one of the places and silently, or out loud, express their thoughts and feelings, addressing the two other aspects. As the dialogue continues, they keep moving physically and emotionally from one aspect to the other. What happens then is a real dialogue among the three aspects.

A client of mine, whom I will call "Pat," was having a hard time communicating with her teenage daughter. After almost a year of strife, they both agreed on certain ground rules of conduct. To name a few, the daughter was to come home before midnight on weekdays. The daughter also agreed to work on a daily basis on her school assignments. The mother agreed to respect the daughter's privacy and honor her autonomy. For example, she would knock on the door before entering her room, allow her to paint and decorate her room the way she wishes, and so on. My client felt that she was holding up to her part of the agreement, but her daughter was not. Her grades were plummeting, and she was consistently coming home in the early morning hours. My client was getting angry and frustrated. She eventually decided to ground her daughter for three weekends. The situation escalated from bad to worse. All communication stopped.

I asked Pat to do the same exercise presented above. She sat down, felt into and wrote the responses of each of her aspects, using their words. After she had finished, she told me that her Emotional Self was feeling hurt and betrayed by her daughter's behavior. Her Defensive Self felt angry and critical, and wanted to control and punish the daughter. And her Expanded Self realized that throughout the entire year of conflict she had not expressed love or appreciation toward her daughter, and that the daughter's behavior may be a cry for loving attention.

In the session, I asked her to sit in each one of the aspects. She sat quietly, and at some point tears were streaming down her face. She was allowing herself to feel both the love she had for her daughter and her hurt. In the next session after the exercise, I asked her to work on an inner dialogue. She started by sitting in the place of her Expanded Self. She sat for a minute with her eyes closed and then she addressed her imaginary Emotional Self sitting to her left: "I know you are feeling hurt and betrayed," she said, "but it seems to me that 'Sue' [her daughter] is feeling the same. She has been going through a rough time in school and socially. She has not been able to focus on her schoolwork, and she has been upset with her two best friends. I think she needs you to tell her that you love her and believe in her talents and skills. Maybe we should have a heart-to-heart talk with her. Tell her your feelings, and ask her to share hers. But most importantly, let's tell her how much we love her."

My client paused to listen to the reaction from her Emotional Self. She then physically moved to the left where her Emotional Self typically sat. Now, she responded to her Expanded Self from her Emotional Self: "I don't think she wants to talk to me. I am hurt, and maybe she is, too. I don't know how to approach her."

Pat moved back to the place of her Expanded Self and responded, "I know how you feel. You want to talk to her, but you don't know where to begin or how. You are afraid that it will end up being another nasty fight, which would cause more pain. Let's think of the best way to go about this. Let's think about what we want to say, how, and when. We will rehearse a little. And when we are ready, we will approach her."

"She is a brat. A spoiled brat." The voice of her Defensive Self jumped into the picture. Now, Pat had to sit in the place of her Defensive Self and verbalize its response, which was anger and criticism. Her Expanded Self had to deal with a criticizing Defensive Self and a reluctant, hurt Emotional Self. The dialogue continued for a while, and by the end of it, Pat was able to soften the critical reaction of her Defensive Self and engage both Defensive Self and Emotional Self in a decision to have a heart-to-heart talk with Sue.

In the next session, Pat told me that she had had a painful but authentic dialogue with her daughter. They both ended up crying. Her daughter admitted that she was involved in a sexual relationship with a married man, and that she had desperately needed her mom's counsel but was afraid to tell her the truth. This was the beginning of a real relationship between them. They needed patience and continued honesty, which were at times difficult to manage. Pat was committed to deepen the relationship with her daughter. Slowly but surely, a friendship developed.

Examples of Inner Dialogues

I have asked two of my clients to write in their own words a short section of a dialogue that they have had. I hope these will help you to better understand the healing power of inner dialogues, as it's done in the Gates of Power® method.

Here is an excerpt from a real dialogue done by a client who has battled various types of addictions for much of his adult life. He was able to find his passion which is being a performer and a professional clown, and to build a creatively fulfilling life free of addictions. This dialogue was one in a series of dialogues done at a point in his process when he was working to weaken the hold of his Defensive Self's on his life.

Expanded: Okay, guys, so what are we gonna talk about today? What is bothering us?

Defensive: Jerk. We're supposed to talk to each other, and that's gonna make our life better? Yeah, right.

Emotional: You ruined me, defensive guy. You stepped on me and beat me up with your addictions. I never had a chance to live or do what I love to do.

Defensive: Listen, moron, I want to stay home, eat spaghetti, watch movies and porn. If you don't like it, learn to like it.

Expanded: I think you should stop that stuff and give him a chance to do what he wants.

Defensive: Do what he wants? Why, so he can humiliate himself? He wants to be a comedian, an actor, a clown. I'm certainly not going to allow that. I'm actually protecting him from humiliation and ridicule.

Expanded: No, actually you are denying him and yourself life.

Defensive: No. Life is the stuff I do—the delicious food, the TV, the porn. Everybody says that that stuff is the good life.

Expanded: That's true—people do say that, but it's really just a defense against the loneliness and isolation that people feel. It's them trying not to feel those things.

Defensive: Loneliness? Who needs people? I don't. People are jerks. I see people I don't even know, and I don't like them.

Expanded: How do you know you won't like them if you haven't met them?

Defensive: I can just tell by looking at them.

Emotional: I think deep down you're in a lot of pain, just like me. I don't want you stopping me from living life anymore. And you, Expanded Self, when are you gonna start protecting me from that monster?

Defensive: Monster? Listen, I am protecting you. Just lie down, and don't fight me. I'm too strong. And you, Expanded Guy, I've got you too, so don't you fight me, either.

Expanded: You're a culmination of bad habits that need to be broken. You are living a lie, and you have become a perpetual machine of self-destruction. You're not a bad guy, Defensive Self, you're just a bit mixed up about what you want. Addictions do have a way of making us believe that they are really good for us. What we'll do is take small steps to healing you and take small steps to allowing the Emotional Self to live and get out there. We'll all work together. And, Defensive Self, with your strength and will, I think at some point you will be a very valuable asset to our trio. Emotional Self, please have some patience and compassion for the Defensive Guy. He needs help, and bashing him does nothing productive. I'm requesting that you let him be, and I'll take care of not allowing him to hurt you any more, okay?

Emotional: Okay, but I will focus on my own goals and not on what he's doing or not doing. I won't bash him, but I still don't like him.

Expanded: That is fair enough. Let's say good night for now.

I know it must sound strange, funny, or even crazy to have dialogue like that out loud. But we all do it internally talking to ourselves. Isn't it better to do it constructively and consciously? Here's a second dialogue, from one of my female clients who works long hours providing administrative support to high-level corporate executives. Her true passion and skill is writing and storytelling. While constantly assisting others, she had a tendency to neglect her own creativity, and her life started to lack adventure and fun. She is learning to make her happiness a priority by carving out daily writing and personal fun time. This dialogue is taken in the midst of that process.

Expanded: I think we all need to sit down and chat. We're all unhappy, and it doesn't need to be this way. So, let's talk. E, what are you thinking?

Defensive: Why does she get to go first?! This is ridiculous. We need to get to bed so we can be at work early. We should be productive and work on our resume, but no, we're supposed to *talk*. We've been lazy all weekend, and you want to talk now? It's the middle of the night!

Emotional: I'm tired and she's mean. This sucks.

Expanded: I know this isn't ideal, but since there's very little chance we're going to fall asleep right now anyway, why not give it a shot?

Emotional: I've had very little playtime this week and frankly, I don't appreciate it. We have just been doing stupid *work* all the time. I WANT MY FUN! And a cute boyfriend. I'm tired of being alone.

Expanded: Okay, I hear you. We should figure out a plan for that.

Defensive: You want fun and a boyfriend? What on earth have we done to deserve that? We're not in good enough shape to be noticed by any man. We aren't nearly accomplished enough to be interesting to anyone; I'm shocked we even have friends. We need to be *doing* more. We've no time for rest. We're behind. We should have done more with ourselves by now. We're old, we're not pretty enough, and we have a dead-end job.

Expanded: Wow, that's a harsh way of looking at things, isn't it?

Defensive: Of course, it is. But lots of people live this way. It keeps us safe.

Expanded: You've done an amazing job in trying to keep us all safe all of these years. But you need to loosen the leash here. It's too much, and you don't need to hold on so tight.

Defensive: I don't believe that for a second.

Expanded: I didn't think that you would. It's a scary world out there, and there's a lot of hurt that can happen. You've been doing this protecting thing for so long, it's going to be hard to let go. But, you know, there's a lot of good stuff out there, too. Don't you want in on that?

Defensive: Well, yeah. But it's too risky.

Expanded: But are you happy doing this?

Defensive: No. It's not my job to be happy. I'm the one who takes care of things.

Expanded: Says who? And why does taking care of things not involve happiness?

Defensive: We don't deserve it.

Emotional: She's right. I want it, but I don't really think we deserve it. That's why I always end up going back to her when I get too happy.

Expanded: Why not try something a little different? You're not happy now, so how about we just try on the idea for a bit that we deserve to be happy?

Defensive: I don't know. It sounds too simple. I don't trust it.

Emotional: Yeah, I'd like to do it, but I'm just not sure I trust you, either.

Expanded: Not trusting anyone hasn't gotten you anywhere in the past. So how about you give this a try and see how you like it? We'll start small. Tell me something right now that you are feeling, that is completely honest.

Emotional: I'm lonely, and sad about being lonely. I want to be loved, but I don't think I deserve it.

Defensive: I'm afraid to get hurt. It reminds me why I don't deserve to be loved. I hate feeling that. It hurts more every time.

Expanded: How about some happy thoughts?

Emotional: I got a sandwich at the deli and the cute grill guy put a smiley face on my sandwich wrapper for me. It made me giggle.

Defensive: I had a very productive day at work and got through one of my lists. I should have done more, though…

Expanded: Hey, no! Stay with the good stuff. So, we did it. We said one thing that made us happy and one thing that we're feeling right now. We can keep doing more of that, and we'll get there. One small step at a time. See, that wasn't so bad.

As you can see these inner dialogues are small steps taken toward creating a sense of inner unity and balance. Just like a team needs many meetings and discussions to become cohesive, our inner team needs to engage in many dialogues to learn to live and create together.

The Art of Connecting and Communicating with Others

Authentic and compassionate dialogue with others can be as trying as the dialogue with ourselves, and at times even more challenging. We all need to acquire communication skills or, better put, connecting skills. None of us is exempt. Since relationships are absolutely essential for well-being and success, we need to keep developing the ability to relate and connect constantly.

Q: What is it that we want most when we communicate with others?
A: We want a sense of connection.
Q: What contributes to a sense of connection between people?
A: The following:
- All sides need to feel heard.
- All sides must feel respected and honored, even in the heat of a disagreement.
- All sides need to feel supported and enhanced, if there is an agreement.
- All sides need to be able to share their experience, knowledge, insight, or feelings.
- Differences need to be accepted, if they did not get resolved.
- All sides must show willingness to continue the communication to further the connection.
- All sides must strive to come to a resolution that is satisfactory to all.

When we connect, we are able to exchange knowledge, support, and joy. We give and receive. Connecting is one of the most fulfilling aspects of living. We long for it, and at the same time we sabotage it regularly.

Q: What are the obstacles to creating true connections?

A: In the same way that our Defensive Self blocks our connection with our Emotional Self, it blocks our ability to connect with others. Here are some of the ways that our Defensive Self prevents us from connecting to others:

- **Resistance:** A reluctance to open up, trust, let in, accept, or share with others.
- **Automatic reaction(s):** A habitual pattern, often unconscious, of avoiding the experience of being present.
- **Judgment and Comparison:** Forming opinions without real knowledge or understanding of whom or what we judge; classifying and stereotyping are some defensive tactics to maintain separation from others.
- **Denial of responsibility:** Lack of ownership for our actions, feelings, or needs.
- **Communication of desires as demands:** Inability to express authentically to others our needs and desires in the form of requests.
- **Blaming and dumping:** The habit of focusing on the other as the cause of one's trouble.
- **Manipulating and Controlling:** Using another as a pawn in order to pursue or achieve our own agenda.

All of these patterns of being originate from a defensive stance. Our Defensive Self has a tendency to withhold true feelings and to keep others at a distance. It creates a separation between ourselves and others and resists the possibility of being vulnerable—all in order to protect us from hurt. When we try to achieve defensive power, we judge, we deny responsibility, we blame, we dump on or punish others. It makes us feel right, versus the other, who is wrong. It makes us feel better than… The goal is to be on top of "the game of life." It is a "me against you," dogeat-dog world perspective. Within this perspective, we try to control, manipulate, pretend, lie, or use force. These are ways of war and emotional violence, and they are not conducive to compassionate communication and connection.

We all have a Defensive Self—it has a protective role—and if we intend to be fulfilled, we need to soften and transform our rigid, contracted, and stubborn Defensive Self into a compassionate protector, a peaceful warrior. This is quite a job. We can use all the help we can get to accomplish it. I highly recommend reading Nonviolent Communication.[6] It's a wonderful book loaded with great tips for creating nonviolent exchanges between people.

The Seven Guidelines for Successful Connecting

The following are my seven guidelines for successful connecting. I will elaborate on each one of these below.

1. Observing as opposed to evaluating
2. Identifying feelings and needs
3. Expressing clearly and honestly
4. Requesting as opposed to not asking or demanding
5. Listening empathically
6. Mirroring
7. Giving and receiving appreciation

Observing as Opposed to Evaluating

Learn to differentiate between observation and evaluation. J. Krishnamurti, the Indian philosopher, remarked that "observing without evaluating is the highest form of human intelligence." For most of us it is difficult to make observations without rushing to evaluate them. We tend to immediately and at times unconsciously form a judgment, categorize, or peg what we are observing. When we witness compassionately, without rushing to evaluate, we develop the ability to truly see, hear, feel, and understand what we are observing in a whole other way. We become available to the actual experience of others, nature, or ourselves. Notice your judgments and interpretations, and practice letting them go. They will continue coming in, but you can drop the attachment to them. Teach yourself to drop the need to "know it all." Create a space for experiencing life rather than analyzing it. Cultivate what Buddhists call a "beginner's mind"—a mind that is not cluttered by past experiences, details, preconceived notions, or existing beliefs. The following are two examples of observation and evaluation:

- **Observation:** The man I met on a date yesterday was continuously looking at his phone and texting.

- **Evaluation:** Men are not able to listen attentively. They are always distracted by their work.
- **Observation:** It looks like she has a wig on. I have seen her real hair, and it's a different color.
- **Evaluation:** Her wig is ugly. It doesn't fit her.

EXERCISE: Writing

Choose three incidents from the last two days and write down your observations and evaluations about them. Letting go of evaluation allows you to experience these incidents in a new and maybe surprising way.

Identifying Feelings and Needs

In the chapter entitled "The Gate of Emotions," I have explained the importance of identifying, experiencing, and expressing emotions and needs. Here in "The Gate of Dialogue" chapter, I would like to stress the importance of communicating these honestly and clearly, as well as learning to listen to others' emotions and needs, even if they themselves are not able to define or express them clearly. I have mentioned the Four Magic "I's"— "I feel," "I think," "I want," "I need." I call them the Magic "I's" because if you stick to them when you speak of your experience, it will keep your communication honest and clear. On the other hand, if you find yourself employing the word "you" a lot, it is certain that your focus is on the other person and you have moved away from describing your own experience.

Most of us confuse the categories of feelings, thoughts, wants, and needs. Let's try to distinguish among them.

Expressing feelings can include the personal statements: "I feel hurt," "I feel afraid," "I feel alone," "I feel relieved," "I feel excited," "I feel encouraged," and so forth. However, note that when we make statements such as "I feel abandoned by you"—or "attacked," "let down," "unsupported," and so on—we are really expressing a personal interpretation of the other's behavior; our interpretations should not be confused with our own feelings.

For example, if I find myself "feeling abandoned," I need to check in with myself to see what I really feel. I might be feeling pain, fear, or anger. These are my feelings. I also need to realize that what I am calling "abandoned" is only my interpretation of the other person's behavior. They might be preoccupied, in a bad mood, busy with a deadline, or getting a cold. They might not be aware of the impact of their behavior. "I feel that you do not love me" is not a feeling; it is an interpretation. "I feel that you are ignorant" is not a feeling; it is a judgment. "I feel that Sam is very generous" is not a feeling; it is an assessment.

Every time we put somebody else in the expression, we're not talking about our own feelings. "I feel hurt because you don't listen to me" is not a real expression of one's feelings. A more accurate way of expressing this would be, "When I imagine or experience that you don't listen to me, I feel hurt." Another example: "When you are late, I feel neglected." In these last two examples, we are making statements that distinguish between our interpretation and our feelings.

Remember to check with the other person to ensure that your perception is real. The statements "You don't love me" or "You don't listen to me" are your perceptions to an extent. You may assume that another person doesn't love you, based on their actions. To you, it seems completely logical that the way they behave means that they don't love you. However, this is an interpretation of their behaviors. For effective dialogue, connection, and communication, it is necessary that you ask the other person questions that can help you understand their behaviors.

Observe this person you are in relationship with as you would an interesting piece of art. Listen to them carefully, find out how they feel, what makes them happy, what inspires them, what they need, and what they hold important. Take them in. Notice when you start to attach your own interpretation of that person's behavior rather than observing yourself and them. For example, you might observe, "Mike doesn't respond to my text messages." It can be very easy to make the next leap into "Mike wants to break up with me because he doesn't respond to my text messages." This may or may not be true. The only way to really know is to engage in an honest dialogue with the person whose actions we desire to understand and listen with as much openness as possible.

Needs evoke feelings, and feelings inform us about needs. Here are some statements about needs:

- I need to choose my own goals and values.
- I need to express myself authentically.
- I need to feel independent.
- I need a sense of community.
- I need care and consideration.

- I need to feel loved and give love.
- I need to contribute using my talents and abilities.
- I need warmth and physical affection.

When our needs are not met, we are unfulfilled. Obviously, we need to know what our needs are first and then find creative, expressive, and practical ways to fulfill them. We are the ones responsible for fulfilling our needs. Real needs are different from addictive needs, which are a compensation for not getting real needs met. When we are not making the effort to understand our needs, and attend to them, we create inner suffering. At that point, we might feel a desire to numb our suffering. The desire to numb our pain creates an addictive need. We begin to use substances, sex, overworking, television, even relationships to avoid the pain that we have caused ourselves by not listening to our feelings and by neglecting our needs.

Putting the responsibility for the fulfillment of our needs in somebody else's hands will create frustration and suffering. Conversely, taking on the responsibility for another person's feelings and needs is enabling them, robbing them from their birthright to take care of themselves. A part of being responsible includes being caring, considerate, and helpful to others, but this should not be confused with shouldering responsibilities that belong to others.

Expressing Clearly and Honestly

The process of learning to distinguish among thoughts, needs, wants, and feelings is continuous and extremely valuable. It is the preliminary part of communication. The second part is cultivating the skills involved in expressing ourselves clearly and honestly and, of course, the third part is cultivating our listening skills.

Here are some examples of clearly expressed statements as they relate to the Magic "I"s:

- When you did not come home yesterday, I thought (*I think*) that something had happened to the car. I felt (*I feel*) anxious and angry. I needed (*I need*) to hear from you. I want you (*I want*) to get a better phone so that you can call me when you are stranded.

- I feel (*I feel*) discouraged by the lack of progress in this project. I think (*I think*) that we are not utilizing the tools and the information available to us. I want (*I want*) to create a brain-storming meeting and come to

some definite decisions about our next steps. I need (*I need*) to talk to Harry right now and get his input about this.
- I feel (*I feel*) excited about our trip. I think (*I think*) we're going to have a great time. I want (*I want*) to see as much as possible, and I need (*I need*) us to sit together and create a realistic plan with as many details as possible so that we can maximize our time there.

Notice that in all these examples, the person speaking uses all Four Magic "I's": "I think," "I feel," "I need," "I want." They are avoiding blaming, attacking, dumping, or judging. The tone of your voice and the music behind the words are as important as the words (or even more). It is ineffective to use the Magic "I's" but have a blaming, emotional energy behind the words.

Requesting, as Opposed to Not Asking or Demanding

Taking responsibility for our needs means at times asking for help, advice, consideration, feedback, and so on. I have found that a great number of people are reluctant to ask for what they need, as they see it as a weakness and are ashamed to ask for their needs to be met. If you are such a person, do yourself a huge favor and learn how to ask for what you need, or else you will forever be missing out on one of the best parts of life—receiving.

Receiving means giving another person an opportunity to give. Giving and receiving are one and the same: when you give, you are allowing someone to receive and when, in turn, you receive, you allow someone to give, and in doing so, you become a giver all over again. It is the wondrous unending cycle of living. It is good to ask, and it is good to be asked. How we ask is the key. Honesty, emotional expressiveness, and vulnerability create openness in ourselves and in others. Demands, defensive reactivity, control, manipulation, guilt trips, and blame will not fulfill our needs—they might provide a momentary satisfaction, but they will fail to truly fulfill our needs. Learn to request using positive language. Be clear and specific. For example, let's say that you need your child to help you with the household chores. A negative request would be: "Don't watch TV before you clear the table and wash your dishes." This is a demand, and you are telling him or her what *not to do*, rather than what *to do*. A positive request would be: "I need you to help me with clearing the table and washing the dishes. lease do that before you sit down to watch TV."

Another example of a negative request: "You always forget to buy spring water before you get home. How many times do I have to ask you to do that?" A positive way of expressing this would be "Our faucet water tastes strange. Can you please remember to pick up some spring water before you get home today? I would love for you to remember to bring it without me asking for it." When requesting, make sure to ask your partner to share with you how they feel about your request. Find out whether they are comfortable, willing, or able to consider it.

Listening Empathically

Just as it is necessary for us to clearly express ourselves, it is important to learn to hear others' feelings, needs, thoughts, and requests. Even when others are not skilled at defining their feelings and are not able to express themselves using the Four Magic "I's," we can train ourselves to listen for these while they are communicating with us. For example, let's take the wife in the previous example, who is frustrated that her husband does not bring spring water home for dinner. In her frustration, she judges and evaluates: "You never bring home what I ask you. You just don't care. I've asked over and over again. I am sick and tired of asking."

If you (the husband) learn to listen empathically to her expression, you will seize the moment by acknowledging first to yourself that she is *feeling* hurt, she *needs* your help, and she is requesting (*wants*) your consideration. At this point, she's unable to use a positive form of communication, but if you listen with your heart and are able to give up defensive reaction, the communication will shift from tense and defensive into a moment of real sharing.

Maybe you will give her a hug and say: "I'm sorry, I know I have become self-involved and absent-minded. I do love you and want to help always." Or maybe you smile and say something that makes her laugh and know that you heard her. Or maybe you drop everything, go to the store and bring spring water that would last for the next month. Whatever you do, you're coming from empathy and care, and she will feel that and soften.

Mirroring

Empathic listening is the key to good communication, and the skill of mirroring is essential when you want to take any connection to a higher level. Mirroring is the ability and the skill to reflect back to another person what they observe, feel, need, and want. It only works if you take yourself out of the way for a minute and really step into their shoes—feel, see, and hear what they experience. Mirroring does not mean giving up your point of view, desires, or convictions. It only means putting them aside for a moment when listening to your partner's sharing. This applies to all forms of communication: personal, work, and social. We all want to feel heard and understood. Messages we send are not always received accurately, and vice versa—the way we receive others' communication can be totally off. When we are mirrored, it helps us determine whether we are actually understood. When we mirror, we are able to determine whether we actually understand.

Mirroring always starts with empathic listening, as explained before. We listen from the heart to the underlying feelings, needs, and requests of our communication partner. We don't interrupt (very hard to do), and when they finish expressing themselves, we reflect their message back to them. Here's an example. Your friend is sharing with you about her new job: "I feel confused as to what my job description is. The company is a start-up, and it feels like everybody is unclear about their exact role. I'm used to structure and clear assignments. This confusion is causing me to be anxious instead of being happy that I finally have the kind of job I was looking for. I dread it." Since this communication is not concerning you, it is easier to mirror. Example of mirroring: "I understand how you feel. You're not getting clear directions from your boss, and it is confusing. You're not sure if you need to define these for yourself, or ask him to define them for you. You feel anxious. You need clarity. And you would like to receive, at least in the beginning, more guidance. Is that right? Did I get it?"

If you missed something, the questions at the end give your friend the opportunity to add or correct your mirroring, or explain further. If you did not mirror your friend, and she was not sure whether you understood her state of being, she could ask you, "Do you know what I mean?" This is a request for mirroring. You could say, "Yes, I do." That might be good enough, but a more specific mirroring will make her feel truly listened to.

Mirroring becomes more difficult when there is an emotional charge or a conflict between the parties. This is also when it is most necessary. Here is an example, Woman: "I am exhausted from getting up to feed and hold the baby several times every night. You just sleep away like nothing is going on. This is not only my child. Don't you think that you need to get up, too, and let me sleep at least once during the night?" Man, mirroring: "I understand that you are really exhausted from getting up for the baby at night. You are angry at me for not waking up and for not sharing the responsibility. You need me to relieve you once during the night and let you sleep. Did I get it?" Woman: "Yes. I'm upset that you don't see my exhaustion. You act like you don't care." Man: "You're upset because it seems like I don't care about your well-being." Woman: "Yes."

At this point, you, the man, can explain your point of view: "The reason why I try to sleep, even though I hardly can, is that I need to operate machinery and drive at work. I cannot afford to be tired and unable to function. It is dangerous. Can you understand my perspective?" If both partners go back and forth and continue to mirror each other, they will eventually feel understood. The conflict will soften, and they can come to an agreement that will serve both.

Giving and Receiving Appreciation

Any loving exchange empowers us. An expression of appreciation and acknowledgment that comes from the heart nourishes and celebrates both giver and receiver. Make it a priority to express appreciation, not as a manipulative tactic to get something back but as an unconditional expression of honest feelings.

Acknowledging someone in order to get better results can be manipulative. If you are a teacher, parent, boss, friend, or lover trying to get someone to be a certain way or to do a certain thing, and you use praise or acknowledgment as a means to an end, you are being manipulative. Even though you are trying to improve their grades, behavior, productivity, or their relationship with you, your expression is conditional.

Praise that comes from the heart should always include your feelings, not just "You did great" or "I think you are the best." These sound more like judgments because they don't include how you, the praise-giver, feel. Why do you appreciate the other person? How did their actions or expression contribute to you personally? For example, instead of only saying "You did great," you can elaborate: "I was really tired. Thanks for picking up your sister after school and playing with her so quietly while I was taking a nap. It made me feel loved. You did great." In this example, the mother expresses her feelings and needs and acknowledges her son for considering them and helping her get some rest. Both parties are truly empowered by this kind of acknowledgment. Mother and son draw closer and feel understood.

Let's take another example: "I think you are the best." When you say that, you're not truly expressing your feelings. What is it exactly that your friend did, how did it affect you, how did it contribute to your enjoyment? Here is more specific and personal way to acknowledge them: "I have been trying for the last three 2 hours to figure out how to put this equipment together with no success at all. I 3 love the way you can zero in and use this complicated manual. You really have a 4 talent for figuring out things. You saved my day. I think you're the best." The more 5 specific we are in expressing our feelings, the more we give, and the more we gain. 6 Nothing feels better than true appreciation.

A few words about showing affection. When it comes to affection, don't be stingy. For many years as a child and young adult, I did not feel my father's affection. He was, for reasons I understood later in life, shut down emotionally. I remember that once when I asked him about this, he said, "I feel the love; I just cannot express it." I see my father in me sometimes, so I commit daily to opening up to the feeling of love and to finding ways of expressing it. As I matured, I learned to see and feel my father's love behind and through his actions and his awkward attempts to express love. I have come to love him unconditionally and to learn to express my appreciation to him in spite of his shy smiles and protests. At any given moment, look around you and find someone or something that inspires your love or affection. Open yourself to these feelings, and find ways to show it. Love is the substance that holds life together. Corny but true.

Traits of Good Communicators

To succeed in any area of life, to reach your potential and find fulfillment, you must become a good communicator. Take it upon yourself to cultivate the connector/communicator within you. Your Expanded Self is a wise and a compassionate communicator. Let it guide you in all of your relationships. Keep the following tips in mind as you seek to improve your communications:

- **Be the cause.** Stay present, which means both committing to creating mutual understanding, mutual benefit, and mutual enjoyment and taking responsibility for the success of the communication.
- **Keep an open mind and heart.** Be flexible, ready to learn, and ready to see things in a new way.
- **Focus on the other person.** Focus on the other person and see their value.
- **Find common ground.** Learn to see things from the other's perspective. Even if, or when, you have a different opinion.

- **Be authentic and clear**. Use all five channels—thoughts, emotions, words, physical expression, and action.
- **Be a contribution**. Find how you can help, support, inspire, create change, or express affection.
- **Use humor**. Playful enjoyment can contribute to almost all communications.

The Ten Commandments for Good Communication

1. **Know Yourself.** Use your Expanded Self to observe and guide your other two aspects. Find out how you feel, what you need, what you believe in, so that you can communicate it.

2. **Commit to Creating Connections.** Take responsibility for the success of your communications. Be the cause, the initiator, the giver.

3. **Avoid Reactivity.** When faced with strong emotions and intense reactions, take a minute to figure yourself out. Get clear and strive to create a constructive way to communicate.

4. **Cultivate Empathic Listening.** Extend that to yourself and others. Empathy helps you understand and accept. It enhances transformation and change.

5. **Be Clear.** Be authentic and expressive, and use the Four Magic "I's."

6. **Show Appreciation.** Do whatever you can to validate your partner(s). Use listening and mirroring skills, and show respect and consideration. You can still maintain your beliefs and go for them. One has nothing to do with the other.

7. **Be Reliable.** Say what you mean and mean what you say. Integrity cultivates mutual trust.

8. **Learn to Negotiate.** Create win/win situations. It is best for all involved.

9. **Tap into Your Humor and Playfulness.** Bring enjoyment into your communications.

10. **Let Go of the Need to be Right, in Control, or on Top.** Connection and the exchange of understanding are so much more fulfilling. Communication is an art. Keep experimenting and go through the trials and tribulations. You will come to enjoy it, and so will all who come in contact with you.

9

The Gate of Creative Expression

*Use your creative ability to express
the highest and the best in you.*

All of us possess three important abilities and gifts that inspire our lives. These three gifts are handed to us by the Great Creative Source as an offering of unconditional love. The first gift is the ability to love and be loved. Even when we are having a tough time loving or receiving love, we are, deep down inside, capable of it, and are actually moving toward love. It is part of our innate nature. The second gift is the ability to feel connected to the whole, the great expression called life. We feel this connection through nature, culture, art, community, spiritual experience, a sense of unity, and the simple enjoyments of our daily lives. The third gift is our ability to create and express. We are all endowed with this ability; some of us make it a vocation, and all of us use it in one way or another.

The Biblical phrase "Created in His own image" is definitely pointing to our ability to create (among other things). It seems like the Creator desires company, teamwork, and inspiration, and He/She gave us the ability to create with Him/ Her.

Living each day is a creative process. We make choices, we come up with solutions, we create small or big things. It can be a letter, a meal, a new way to dress up, a design for a new building, or a treatment for a movie. This Gate inspires you to embrace creativity and expression as a way of life. Our Emotional Self loves to play, to be silly, to create, express, and discover new things. All of the above enhance our happiness, and happiness is the jewel of life. This Gate, more than any other, leads us to the experience of joy.

We're aware of fears, doubts, self-criticism, and emotional trauma that hold us back. All of the Gates lead to liberation of joy and freedom of expression, but the Gate of Creative Expression takes us there, via the winding path of childlike, creative fun.

I can feel your Emotional Self going, "Yay!" and possibly your Defensive Self going, "What the heck does that mean, 'creative fun'?"

My Creative Journey

As I mentioned earlier, I was born in Israel at the time of the country's conception. My childhood's simple pleasures were overshadowed by the wars. For the first five years of my life, my father was not around. He spent two years in different hospitals after being shot in the war and then three years in the mental ward suffering from severe post-traumatic stress disorder. When he returned home he was a broken man, physically and mentally. To my child self, my father was a scary stranger, with bouts of silence and anger. My mom, who expected to have a husband to care for her, was left grieving, confused, and panicked. Being the eldest, I was supposed to be her helpmate, the one she leaned on. I learned at a very early age, reluctantly and under a thunder of screams and blows, to clean, organize, shop, run errands, and babysit my siblings. There was no place for leisure, play, or fun in my schedule. There were no ballet lessons, no swimming, and no flute playing. These were out of budget and out of the question. I excelled in school—I guess I had to do something to get attention and recognition. Like all young people in Israel, I served in the army, after which I decided to go to the Academy for the Performing Arts—a "crazy" decision no one in my family, including myself, understood.

In the academy, I started my creative journey. Looking at it now, I realize that my soul was crying out for expression. I felt jailed in my caretaking obligations and my efforts to excel. These left me no room to be expressive. I realize that creative expression saved my life, literally. I was dying a slow death, a shattered and lonely child living in a grownup suit, muted and obedient. The academy started my liberation, painful as it was. I slowly learned to let myself be. I learned to move, scream, cry, laugh, speak my mind, and maybe most importantly, feel the sadness that lived within me. It was the beginning of my creative journey of transformation. I proceeded to work as an actor on some of the best stages in Israel. Later, I came to New York on a grant and continued studying acting and dance. In New York, I discovered my passion for dance and immersed myself in it. I started writing and directing my own theater pieces, weaving together theater and dance. The themes that moved me again and again were connected to the desire and the struggle for inner liberation.

At some point, I founded a dance performance company called Inner Landscapes. It was a collective of directors and choreographers dedicated to innovative, multimedia performance art. Creative expression helped me reclaim my aliveness, my strength, and my spirit. It gave me joy beyond words. Nowadays, I only dance in my living room, but once you know creativity, it lives with you, as close as your breath. Today, living life is the creative project I'm dedicated to. Writing, counseling, lecturing, having a fun time, or doing nothing are all creative outlets for me. Living moment to moment with heart and senses wide open, appreciating and enjoying life, is the creative way of being I practice.

On Creativity

I remember myself at 13 years of age, standing in one of these big aquariums; I believe it was in Eilat, a town by the Red Sea in Israel. I was awestruck by the endless colors, shapes, and variety of sea creatures floating in front of my amazed eyes. I recall thinking: *How could God come up with so many variations of fish? How could He [God was a He at that point in my life] invent so many shapes and colors? Where are all these ideas coming from? He must be unbelievably creative. I wish I could have one-quarter of his talent.*

Later, I started noticing the endless shades of yellow, gold, red, and brown painted on the falling leaves. I began noticing faces of people and shapes of clouds. I kept being amazed at God's talent and creativity. Some years later, I started to suspect that a little bit of this talent for the creative lived within me, a gift I was supposed to cherish and cultivate. Maybe, I thought, this is my way of playing with God and creating for Him. It was fun to create, and I liked to imagine that it was making Him smile with pleasure.

The young version of myself got it right. The Great Creator loves creating, and we love creating *for* Him/Her and *with* Him/Her. When we create, we are in a dialogue with universal energy. We are realigning and transcending our limited notions. We expand. We dip into the mystery. We discover the unexpected. We find our wings. You are creative; we all are. Take yourself by the hand and commit to a creative way of being. You will instantly feel more excited about living— maybe a little scared, puzzled or doubtful, but tickled and curious.

Living Creatively

"What does it mean exactly, to live creatively?" you might be asking. The first thing I want to say about it is that it does not mean to be an artist or necessarily create anything that falls into the category of artwork. It means to live intimately with your childlike nature, your Emotional Self. Even when it is pained by unresolved past experiences, it longs for creative expression. It loves adventures. It loves nature. And it is up for fun and silliness, if given the permission and the opportunity.

Our creative and expressive nature endures many blows, from childhood on. We are told not to cry like babies when we are only two or three years old. We're told to sit still, stop giggling, stop being silly, stop screaming, stop singing, stop making faces, and so on. In other words, the message is: Stop having a good time. Stop experiencing your feelings.

Our ability to live creatively begins to diminish early on. We must learn to be "good." We cannot take the risk of losing love, so we begin to cultivate our Defensive Self—tactics for emotional survival. If being expressive and creative is not approved of, we learn to repress it. Slowly and surely, we forget the feeling of expressive freedom. We comply with our parents' demands and expectations and then those of teachers, peers, bosses, lovers, neighbors, and even strangers. We learn to be what we are expected to be. We learn that it is important to get ahead, make money, raise a family, and be responsible. There is nothing in this script that tells us to "be ourselves."

One of my clients came to see me because his marriage was falling apart. He asked me, "Being myself. What is that? Who knows? Where do I find that self and why should I?" Lack of intimate communication was his wife's complaint. "I'm doing everything for the family… making good money, getting ahead. I'm responsible and loyal. What does she want?" he wondered. "She wants to hear your feelings. She wants to tell you about hers," I said. "I don't know what my feelings are," he told me. "Feelings about what?" This very kind and truly responsible man had buried his Emotional Self so deeply that it took a long and much-needed archaeological dig to find it and resurrect it. Your Emotional Self is the one who can bring in the enjoyment, vulnerability, and love that you need.

Most of us are reluctant to experience the intensity of our feelings. We know that underneath the surface of safe emotions there are layers of difficult and possibly painful ones. Naturally, we resist them, but when we don't feel deeply, we don't heal, and we don't find that lost self that we need to experience life and enjoy it. To me, living creatively means allowing ourselves to rediscover and express our Emotional Self in all its colors and states. Painful, silly, loving, outrageous, innocent, angry, curious…

This is a tricky process. We descend into scary realms, we grieve, we release, we soar, we give birth to ourselves, and we learn to be. It is also a creative process that teaches us courage and inspires us to keep living life as an adventure.

Tending To Our Emotional Self

Your Emotional Self is a source of magical possibilities. Yes, it needs loving attention; when it receives that it flowers, releasing a childlike perfume of warmth and playfulness. What follows are five ways to attend to our Emotional Self and nurture it into a creative, joyful power. I have expanded on each one below.

1. Daily Intimate Attention
2. Creative Expression
3. Adventure
4. Lazy Time

Daily Intimate Attention

Just like you would make time every day to be intimate with your child, mate, or loved one, you must make time to sit, be, feel, or dialogue with your Emotional Self. Set aside half an hour every day, preferably toward the end of the day. Put yourself in a private setting—your study, the bedroom, the couch, the porch, or a bench in the park. I recommend having your journal with you, and maybe a box of colored pencils. Close your eyes, and take a few minutes to consciously relax. Soften your jaw and face muscles, your shoulders, your chest and stomach. Let your thoughts drop away as much as possible. Focus on your breath, actually feel it going in and out, and let the rhythm of it relax you further.

After this short relaxation, draw your attention into your emotional center. Physically, it can be located in the chest or the gut area. After doing this for a minute, connect with the place that I call "The Home of Your Feelings." In the beginning, you might wonder whether you are actually there or not, and what it is that you are supposed to feel there.

Start by asking your Emotional Self, much like a parent would ask a child, "How do you feel?" (In this case you are both the parent and the child.) Listen for feelings; let them just pop up. For example, *"I feel tired," "I feel anxious," "I feel giddy," "I feel sad."* Refrain from judgment or comments, just like when you're listening to a child.

If you hear a feeling you don't understand, or need more information about, ask some questions. For example, let's say you hear, *"I feel anxious."* Ask, *"What are you (Emotional Self) anxious about?"* Your Emotional Self will tell you, if you're truly open to hearing. If you ask the same question, annoyed or disapproving, you will not get an honest response. Let's say you hear, *"I don't know why I'm feeling anxious."* You can help your Emotional Self discover more by asking further questions like, *"Are you anxious about the trip that we're going to take?"* If the answer is no, keep investigating and intuitively guessing. *"Is it the new project that we're doing at work?"* And so on.

Once you discover the underlying reason for the anxiety, express empathy— do not judge. Let your Emotional Self know that you are going to figure out ways together to alleviate the anxiety. Even if you have no idea at that moment what would be helpful, your Emotional Self will feel better knowing that it was heard and understood. What's important in this intimate listening is creating a loving bond between your Expanded Self and your Emotional Self, just like between a parent and a child (as a general rule, the same loving bond should be cultivated also between your Expanded Self and your Defensive Self). By listening, asking questions, and accepting your feelings, you are becoming a supportive parent, and your ability to guide your Emotional Self from a place of compassion and wisdom will develop. Here are a few ways to go about this process:

- You can do this as an emotional meditation. Sitting the whole time with your eyes closed, silently going through the process.
- You can use your journal and do the process in writing.
- You can use the colored pencils and draw and write.
- You can mix and match. Start in an emotional meditation and move into writing and drawing, or vice versa.

My clients tell me that this daily intimate sitting, which feels silly, awkward, and useless at the beginning and is only performed at my prompting, slowly becomes one of their most favorite activities, even when it brings up difficult feelings and haunting thoughts. There is a comfort in revealing one's feelings to oneself. And the loving attention from the Expanded Self to the Emotional Self feels soothing and is healing. If you want to know yourself and express and actualize your potential, you must sit with yourself—all three aspects of yourself. And you must definitely nurture your Emotional Self (nurturing does not mean indulging or enabling).

Creative Expression

Creative expression is not just the domain of artists. Every profession has its own form of creativity and every ordinary day is filled with creative opportunities. Being creative and expressive is a state of mind, one that you already possess. Look for everyday creative and expressive outlets. It can start with the way you choose to dress in the morning, or the way you put together your lunch, and can continue with an expressive conversation, a note, or a short e-mail to someone you like. At work, whatever it is that you do, look for creative possibilities. Think outside the box, play around with new ideas, engage your team—make it interesting for yourself. Evenings also present a playground for creativity: an interesting dinner, program, or lecture; a great conversation; a book, art, or culture; laughter—these can all tickle your creative sensibilities, if you let them.

Make a commitment to a creative and expressive life, and be creative about creating it. If you are an artist, creative expression is a natural part of your day. Let it spill over into the rest of your life, if you're not doing it already. Watch for your Defensive Self's reactions—as you open yourself to expression and fun, it can feel very threatened. Expression leads to freedom and vulnerability, and your Defensive Self is not keen on those; openness might lead to hurt. Your Defensive Self will try to sabotage, contract, or criticize you in order to keep you safe. Your Expanded Self needs to reassure and relax your Defensive Self (this can be quite a job). Eventually your Defensive Self learns to be more trusting of life and living.

Playtime

How much time do you spend just playing? Playing is for kids, we think. "I hardly have time to wash and set my hair or do my nails," said one a client, a full-time businesswoman with two kids. "You must be joking. I don't even have time to eat calmly or read for pleasure." I totally identify with her. I live in New York City, where the pace of life runs at least double speed. Most active and working adults work from nine in the morning to seven or sometimes eight o'clock in the evening, with not much of a lunch break. Late dinners are many times accompanied by the residue of take-home work. The household chores and attention to the kids usually take the little time that is left. Who can even think of playtime?

I have personally found that if I don't strongly commit to playtime and schedule it, I never get to play. Playtime has an amazing effect on my spirit. It is a great remedy for stress.

What is it that I mean by playtime? It means doing something that is purely pleasurable or silly and lighthearted, just for the sake of having a good time. This means different things to different people. For some, it's sitting around with friends, joking, laughing, and generating silliness. Others love the quiet of a chess game, puzzles, or board games. Yet others love to walk in nature or just sit under a tree or on the beach, watching the clouds and listening to the birds. There are also people who love to expend a lot of energy during their playtime activities. This might be a vigorous game of football, mountain climbing, rock climbing, or scuba diving. In one of the creative exercises that follow, I suggest making a list of your pleasures. Be sure to make this list, and do your best to schedule playtime with yourself and your loved ones. Daily mini playtimes and longer ones on the weekends are as necessary as food. Ultimately, you are here to experience joy and follow your bliss. Playtime is a must on the road to enlightenment.

Adventure

Adventures keep us young in spirit. They water the soil of the soul and fuel our aliveness. They keep our brain functioning better and our hearts excited. What constitutes adventure is unique for each person. Some of us might want to climb the Himalayas, skydive, or take a long sailboat ride. For others, it can be new museums, a new opera score, a different jazz class, a new course, or the zoo, if we have not been there for a while. An adventure is anything new—or old—that feels new and exciting. Every day should have a little adventure in it. A new dish for dinner, a possible new friend, a new or different route to get home, a new book, a new idea, a new plan. Keep generating adventures for yourself. I recommend keeping a running list of adventures experienced and desired. Remember, adventures don't have to consist of a trip to China; they could be as simple as a new song on your playlist.

Lazy Time

Lazy time was definitely one of the most difficult things for me to get used to. Just thinking about it used to get me anxious; the overachiever in me would panic. If you are like me, lazy time is a must. I always admired people who could lounge around, being deliciously lazy for hours. I also used to think that they were wasting their life away. I had a love-hate relationship with laziness. Later, I realized that laziness, like most things in life, needs to be kept in balance. A person also needs to assess why he or she is being lazy. Is it resting, or is it avoiding? The lazy time I am suggesting is a conscious choice to rest, relax, and replenish. This doing nothing is not an avoidance tactic but a pause, an energetic slowdown, a full permission to let go of doing and thinking. Lazy time is on my personal list of pleasures.

Check with yourself—are you resting or are you avoiding? Do you allow yourself some lazy time, or are you compulsively doing, doing, doing, and more doing? It's a question of balance, giving and receiving, inhaling and exhaling.

Fun, Creative, Expressive Exercises

Movement and Sound Meditation

Put on a piece of music that you love and move in time with it. Drop the thinking mind, and let your body do the moving. With eyes closed or half-closed (if you don't want to bang into the furniture), surrender to the music and the movement. Allow yourself to make sounds, say words, or sing. Your Defensive Self might try to make fun of you and criticize this activity in order to stop the "silly behavior." "You are not 12 years old," it might say. "What are you doing?" You can answer, "I am 12, and I like it." And keep enjoying yourself. You don't have to go to a club and/or drink to feel wild and free.

Writing and Drawing Meditation

Take a large piece of drawing paper (I recommend having art paper and crayons at home at all times) and write on the top of it a question or a theme that occupies your mind. Then, without thinking, start drawing. Let your hand guide you. Your subconscious mind will move your hand to draw something that is connected to your question. Enjoy being led, and drop all expectations or preconceived notions about the drawing. Don't grade or manipulate it. Let it become what it is. Once you feel it's finished, take another piece of paper and write spontaneously a few lines about the question or theme. Again, with minimal thinking. Now that both drawing and writing are done, look at them and see what they reveal to you.

Your Optimal Self, Your Optimal Life

Take yourself out of life for a good hour. Commit to silence and privacy. No phone, no talking, no work. Sit or lie down comfortably; close your eyes and relax. Ask your Expanded Self to help you create a clear vision of you in your optimal state of being and of your optimal life. You can start by asking yourself, "Who would I be without my anxiety, worry, self-doubts and criticism?" In other words, who would you be without your defensive structure?

I know that this is not an easy assignment. Our defensive patterns have become part of us, so much so that they feel like us. We identify with them and have become attached to them. Do your best in this visualization to let go of your fear and survival-based state. Imagine yourself free of self-doubts—confident, loving, expressive, trusting. Let yourself feel the ease of this state of being. This is the potential you. See yourself interacting with other people, doing your work. See yourself enjoying your moments, your hobbies, exploring different activities, and going on adventures.

In this visualization, let yourself live the best life you want for yourself. Be as specific as possible, and imagine the smallest details. How do you see the world, others, your work, your passions? What are the things that you are accomplishing? Go for the highest vision of yourself and your life. Be courageous and outrageous. Step into uncharted territory, away from your comfort zone. After about 30–45 minutes of visualizing, write your vision down under the headline "My Optimal Self, My Optimal Life." This exercise is emotionally liberating as well as an indicator of areas that still require expansion.

Delight in Being/Sensory Exploration

Choose a day and dedicate it to indulging in your senses. On that day, commit to experiencing all your regular daily activities with extra-open senses. For example, noticing how the light hits your eyes first thing in the morning. How your body feels under the covers. How does that first step out of bed feel? The water on your face, the sounds of the street, the taste of the first tea or coffee, and so on. This is a great practice in being present in the moment and in the senses. It teaches you to appreciate being alive. You will be distracted. Don't let it discourage you. Keep coming back to your senses.

Using Your Hands to Create

There are many ways to enjoy creating things with your hands. You must admit that it is satisfying to see the end results of these creative activities. Start by looking around the house for possibilities. For example, I painted patterns of red and gold inside all of my lampshades to achieve a certain atmosphere, and I love it. I created an angel out of strings of gold and silver wires and gemstones to put above my bed. I had never done that before or since. I created earrings and necklaces, changed or added fabric on my decorative pillows, and the list goes on. Get your hands busy. Repaint a picture frame or a room. Cook, knit, build a bookshelf, or mount one. Rearrange the furniture, mend the broken chair, and give it a new look. Clear the closets and reorganize or renew their compartments. Repot plants. These simple, creative projects are "doing" meditations. They quiet the mind and enhance your environment.

List Your Healthy Pleasures

Start by listing all things that give you pleasure (healthy pleasure, as opposed to destructiveness; I hope you can tell the difference). You should be able to list at least 20 things. Suggestions include: foods, activities, movies, music, books, arts, crafts, travel, play, sports, working out, dancing, lovemaking, sleeping, baths, singing, laughing, surfing the net, the beach, the mountains, and so on.

Next, list what would be fun to do if you dared to be out of your comfort zone. Some examples are skydiving, belly dancing, drumming, rollerblading, scuba diving, rock climbing, dressing up for Halloween, karaoke.

Finally, make your bucket list. List all the things you would like to do before you pass out of this world. The list may include places you'd like to visit, projects you want to accomplish, skills you want to cultivate, people you want to meet, and experiences you want to have.

Look at all three lists and commit to doing at least one of your pleasures a day. Make sure you vary your pleasures to cover all three lists. Pleasure is good for your soul and for your looks. It puts a smile in your heart and definitely moves the chi in your body. Go for it.

Childhood Fun Memories

Write down, maybe one at a time, a record of your childhood fun memories, small and big. For example, the smell of a guava tree in my backyard comes to my mind, or the memory of me and my girlfriends sitting by the tree in the park on the way from school, giggling about the boys. The taste of dark bread, butter, and anchovy paste, one of my favorite childhood foods. This exercise will warm your heart and connect you to your childlike self, its innocence and openness to simple delights.

Victories and Magic Moments

One of my most favorite activities is recalling at the end of a day my magic moments and my tiny or substantial victories. I highly recommend doing this. Reliving a magical moment or acknowledging a victory replenishes your trust in yourself and in the goodness and beauty of life. A magic moment can happen when you are looking at the moon or at a sunset. Or it can happen when you are playing with a child, giggling with your friends, or feeling playful at work for no reason. It could be a moment in a movie, in a concert, in nature, or on the subway.

A magic moment can happen anywhere, anytime. It is up to us to be available, still, and open enough to experience it. Acknowledging our victories enhances our ability to create more of them. Getting to a yoga class when you didn't feel like going is a victory. Being able to work through a reactive feeling without attacking shutting down is a great victory. Saying no when it's difficult but appropriate, or saying yes when you feel like running away. Speaking your mind in a meeting or in an important conversation. Taking a bath when you need it, in spite of more work that needs to be done is a victory for the overachiever. Doing work into the night when it is a must in spite of a lazy tendency is a victory. The list is long. We're not used to acknowledging ourselves for the so-called little victories (or for the big ones). All victories count; they all give us strength.

Letter Writing Exercises

Important Letters

These letters are an opportunity to express everything you ever wanted to say. They are private and are not meant to be sent out. They are simply vehicles for personal expression, not for sharing. The list I'm providing may seem intimidating, so feel free to pick and choose the ones that resonate with you at different times:

- A letter to a difficult parent
- A letter to a wonderful parent
- A letter to a helpful teacher
- A letter to a discouraging teacher
- A letter to your child self, addressing a crucial time
- A letter from your child self to you
- A letter to a friend whom you feel betrayed you
- A letter from your Expanded Self to your Defensive Self
- A letter from your Expanded Self to your Emotional Self
- A letter to a stranger whom you feel has changed or saved your life

These are some ideas for letters. Writing them can possibly help you process unspoken or uncompleted experiences and achieve better resolution and clearing. The exercise also provides you with a great opportunity to express yourself. Feel free to add other themes to the list, and keep writing as you feel inspired.

The Love or Hate Letter

Most of us have had the experience of loving someone madly without being able to express to them fully the intensity of our feelings. This kind of love, even if it happened 20 years ago, keeps living in our emotional memory. Dare yourself to write the ultimate love letter, all that you could not say then. Be bold, passionate, and unreasonable. It would free and empower you. You will also get a kick out of the lover in you that would show up, maybe to your great surprise. On the other hand, most of us also have had the experience of hating someone madly, without being able to show them the intensity of our feelings (in this case, maybe it was better that we didn't). Feel free to write a passionate hate letter. Put it all on paper. Revel in the bitterness and the anger. After you're done, don't be surprised if you have a grin on your face. You will feel lighter and will be able to let go of some of the bitterness. You might even laugh at yourself.

Self-Appreciation Note

This exercise can be uncomfortable for many of us. We are not taught to consciously articulate a list of all that we appreciate in ourselves. We might kind of, sort of, know that we are okay, or that we're good at certain things. But how many of us have sat down and actually detailed all the small and not-so-small elements that we appreciate in ourselves and in our lives? So, this is it. If you're ready to acknowledge, appreciate, and honor who you are, start building this appreciation list. It might start with three things and slowly grow to 30. There's no need to feel guilty, selfish, vain, or out of line. Self-appreciation is not an ego booster or an "I'm better than you" competition. It is just what it is: appreciating the person that you are—your talents, abilities, gifts, struggles, lessons, victories, vulnerabilities, dreams, achievements, and so on. If you're resisting this exercise, you might especially need it. If you're open to it, you're going to have a lot of fun.

The Love Gifts

Make a list of the people you love most. Write down under each one what it is that you love about them, how they move or inspire you, the special way you care about them, and how you feel they share their love with you. When you do this exercise, you will notice that love takes different colors. One person you love might evoke a desire to protect them, while another will evoke in you a sense of amazement. We love people differently, and our love takes many forms. Once you have the list, with a few lines underneath each person, think of a gift that you want to give each person. It can be something physical, spiritual, or emotional. It could be given to them directly or mentally. Define the gift you are choosing to give each person on your list, and now that you are clear about it, start giving. You might decide to buy or make some tangible gifts, write and send them, speak them, or show them by doing an action. You can even send thoughts and feelings silently. Be creative. Love's energy is best expressed.

A Day of Stillness

This exercise is done best on your day off. Choose a weekend day, or any off-work day, and commit to minimal talking/listening and minimal doing. For example, when you get up in the morning, if you're used to putting on the radio, music, or television, refrain from doing so. Most of the time, even on a day off, we still look at the list of things we need to do. Even though we're not working, we begin to attend to all the phone calls and errands of the day. Instead, decide that this is your vacation day. In a way, you're out of town. Take yourself for a long walk. Have lunch by yourself, quietly. Turn off your cell phone, or leave it at home.

Use your afternoon to do light reading, journal writing, or any solitary activity that appeals to you while being conscious not to crowd or overstimulate your mind. This restful exercise is a challenge for the overdoers among us. It forces you to be still. At first, it might bring up anxiety, restlessness, or even disorientation, but if you stick to it, you will slowly relax and begin to experience life from a more meditative perspective. Insights or underlying feelings will float up, and in the silence, you will notice, and maybe accept them, with greater ease. Creative ideas like stillness. Interesting things happen in the quiet. You might become very fond of it.

Write Down Your Dreams

Our dreams are a source of information and inspiration. They show us layers of ourselves we might be ignoring. Writing down your dreams and intuitively feeling into their meaning is wonderfully creative. There are many different methods of interpreting dreams. In this exercise, my suggestion is to try to tap into the feelings that you experienced in the dream, or at least one main feeling. An important part of this exercise is allowing yourself to re-experience, in a waking state, a feeling that you had in a recent dream and to follow the emotional associations that might be accompanying this feeling. "That reminds me how I felt when…" The exercise is not about analyzing your dreams but experiencing their emotional reality. Sometimes, our dreams stay mysterious; other times, we can intuitively understand them. There's no need to try too hard. You might want to draw, use colors, or if you have had very vivid images, you might want to sit with them for a while before writing.

Creative Gatherings

Creating with others is a lot of fun, as we all know. It expands the pool of creative ideas from which we can draw and produces unexpected results. I highly recommend creating opportunities to enjoy creating with others. These might include cooking, painting the house, playing games, planting, creating videos, making music, taking pictures and organizing them, making collages, creating musical playlists, making jewelry, planning a trip, or working on a play. You might want to consciously schedule, at least once a month, something creative and fun that is done with other people.

The Ten Commandments for Creative Living

1. **Connect with Your Emotions:** Take time to be with your Emotional Self. It is your best creative ally. It helps you realize your needs, your desires, and your passions. It inspires you to live a full and expressive life.

2. **Make a Commitment:** Realize that creative living requires commitment and structure. Promise yourself to use the exercises in this book or others, or feel free to invent your own.

3. **Make Time for Play:** Schedule specific times for play and fun on a daily and weekly basis.

4. **Join Creative Gatherings:** Initiate or get involved with groupsdedicated to creative expression. Sharing new activities and new ideas will generate more of them. It can be a book club, a drawing class, a cooking course, antique hunting, bird watching, and so on.

5. **Generate New Adventures:** Keep your life adventurous. Create small and big adventures to keep you growing, learning, and discovering.

6. **Use Your Hands:** Make a list of creative projects. Small or big, it doesn't matter; just keep your hands busy.

7. **Enjoy Laziness:** Take time to do nothing. Relax, release, recharge.

8. **Express Yourself:** Find ways to be expressive in your daily communications. Authentic sharing of yourself is a constant learning experience. Like a good wine, it gets better over time.

9. **Schedule Time for Art and Culture:** Give yourself a good dose of art and culture. From craft shows to performances and museums, enjoy the creative expression of others. Open your heart, and let yourself be moved, inspired, and challenged.

10. **Appreciate the Unique Expressions of Yourself and Others:**
Be generous with yourself and others. Creativity and expression need a receptive space. As much as possible, refrain from harsh judgment and labeling. People and cultures have different ways of expressing and creating. There is no right or wrong when it comes to creative expression; it's all a question of personal point of view. Stay open. Give yourself a chance to play. Even if a certain genre of art is not to your taste, you can use it as a creative source to inspire you to do different.

10

The Gate of Life Path

*Use your life path to express the
highest and the best in you.*

The universe seems to be purposefully initiating constant change, growth, and evolution. We witness its purposeful motion in nature and in our lives. The energy and consciousness within an apple seed propels and guides it to grow into a flowering plant. The same energy and consciousness propels an embryo to develop, a child to grow into an adult, and a creative project to manifest. The human soul is also a seed. Its purpose is to grow into a powerful tree that expresses the Creator's consciousness. Just as one apple seed can bring forth a tree bearing hundreds of apples over many years, a single human soul can inspire and enlighten generations of human beings. There are many varieties of apples; similarly, each of us is a unique soul fulfilling our purpose in diverse and original ways. We all, however, share the same purpose: to realize and actualize our true nature.

One of our most important lessons involves learning to express our best self amid the reality of our daily life. It is through our humanity that we express our spiritual nature. It sounds contradictory but is really complementary. Our knowledge of how we as individuals fulfill our life purpose is not an intellectual understanding; it is a heartfelt, intuitive experience coupled with a desire to share and contribute.

Allowing your adult child to make mistakes requires unconditional love and respect for their free will—indeed, by so doing, you become a reflection of what gave the human soul free will in the first place. It is up to each one of us to honor, discover, and follow our true purpose. Guidance and support are always available, but each one of us needs to reach out for these, make a connection with our true soul's desire, and take responsibility for actualizing it.

Connecting To Your Personal Purpose

I have been asked by many clients, "How do I find my personal purpose?" In other words, "How do I define my life path?" My answer is always, "Ask this question as many times as needed in your meditations and listen to the answers." Answers can come through a feeling, an image, a word, or a combination of all these things. Some of us are very clear about our life path. My brother, for example, who is a brilliant mechanical engineer, started taking things apart and putting them back together when he was four or five. He loved nothing more than finding out how things work. To this day, this is what fascinates him.

On the other hand, I was led to pursue acting by a strange pull that came over me when I was looking at the advertising for the Academy of the Performing Arts. I remember being glued to the words dance and acrobatics that appeared on the list of subjects. I had no dance background, and actually I was one of the worst students in my high school gym classes. I also showed no acting talent whatsoever. I cannot explain my attraction to the ad, other than to say that my soul was calling. It knew that this was the path to follow.

Twenty years later, after a long and successful career in acting and dancing, when my therapist at the time told me that I am a born counselor and that I should join his training program, I got very upset with him. "I am an actor," I said. "I don't think you appreciate that." It took two years for this message to register. One late night, I heard the small inner voice whisper, "He is right." In fact, we were both right. I continued my work in the theater while also training as a psychotherapist. In my case, I was nudged into my life path. I was literally given instructions to pursue it, twice, in spite of my emotional resistance. Needless to say, I'm grateful for the instructions and grateful that I followed them.

"How Do I Know If I Am On My Life Path?"

This is another question that clients often ask me. I also hear it from friends and acquaintances. Here are some helpful tips to answer this question for yourself:

1. Your true life path incorporates your gifts, talents, and abilities.
2. Your life path feels natural, and you have a feeling that you belong there, even in spite of difficulties or challenges. Level of comfort may vary from person to person; some people may feel fully comfortable, while others may feel awkward and nervous, but still know that it's the right place for them.

You may find yourself thinking or saying, "Yes, this is what I'm supposed to be doing."
3. Your life path brings you deep satisfaction and a sense of fulfillment, even when you are struggling with obstacles and setbacks.
4. Your life path is not something that you do to impress, look good, please your parents, achieve status or money, prove your worth, or get acknowledged. These traits of our defensive self might be mixed in, since we are human, but they are not the propelling force behind choosing a true life path.
5. Your life path gives you the opportunity to share your talents and abilities with others, and it feels good to do so.
6. Your life path is aligned with your spiritual and emotional evolution as well as with your spiritual path.

Thinking about these indicators and reflecting on how you're spending your days can give you valuable insight as to whether you are aligned with your life path or not.

I had a client who was a highly paid lawyer. He told me that what he really wanted to do was to be a high school teacher. "My father will kill me," he said. "There is no way I could do that to him or to myself." His father was a lawyer and actually found him his first job. It took almost two years of counseling to make this transition. First, he had to emotionally accept the cut in salary and the change in status and lifestyle. Then, we had to deal with his relationship with his father—how to present this choice, how to stand up for it, and how to go about life in spite of disapproval. It all eventually worked out, in spite of many challenges. His courage was necessary every step of the way. There is something magical about a true life path. It is aligned with the greater order of the universe, and that gives it tremendous power.

EXERCISE: Helpful Inquiry About Your Life Path

1. **Make a list** of all your talents, abilities, and skills. For example, mine would include creative thinking, acting and dancing ability, analytical thinking, communicating, listening compassionately, and writing. Make a second list of your passions—things that give you pleasure and fulfillment and things you love to share with others. This might be a long list. Don't

be alarmed. For example, my passion/pleasure list would include dancing, yoga, theater, art, nature, meditation, counseling, leading workshops, research, reading, writing, and so on.

2. **Look at your lists** and identify the "through-line," the dominant elements that emerge. To come back to my own example, the through-line in my lists is arts, communication, and transformation, all of which I am really passionate about. Make sure you write them down.

3. **Ask yourself, "Am I practicing, enjoying, and sharing some of the elements on my lists in my work life?"** If not, why not? Here are some reasons I gleaned from my discussions with clients:

    - "I am not sure what my talents and gifts are."
    - "I don't see how I can make a living using my talents and my gifts.

They are not practical."

    - "I am afraid of failing, so I don't use my talents and skills."
    - "I am afraid of making a mistake that I will regret forever."
    - "I have some talents and abilities, but I am not really good enough to excel and stand out."
    - "I love working with kids, but I was trained as a mechanic. I make a good living, and I don't think I can change the course of my life now."
    - "Making a living is different from hobbies. I prefer to keep it that way."

Write down some of your own reasons for not utilizing your talents and abilities in your work life.

1. **Ask yourself, "am I practicing, enjoying, and sharing some of the items on my lists in my personal life?"** If not, why not? Here are some reasons I gleaned from myself, friends, and clients:

    - "I don't have time to pursue my hobbies."
    - "I don't have money to indulge in my talents and gifts."
    - "I don't think it is important that I do. I need to stick with making a living and paying the bills."
    - "I never cultivated my talents and my gifts. Neither of my parents thought these were important, and it feels like it is too late now."

- "I am not sure what I might enjoy doing other than what I'm doing now."
- "I have been trying to integrate these into my busy life, and I find it frustrating."
- "I am afraid that if I enjoy some of my talents and gifts, I will not want to do anything else and my life might fall apart."
- "I feel confined by my current environment and circumstances. If my living conditions were different, it would be easier."
- "I feel limited physically."
- "I feel limited emotionally and mentally. I'm held back by fears and phobias."
- "I don't feel I deserve to have fun and engage in pleasurable activities when so many other people are suffering."

Write down your own reasons for not making time for your passions and interests in your personal life. Once you have them written down, use the tools available to you to clear out what is holding you back.

Follow Your Bliss

If you have defined your talents, gifts, and pleasures, and you clearly enjoy engaging in certain activities and projects, it means, simple and clear, that you are supposed to do so. The famous quote by Joseph Campbell, "Follow your bliss," is not some new age fluff. It is a guiding principle for living a purposeful life. You are here to be fulfilled and to contribute. These two are your rights and your responsibilities. Your talents, abilities, and passions live within you like the seeds of an apple tree, waiting to become fruit. It is wise to support and nurture them. Doing so, you are giving to yourself and others.

Many of us lack the courage to follow our bliss. We are taught that we should have a good job that pays the bills and that fulfillment is secondary. Not true. Fulfillment is primary. Ideally, we should find a creative way to marry our fulfillment with a good job that pays the bills.

A client of mine, a successful actor, never had to ask himself what his talent and abilities were and what he enjoyed doing. It had been clear to him since he was 15 years old that theater was his bliss. Another client found, at the age of 20, that she liked working with children. She was tutoring kids in an afternoon program, but that did not cover the bills. She looked for something else that she could enjoy doing that would bring her income. Her secondary passion was beautiful homes and interior design. I encouraged her to invest in studying. She had to overcome self-doubts and fears, and she did. She graduated and became an accomplished interior designer. Two years down the line, she was making a good living and did not need to teach anymore. She insisted on keeping her teaching job because, as she told me, the kids touched her heart in a way that beautiful things could not. She was able to weave both passions into her life while earning the money she needed.

Another client was a manager of a few stores when he came to me. He enjoyed his job and made good money, but all along, he kept telling me, "I feel that there is something else I am meant to do, but I don't know what that is." I asked him what gives him, other than his job, the most joy. And he said, "Physical activity Football—playing and coaching." I said, "Go for it. Find some time to play." He did. He found a group of adults that met once a week and played football. One of our sessions, he arrived complaining that his back was sore from playing football. I suggested that he tries yoga to help him stretch. He did, and fell in love with it. Today, five years later, he is teaching yoga and coaching football. He left his job and is investing in his own wellness business.

EXERCISE: Identifying Neglected Skills

Look at the list of your abilities, talents, and skills. Which one of these are you not utilizing? Take each one of the talents and abilities on the list and write down your reasons for not engaging with it. I invite you to make a commitment to each of these abilities and find a way to enjoy them. If you are determined and creative, you will surprise and delight yourself. For example, at this point, I cannot take a dance class every day the way I used to because of physical injuries that occurred as a result of years of dance (thank God I can do my yoga). So, what I do is take a dance class once a week or once every two weeks. I "mark" the big jumps and turns instead of doing them full out. Taking a dance class, even though I'm not doing it fully, gives me tremendous joy. I also think that it inspires the younger dancers.

Let's take another example. Let's say that you love gardening but live in the city, with no space for an outside garden. You can still have a garden of plants in the house. You can volunteer to work in one of the public gardens, or you can help a friend with a garden. A friend of mine has a real knack for marketing. He headed up the marketing department of a big firm for 20 years. All the while, he was painting here and there as a hobby. Three years ago, after his two grown-up daughters left the house, he decided to make a commitment to his painting.

To day, he's doing that full time and is using his marketing skills to sell his paintings as well as the paintings of two of his friends. They created their own "marketing team" for their work and are having a ball.

Each one of your talents is a contribution waiting to happen, and an experience of joy. Your life path should include all the things that are truly important and fulfilling to you. If family is important to you, then it is part of your life path. If you are passionate about creating a successful business, it is part of your life path. If you are an artist, it is in your life path. Each one of us has a few important elements that are woven together to create our life path. All elements should be honored and given energy and attention.

Of course, it is a balancing act. It takes skill and commitment to keep all elements flourishing at the same time. Family/relationships and work/contribution are two of the main elements. The third element can be our spiritual and emotional growth, and the fourth can be learning/discovery/travel. There are other elements. Each one of our paths is a unique combination of elements. We are the weavers of the tapestry of our life. We create it according to our needs, passions, desires, and abilities. Each of our creations contributes to and enhances the greater tapestry of life.

EXERCISE: Defining Your Life Path

PART ONE: Write down 3–5 of the most important elements that pave your Life Path. If you need help figuring them out, here are some fun ways. Ask yourself: what would you do if you won, tax-free, $10 million? Your money concerns are over. Now, what would you want to do with your life? Entertain that for a minute, and write down what comes up. The second scenario that might help you is to imagine that you only have two years to live. What would you do? Hopefully, you came up with 3–5 important elements that you're deeply passionate about.

PART TWO: Evaluate each one of the elements, and write down an honest report. How much are you cultivating each one? In what ways are you neglecting or postponing them?

PART THREE: Write down three specific choices and commitments leading to actions to enhance each element. Pay special attention to the ones that are least attended to. Start making a dedicated effort to take care of all the important elements of your life path.

The Four Magic "C's"

Since I mentioned commitments and choices, I will share with you what I call the **four magic "C's"**: **Choose, Commit, Contribute**, and **Celebrate**. These, like the Four Magic E's, unfold in this order.

Choose

Choose your thoughts, beliefs, feelings, and actions very carefully. They translate into vibrations. We are energy, and we vibrate on the frequencies that reflect our state of being. Whatever we emit as vibrating beings, we attract to ourselves. Most of us are aware by now of the Law of Attraction, which means "like attracts like." As you think/feel, you become; what you become, you attract. We attract to ourselves people, situations, and events that match our vibration. It behooves us to work diligently toward shifting negative thoughts, feelings, and behavior patterns into positive, life-affirming ones. Consistently and daily, we must choose to transform. It is a discipline and a choice that we can make, or not. Well-being is a choice. Success is a choice. Love and commitment are a choice. Being a contribution is a choice. Achieving these might be what is called the "hard work miracle," but they all are fueled by the power of choice.

Commit

Commit to the discipline of shaping your inner reality. Commit to realizing who you truly are and why you are here. Commit to the connection with your higher wisdom. Commit to being honest and open with yourself and others. Commit to respect your unique contribution. Commit to your happiness and to your well-being. Commit to your expression and growth. I could go on and on. What I'm saying is: Commit to experiencing and expressing the best in you. Without commitment, focus, and a burning desire, we don't get there.

Contribute

We find deep joy in giving. I am not saying anything new. It is a well-known fact that we love to share our gifts and abilities with others. We love to feel appreciated, useful, inspiring, and helpful. There is a need within the soul to love and be loved. Living a life of contribution answers this need. Sometimes, as young people, we might not yet be ready to live life from a giving perspective. We want love. We need approval. We want to look good, to impress others, and to be noticed. That is normal. As we mature emotionally, we begin to find fulfillment and satisfaction in contributing. This yearning to make a difference is like a good wine: it tastes better the older we get.

Celebrate

I can't think of anything more important than to enjoy our daily moments and feel the magic and the beauty within them. Open yourself to the moving, playful, funny adventure of being alive. I actually tell myself to do that every morning. Celebrate being here—the challenges, difficulties, and miracles … all of it. It is possible to embrace, accept, and surrender to life and, at the same time, change and contribute to the creation of a better world. Tap into trust, gratitude, and humor. It's not always easy to do, yet it's always uplifting.

The Four Questions

The following four questions have inspired people's lives since the beginning of time. Who am I? Why am I here? What is in my way? How do I get there? **(How do I realize who I am and fulfill my purpose?)**

Thousands of books were written in an attempt to answer these questions. I suggest that if you have not pondered these, start now, since it might take you a lifetime. I have been asking myself these questions for the last 40 years, and my revelations keep coming. I will not delve into a long exploration of these in this book. I have touched on them lightly in the other chapters. But I would like to relate a story of a client who spoke to me about her exploration.

I asked her, "Who are you?"

She answered, "I am a multi-leveled being."

"Tell me more," I said.

She responded: "I am an incest survivor who is learning to take responsibility for my rights, my boundaries, my lessons, and my strengths. I am an artist—an actress, singer, and a vocal coach. I am a mother and a wife. At the same time, I feel that I am none of these. These different roles feel like assignments that I am completing with deep sincerity and dedication for the purpose of growth."

"Then, who are you really?" I asked again.

"I have a sense that I am consciousness witnessing itself," she replied. I loved her answer. "Why do you think you're here?" I asked.

"To experience myself as that consciousness, and to express joy and creativity," she said.

"How do you get there?" I asked.

She smiled and said: "By releasing all that is not that, and I have a lot to release. That is why I like sitting with you. It is easier to let go in the company of a witness other than myself. Your compassion helps me release my anger, my tears, and my fears, all that I don't wish to hold onto."

This is a peek into one person's exploration of the four questions. Each one of us needs to experience the answers first hand. Reading the masters helps, as do discussions, meditations, being in the presence of great teachers, and learning from our life experiences. Most of all, knowledge speaks in the stillness of the heart.

Manifesting Your Life Path

The four questions are effective guidelines in the process of manifesting your life path.

To answer the first question ("Who am I?"): Spiritually, you are pure awareness, one with the Universal Consciousness, but on the human level, each one of us is here to discover what moves us, what we feel, need, and love, what makes us happy, and what we are passionate about. At the same time, we also need to face our fears, heal our pain, and learn to accept and honor who we are in this human form, this time around. Knowing who you are means becoming friends with your soul and understanding the secrets of your heart.

To answer the second question ("Why am I here?"): After answering the first question, you can listen to the inner guidance that reveals to you why you're here. Spiritually, you're here to realize your true nature, which is pure awareness—never born, never dead—and an expression of the Creative Source. On the human level, each one of us needs to embrace our lessons and our purpose, the knowledge of which helps us create the vision for our lives. A great indicator for our purpose is a sense of "bliss." What gives us deep pleasure and a sense of fulfillment? On the other hand, difficulties and challenges are great indicators of our lessons.

To answer the third question ("What is in my way?"): Embracing both the difficulties and the bliss helps us address the question.

To answer the fourth question ("How do I get there?"): I will be simplistic and say that the recipe is: follow your bliss, learn from your challenges, and keep releasing and dissolving all that is in the way of your inner freedom and openness.

The Process of Manifestation

The process of manifestation is another subject about which much has been written. As with all great subjects, there is room for more to be written about it, and it could make a difference. Here is the seven-step process I have defined and work with:

1. **The Inner Paradigm**: Creating an open, receptive, and positive state of being
2. **Your Soul's Calling:** Discovering and creating the vision for your life path
3. **Partnerships:** Creating teamwork, giving, receiving, and acknowledging
4. **A Plan:** Making choices, charting your steps
5. **Commitments:** Staying on target, cultivating focus, integrity, and accountability
6. **Actions:** Being proactive, taking initiative
7. **Celebration and Gratitude.**

Let's explore them one by one, below.

The Inner Paradigm

Creating a positive state of being is the most important step in the process of manifestation. Everything in the universe is actually consciousness and energy. The universe is expressing itself by pulsating energetically. We are part of, and one with, this ocean of pulsation. We can change the frequency of our vibrational combination by changing our feelings and thoughts. We are endowed with free will, and we have the ability to shift our vibrations. In this way, we are co-creators with the Universal Mind. This ability to create our vibratory field is a gift deserving of our responsibility and attention.

What we think, feel, believe, and do creates our reality. Our state of being, the combination of energetic vibrations we emit, affects others; at the same time, we are affected by the vibrations of others. Our personal vibratory combination attracts to us similar vibrations (the Law of Attraction). We consciously or unconsciously transmit and receive frequencies all the time, and we magnetize to ourselves what we feel, think, and believe.

I have written this book with the intention of giving you tools to create a more enlightened state of being. It is your responsibility to do whatever you can to move toward a state of wholeness and use whatever tools you find helpful. Your state of being is the base of your life, the roots of your tree, or the building blocks of your inner home. A positive sense of self, a trust in one's abilities, an expressive and creative spirit, an understanding of one's soul direction, and an open heart all contribute to the creation of a confident, loving, and joyful state of being.

When you accept, respect, and understand yourself, you are more open to re ceive. You expect good, you allow yourself to feel joy, and you naturally choose fulfillment. Self-appreciation allows you to be in the moment and trust the unfolding of life in spite of sadness, difficult lessons, and challenges.

Your Soul's Calling

As I mentioned before, our life path is a combination of our lessons and our passions. In other words, this is our evolution and our contribution. Use the exercise Defining Your Life Path on page 169 to define the important elements of your life you are passionate about. You can identify these elements by the fact that they make you deeply happy when you imagine being, doing, or having them. If you have not done so, begin a process of imagining, dream-building, and visualizing the different facets of your life. Create a vision board, create a dream book, with pictures, words, colors. Make time to visualize yourself being, doing, and having what you want. Practice feeling as if it is already happening. Enjoy it. Live your dreams emotionally, as if they are happening now. Expect them to unravel. Look forward to their unfolding. Don't get stuck on doubting and questioning as to how exactly things will happen. Take the actions you need to take without trying to control the process. Allow the Mastermind to work with you and for you. Listen to inner guidance. Follow your intuition, and relax into your daily activities. The main thing is to trust and tap into a sense of an already existing bliss. Obviously, keep dissolving what is in the way of your receptivity.

EXERCISE: Visualization/Writing

Choose one element from your life path vision and, while sitting down, either imagine it or write about it, clearly seeing yourself engaged in a specific part of this element. For example, let's say you have chosen writing as one of your vision elements. Imagine yourself writing as clearly as you possibly can. Where are you? Are you sitting at a desk? What does the desk look like? Is it neat, cluttered? Are you surrounded by books? What types of books? Are you typing on a laptop, or are you filling page after page with your favorite pen? Is there a window in front of you with the breeze blowing onto your face, or are you tucked away in a dark, quiet study far away from other people?

More importantly, how are you feeling while sitting at your desk, writing? The feelings of joy, peace, and contentment, are what most powerfully seeps into your subconscious mind and move it to action. This is not always easy because we're not necessarily used to feeling happy and fulfilled, but by practicing the exercises in this book, as well as committing to any other growth discipline, you can clear blockages and expand your ability to tap into your inner happiness.

Here's a scene from a visualization by one of my clients, someone whose major life path elements were yoga, writing, running, cooking, and family:

■ ■ ■

I wake up to sunlight pouring in through huge French windows. I kiss my husband, put on my robe, and go sit at my writing table on our third-floor balcony. The morning air smells salty and delicious, and I hear the hypnotic roar of the ocean. I turn on my laptop and load up my book file. I'm working on my first novel and also developing my food, style, and lifestyle blog. I upload a new post for my blog. I'm thinking about what to cook for dinner that night, while also putting the finishing touches on my cookbook, which will be published in a few months. After about an hour of work I go downstairs, put on a pot of coffee, as my cat brushes against my legs and the dog excitedly patters across the floor. I happily welcome the opportunity to take him out for a leisurely walk…

Albert Einstein said, "Imagination is greater than knowledge." I cannot emphasize enough the importance of cultivating and developing your imagination for this exercise. People have different capacities for imagining; some of us are more visual than others. If your imagination feels weak, perhaps it's because you're dulled by the surroundings and circumstances of your everyday life. Take yourself to new places. Pick up new magazines, flip through the pages, and cut out pictures that appeal to you. Give yourself permission to imagine yourself in circumstances completely different from the ones you're in now.

This process should be fun. It opens your subconscious mind to the experience of whatever it is you're imagining. Your whole self participates and accepts this imagined reality as truth and before you know it, it begins to manifest itself. Your life's vision has a life of its own. It keeps shifting, expanding, and redirecting itself. What we want at the age of 30 is not the same as what we want at the age of 40, 50, 60, and so on. Your heart tells you what makes you happy and what you truly need. Follow it closely.

A burning desire to manifest what you want must be coupled with consistent dwelling in the feeling reality of your desired vision. Think of how excited you were as a child before you went on a trip. You imagined everything that was going to happen; you ate, slept, talked, and dreamed about it; you burned with anticipation. That kind of enjoyment, when practiced consistently, has the power to create reality in the same way as anger or fear. Many of us learned to accept negative outcomes or become paralyzed emotionally with fear or anger. We forgot to dream and believe, and we need to rekindle the ability to do so. Dare to dream big, and trust the outcome.

Partnerships

Think about the things in your life that you enjoy most and cherish. How many of these do you do with others? We are partnering all the time. Life is a big canvas of teamwork, giving and receiving.

EXERCISE: Writing

Write down all the partnerships in your life. The list of partners can look like this:

- My husband
- My friends (each one is a partnership)
- My kids (each one is a partnership)
- My team at work
- My co-writer5 My therapist
- My accountant
- My doctor
- My lawyer
- My siblings (each one is a partnership)
- My parents (each one is a partnership)

- My spiritual group My tennis partner
- My jazz group
- My teachers
- My students
- And so on.

Look at your list. As you can see, your life is rich with partnerships of all kinds. Each partner brings out something different in you, and each partner gives you something unique. There is a constant exchange of knowledge, love, support, fun, and challenge. Partnerships keep you growing and giving. People who know how respect and enjoy their partnerships evolve faster and achieve more. To manifest your life's vision, you need to be a good team player, a good partner. You need to inspire and be inspired. You need to give and enjoy receiving. You need to reach out and be there for another. You need to discover and create with others. Our power lies in our ability to relate and partner with ourselves and others. The three inner aspects of yourself form a partnership; when this union is solid, you are centered.

> ••• **Reflection Pause** •••
>
> Take a look at your partnering abilities. Even though we feel and behave a little differently within each partnership, we can still notice general tendencies. What kind of a partner are you, in general? Here are some questions to ask yourself: Am I a generous or a withholding partner? Am I expressive and honest, or am I inauthentic? Am I a team player, or do I need to be in the center, making my partner my audience? Do I know how to listen? Do I get easily defensive? Do I respect my partner? Do I show appreciation? Do I support and encourage, or am I quick to analyze, criticize, or judge? Do I love cooperation, or am I a loner? And so on. What do you need to pay attention to in order to be a better partner?

I hope you got an honest picture of your partnering style. If it is not optimal—and none of us can honestly say that we have mastered the art of partnering—then get to work. Realize that who you are as a partner (to yourself, as well as to others) shapes who you are and affects your destiny.

A Plan

A plan of action is a natural outcome of a clear vision. If you're not sure about what is important to you now—meaning what you passionately want to create and why—then you are not ready for a plan. On the other hand, if you are emotionally clear and are imagining and enjoying your vision as explained in Step Two, you are ready and probably eager to create a plan so that you can ground and actualize your vision.

EXERCISE: Writing a Plan

Choose one specific area of your life for this exercise. Write down the necessary steps that would take you from where you are now to the fulfillment of your vision. Organize the steps by their priority order. Example: Let's say that your vision is a deep and enjoyable romantic relationship, and let's say that you are single and ready. There are a few obvious steps that you must take to achieve your vision, such as maybe getting on a dating site or taking time to attend single events. The next step would be conscious dating with the intention of finding a mate, which means not lingering in relationships or long dating periods with people who you know are not a real possibility for you. If you find yourself doing that, then the next step might be to get some counseling and find out why you are sabotaging your success. Every project needs a plan of action. Every vision needs a solid ground of choices and priorities.

Once you have created a specific plan for one area, go ahead and make one for all the other important areas of your life vision. A word of caution: the plan has to be grounded and practical, but at the same time flexible. It's important to maintain an inner ease, in order to navigate within the plan, making adjustments as necessary. Be aware and open to what presents itself while you are walking the walk. Learn from what doesn't work, and shift. Don't get stubborn. Don't get self-righteous. Don't get stuck. Work with your inner guidance. If we co-create with the universe, we learn to allow, receive, and let things happen. Adopt an attitude of relaxed determination. Organic actions work better than forced ones. Stay playful and passionate—playfulness and passion, coupled with lots of intuition, is a potent combination.

Making and Honoring Commitments

Your plan might end up sitting on your desk or in a file in your computer, getting old and neglected, unless you make specific commitments to support the steps and the choices you have created. Let's get back to the example of the single guy or girl who is passionate about creating a great relationship. If he or she does not follow through on a commitment to go on some dates on a weekly basis, his or her vision might not materialize. When we make a commitment and stick to it, we are emitting the energy of, "I am serious about this," "I am dedicated," "I mean it." This kind of powerful action/intention can move mountains. A commitment is a road paver. It can put a dancer or an athlete with a severe injury back on their feet. It can move a nation to freedom. It can make an artist create against all odds. And it did take a man to the moon. It is all about intention, translated into commitment, and from there, to action.

Make specific commitments in all areas of your life's vision, following your plan, and do whatever it takes to stick to them. My clients and I have specific commitments under each Gate. At the beginning of a year, we each create a vision for the whole year, guided by what we call **The Five Major Goals**. These goals relate to different areas we each find most important to us. Here are the steps to follow. Please note: the last chapter will provide more details about the process of making commitments and taking actions:

1. Define your five major goals for the year.
2. Create a detailed plan for each one of your goals.
3. According to the plans, chart specific commitments and place them under the corresponding Gates.
4. On a weekly basis, consult the chart and choose weekly, committed actions that need to be taken, one from each Gate.
5. Do your best to stick to them. Create a discipline, and honor your commitments. I frequently say to clients and to myself: If you fall off the horse, don't waste time and energy yelling at yourself—brush off the dust, and get back on.

For example, let's say that one of your major goals is to create a committed, intimate relationship. After you've created a plan, you write down your commitments. Any one commitment might relate to one, two, or even more Gates. In the dating example, a commitment might be to sign up for a dating website and make a daily effort to communicate with other members. You would place the commitment to chat under the Gate of Dialogue and a commitment to observe your emotions while dating under the Gate of Emotions. You might have a third commitment, let's say to actually meet people regularly for dates and still get to bed at a reasonable hour so you get enough sleep. This commitment belongs in the Gate of the Body. As you can see, three Gates are involved in the main goal of creating an intimate relationship.

One of my clients, a young man who had never been in a serious relationship, was petrified by the thought of approaching women. One of his major goals was to overcome the fear and be able to date. That goal was related to the Gate of Dialogue and the Gate of Emotions. He made a commitment to approach at least three women in a span of a week and to engage in a casual dialogue with them. It could be anywhere—at work, at a bus stop, or a party. His fear of rejection was paralyzing. I asked him to "collect rejections"; in other words, to train himself to accept "rejections," if they happen, so he can learn to survive them. The first couple of months were very difficult. He would freeze and wouldn't be able to carry the simplest conversation, but he stuck to his commitment and slowly began bringing "rejection stories" to our sessions. We called them "rejection stories," even though they were stories about attempts to connect, some successful, and some not so.

Over time, the stories began to be about good moments—a smile, a chat, a phone number… It kept progressing, and at some point, he became so comfortable with reaching out to women that I would jokingly call him the New Age Casanova. Today, he is in a committed relationship, and the past is history. That is the power of commitment. I am sure that you have experienced it in your life. All great deeds, achievements, and discoveries come to be because of the power of commitment.

Actions

Just as marriage vows need to become daily actions of love and friendship, commitments need to translate into actions. We can think of actions as the twin part of making commitments: commitments represent our resolve; actions represent the implementation of our decision. When we make commitments, but don't act on them, we are stuck. On the other hand, when we act without a sense of direction, choice, and commitment, we can get lost. As I said before, it is a discipline that becomes fulfilling and creative. Plan, prioritize, commit, and act.

If you have created a plan and a set of commitments, make sure to act on them on a daily basis. Become aware of the ways that you do and the ways that you don't follow up. If you have a tendency to procrastinate and avoid or delay taking action, take a good look at the reasons why. The opposite is also true. Some people are nonstop doers. They don't allow themselves to rest. They are driven by their to-do list. They, too, need to examine their behavior. I believe that healthy doing is constant and relaxed, like a peaceful breath, with pauses and a sense of balance between doing and nondoing.

Celebration and Gratitude

The ability to celebrate life and feel grateful for all that it brings is a direct path to bliss. To me, celebration means the conscious enjoying of our moments. Viscerally feel the life force in and around you. Enjoy the energy, colors, shapes, smells, and textures of life. Enjoy people, animals, and nature. Trust yourself and life enough to relax, be playful, and grateful for the challenges, the adventures, and the gifts. In terms of the process of manifestation, this seventh step must permeate the whole process.

The best way to manifest anything is to live with the feeling of celebration and gratitude, as if you already have all that you are wishing for. The continuous feeling of enjoyment and trust magnetizes to you more enjoyment and trust. It is an open state that renders you receptive of good. If you grew up, as I did, in a household that did not celebrate victories and magic moments, you need to teach yourself to do so. Some of us grew up with very demanding parents. A score of 90 on a test was not good enough, and maybe helping around the house or completing a creative project were not acknowledged or celebrated. When that happens, we don't learn to feel fulfilled by our little or big achievements. We keep ourselves in the "I am not enough" state, unable to celebrate our victories, thus perpetuating that state. I impress upon my clients the importance of acknowledging their victories and enjoying their daily magic moments. It helps you live in a state of gratitude. Counting your blessings, no matter how few they might seem, creates more blessings, and enjoying your victories, no matter how small they appear, creates more of them as well.

The Ten Commandments for Fulfilling Your Life Path

1. **Honor Yourself:** You are a spark of the Great Spirit, here to realize and express that. Learn to let go of all non-truths about yourself, and open the eyes of your heart to your true nature.

2. **Follow Your Bliss:** Commit to happiness, health, and fulfillment. Consistently and compassionately weed out feelings and thoughts of unworthiness. You are a child of life, and life is not the same without your unique contribution. No matter how confusing things may become, if you're committed to your bliss, you will learn to glean the lessons, get stronger, and redirect your life toward your optimal state.

3. **Be Impeccable, Strive for Excellence:** You gain nothing by doing haphazard work—you need to radiate excellence if you want to attract it. Give 100 percent of yourself to all your endeavors. You receive what you give.

4. **Uphold Honesty and Integrity:** Encourage honesty and integrity in all your actions and non-actions. Be your word—be accountable, reliable, and responsible. Authenticity and integrity are strength. These are the attributes of good leaders. You are the leader of your life, and in many cases, the leader for others. Don't shortchange yourself. Live by example.

5. **Create Partnerships:** Learn to be a good partner in all your life's situations. You will enhance everything you do. You will receive the help, support, and knowledge you need, and you will enjoy giving. Operating daily as part of a team (this includes a team of two) is much less lonely than operating solo, and so much more fulfilling.

6. **Honor Your Goals and Dreams:** These are the expressions of your true self and your path of contribution. Do not compare yourself to others. Don't try to be, do, or have what is not right for you. Honor your unique talents and aspirations, no matter how humble. You never know the possible effect of your creations. Something as simple as sewing pillows with your mom can inspire you to be a great designer.

7. **Stay Focused and Consistent:** Cultivate a relaxed, unwavering mind and a constant process of moving forward.

8. **Enjoy and Play:** As you continue to discover your truth and become comfortable with yourself, you will relax into your natural playfulness. Keep enjoying your moments.

9. **Be Grateful:** Find joy in life's simple pleasures and moments. Appreciate what you have and those in your life. It is easy to take our loved ones and the things we have for granted. Each moment offers an opportunity for insight, growth, and overcoming challenges. We have a choice to create new possibilities and find inspiration wherever we go.

10. **Celebrate:** Celebrate your achievements and your learning. By doing so, you're celebrating your life.

11

The Gate of Silence

Use the silence to reach the highest
and the best in you.

What is silence? The answer is seemingly simple: the absence of noise. Sometimes in the middle of the night, one might wake up and hear silence. The world is quiet.

But there is another kind of silence that is rare and hard to tune into—a deep stillness inside, in which you hear eternity. You feel a peaceful merging into all that is. In this inner quiet, you experience a melting, expanding, and dissolving sensation, as if you lose and find yourself all at once. Time stops, or maybe it stretches, and all that you think you know disappears into yet a deeper knowing. Your personal river of energy finds the sea. A great, sweet calm takes you over, and you embrace it like a lover finding a long-lost love. That is the silence of the soul.

In that sanctuary, we feel the pulse of life and the presence of the One. This is a place of true knowledge beyond words and thoughts. Meditators who experience the beauty of this state cannot wait to be there again and again. Those who have mastered it are cloaked in peace as they walk among the rattling, restless world. Why is it that it seems like we do everything possible to avoid this nurturing peace? The quiet seems to scare us. Does the stillness confront us with all that we have not yet faced? We keep running from ourselves—through overdoing, overchatting, overbuying, overeating, over-fighting, and so on—to numb the truth. The very truth, with all of its possibly painful shades, sets us free if we can walk into, and through, its flames.

> **••• Reflection Pause •••**
>
> Do you allow yourself stillness? By that, I mean a time when you're doing nothing but resting your mind, just breathing and being present. If your answer is no, or not enough, the Gate of Silence is an invitation to cultivate a practice of stillness and mindfulness.

Mindfulness: A Path to Stillness

Mindfulness is the art of attention and awareness. It lives in the present moment, which is the only moment we have. It is a form of nonjudgmental, relaxed awareness. When we are mindful, we are paying attention on purpose to the contents of this moment. We are noticing feelings and sensations. We are taking in the details of our external environment as well as the emotional and mental currents flowing within us. It also means cultivating a relaxed acceptance of what is. We learn to allow what happens to just "be" and observe it with compassion. We are witnessing rather than resisting, controlling or fixing.

Sounds easy? Not at all. Mindfulness takes tremendous practice since we all are, to various degrees, anxious and reactive. We tend to live in the past, or in the future, going back and forth from one to the other in an effort, mostly unconscious, to manipulate life and outsmart it. Just being in the present moment feels very open and vulnerable. Most of us are too restless to fully relax into the moment. As a result, we end up being absent in our own life, a guest rather than the host.

Isn't it interesting that we forget that we are here in this life temporarily? We might not be here tomorrow. Our moments are precious, but we're not living them fully. We are doing things automatically, half asleep, taking life for granted. Mindfulness reduces stress and enhances our ability to enjoy and appreciate life. It opens our hearts and minds to an expanded experience of life, and relaxes our tendency to contract away from what is.

Mindfulness Is to Be Experienced

Many books have been written about mindfulness. Many lectures and discussions have been held. None will truly convey to you the actual experience. Much like words cannot fully describe the experience of oneness, which is beyond words or thoughts, the experience of life through mindfulness is a personal one to be discovered and felt through practice.

Have you ever observed someone or something in a neutral way, without judging, rejecting, or analyzing but simply accepting? No commentary, interpretations, or expectations. If you did, then you know what witnessing is. The experience of witnessing is rare unless practiced diligently.

Our monkey mind is part of our Defensive Self and is relentlessly commenting on everything we come in contact with. We file things in drawers according to our perceptions and categories. We have the "good" drawers and the "bad" ones; here we collect our likes and dislikes. While going through life, we are constantly hoarding emotions, ideas, information, and memories, putting them all in our overstuffed inner drawers. We are constantly bouncing between rejection and attachment. We reject what we think is bad and put it in the bad drawers, and we get attached to what we judge as good. It's as if we need to know, on a moment-to-moment basis, what to discard and what to cling to. This reactive way of being does not allow for observation, awareness, or witnessing.

When we are driven by a sense of survival steeped in duality and fear, our mind can feel like a zoo and life like a circus. However, our inner witness, the cosmic "I Am" within our consciousness (the essence of our Expanded Self), is the real ringmaster of the circus, and it does not identify with the shifts of the body-mind, the various dramas, stories, and interpretations flowing through. So, by cultivating our witnessing ability, our perspective widens, our mind relaxes, and eventually the whole universe becomes our home, or to put it differently, the whole universe comes to live within our mind, and we can observe it peacefully, in a nonreactive way.

Benefits of Meditation

Mindfulness is one way of cultivating a meditative state. There are many forms of meditation: sitting, lying down, moving, drawing, writing, breathing, chanting, creating, and so on. In my practice and workshops, we experience all these forms of meditation, and more. The two common threads present in all these forms of meditations are (1) dropping the "Monkey Mind" and (2) being in the moment.

Dropping The Monkey Mind: The Monkey Mind refers to the obsessive, compulsive currents of thoughts that race across our minds. They are called the Monkey Mind because, as the name suggests, they are restless and jumping. When we are in the throes of the Monkey Mind, it is as if we are tied up and dragged around by the monkey's tail, pulled helplessly to places we don't even wish to go. There is very little respite or inner quiet in that place. Meditation teaches us to disengage from the Monkey Mind and detach from its frantic pace. Slowly, we learn to free ourselves from its grip. Underneath the Monkey Mind lies the creative mind, and beneath that lies the Zen Mind, or the True Mind. The True Mind is still, accepting, and observing. It is nonreactive. It is peaceful. Needless to say, it is a great relief to abide in that mind. It is just that it takes practice and mindfulness to get there.

Being in The Moment: Being in the moment is the ability to be fully engaged and focused in the present moment, whether we are in the midst of an activity or at rest. When we are in the moment, we are enjoying, accepting, and flowing with what is. We all long to experience our moments and enjoy them, but hypnotized by a sense of urgency, we frequently forget how. We feel we must be [better, prettier, smarter], must do [more, less, different], must have [a bigger house, a nicer car, a new job], and everything needs to happen *right now*. We stress ourselves out, and many times overwhelm ourselves, with our lists of "musts." It is difficult to simply smell the roses when we are jogging breathlessly on the treadmill of self-imposed, and at times unnecessary, expectations and demands. We long to live peacefully within our skin, challenging ourselves, but from a place of love and self-acceptance. We long to be, to breathe, to take in life to smile with it, to gently flow and feel the rhythm of nature. Meditation helps us learn the art of being.

EXERCISE: A Moment to Be in the Moment

Two or three times a day, stop for 3–5 minutes and step away from the treadmill of life to take a break. Sit or lie down, or just be where you are. Take some deep breaths. Feel the air going in and out of your nostrils. Look around and see the shapes and the colors of objects around you. Really see them. Take in the play of the light merging with the shadows. Listen to the sounds. Keep relaxing into your body. Feel the different ways that your energy is flowing. Sense the vibrations pulsating in your hands, your feet. Listen to your heartbeat. Witness your feelings. Maybe you feel giddy, maybe you feel stressed. Just notice, without judging.

Also notice your physical sensations. Maybe you have a slight headache, or you're a little hungry. Take in as many elements of the moment as possible. Allow it to be. See if you can drop any desire to have the moment be different.

Can you just let it be what it is? If you find that you are judging, anxious, or stressed, then witness your feelings and accept them as part of this moment, an element of it.

Mindfulness is the only activity that is not about *doing* but about *being*. We're not trying to produce any results, not trying to improve anything or get anywhere; we are just resting in the moment. The non-action of resting is what teaches us to be more serene, it allows to accept, and embrace life as it is. This does not mean that we become passive, dispassionate, or resigned. It means that we're able to flow with and work with life and not brace against it, or try to manipulate it.

If you are a fish, you intuitively know that it is best to cooperate with the ocean. Fish do not try to control the ocean. They are life-smart. They naturally relax and flow with the currents. We can learn to do the same. There is power in cooperating with life. It is referred to as "effortless effort" or "desireless desire," which simply means ease of being. Sometimes, the best way to get somewhere is to let go of trying too hard and open yourself to receive. Ease of being helps us make deeper, more informed choices from a place of inner trust and self-confidence.

Why Are We Resisting the Moment?

Why do we resist the moment? The simplest explanation is because we resist ourselves. I have heard this over and over from clients: "I don't feel that I am good enough." "I am not capable enough." "I am not talented enough." This sense of not being "enough" drives us in an unhealthy way to "fix" ourselves. The truth is that there is nothing "wrong" with us, other than thinking there's something wrong and living with the continual fear and stress that this belief evokes.

Yes, we all have lessons to learn and growing up to do, but that does not mean that there is something bad, missing, or wrong with us. We're just human beings in progress. We are evolving. If we accept ourselves, lessons and all, we can accept others, and life. We can stop the fault-finding and the criticism that we torment ourselves with, and in so doing, we can stop the judgment we spill onto others, and life.

Self-acceptance is a key to inner peace and relaxation. Mindfulness helps us accept the moment and what is. I remember thinking as a young person that accepting meant giving up. It took me a while to understand that it is quite the opposite. Acceptance is the courage to sit with what is and appreciate it. Out of that wisdom, right choices and right actions emerge.

EXERCISE: Following the Breath

Our breath is our best friend, a constant companion, a real ally that never leaves until we die. How would you feel if you had a great companion and you never paid attention to him or her? That would be strange. That is what we do with our breath. We take it for granted. Befriend your breath, acknowledge it, enjoy it, and feel it.

Find times during the day to say "hello" to your breath. You could be on the train, in a meeting, or reading or watching a movie. It takes just a minute to follow your breath—feel its gentle movement in and out, relax into its rhythm, and feel grateful for the privilege of breathing.

If you have a couple of minutes where you can actually be with your breath, follow the air going in and out for a count of 20–30 breaths. Then, continue with your day. There is a beautiful saying by the poet Kabir: "Student, tell me what is God. He is the breath inside the breath."

Mindful Practice

Practice can mean doing something over and over to achieve, improve, and excel. Meditation practice is different. It is a gentle relaxing, non-trying, nondoing. It is a commitment to take time to dwell in stillness and rest from our hectic patterns of living. To me, it feels like soaking in a tub after a long dance rehearsal and letting myself just be.

Meditation is my favorite activity because it is restful, nurturing, and spacious. Time seems to stop, and with it, the rushing, the doing, and the attaining. What a relief. In the stillness, we can see forever. We can discover beautiful gems just by being. I encourage you to create time for this delicious experience. Treat yourself. Create a physical space for your meditation practice: a chair, a pillow, a meditation bench, the floor, or even your bed. When you're first starting out, you may want to avoid practicing in your bed; less experienced meditators may tend to fall asleep. Designate a time during the day, or even twice a day, to stop and meditate. Start with five minutes and slowly stretch the time into 15–20 minutes. Try different kinds of meditations.

Suggested Meditations

Drawing Meditation

I have noticed that some of my clients love this kind of meditation, while others find it difficult in the beginning. They feel that they should be able to draw, and since they have not done any drawings in their adult life, they get intimidated by it. I want to reassure you that you do not need to know anything about drawing. The opposite is true. Being a novice helps you, because you don't have any expectations from yourself.

Take a piece of art paper or simple computer paper and a pack of crayons, sit comfortably, and first take a few minutes to breathe with eyes closed, or open. Relax into the moment. Help your whole body to relax by suggesting to it: "My dear body, we are resting. You can relax." I know it sounds strange to talk to your body, but trust me, your body listens to you all the time, so why not give it permission to relax?

Next, relax your heart, your Emotional Self. Put your hand on your physical heart and tell your Emotional Self, "My dear heart, we are resting. You can relax."

Now, tell your mind, "My dear mind, we are resting. You can relax." The mind has a tendency to overwork and overthink; a general reminder helps it slow down a bit and eventually calm down.

After a few minutes of just being and breathing, you are ready. Now, let your hand intuitively put shapes and colors on the paper without knowing what you might draw in the next minute. Let it be a mystery revealed, piece by piece. Just follow your hand and your impulse, no thinking, no analyzing, no criticizing. Enjoy the act of drawing for its own sake, unattached to results. Become a four-year-old doodling. It's a lot of fun. By the end, you will feel present, and if you look at what you drew, you will see that you have expressed something real and interesting that came through your hand onto the paper.

Moving Meditation

Moving meditation is another meditation that is not widely practiced, unless you happen to be in a workshop or a specific training that incorporates it, but it is a wonderful way to move your body and open up your energy field. It also helps you drop your mind and become present. This meditation, like the Drawing

Meditation, might feel a little awkward in the beginning, but once you experience it, you might want to do it again and again.

Standing up, start in the same way you started the Drawing Meditation, by taking a few minutes to relax. Make sure you have room around you. You don't need much, just enough room to move your arms and your legs freely and take some steps. Standing up, semi-close your eyes, take some breaths, and gently stretch in any way that feels good. While stretching, slowly begin to drop thoughts and perceptions, reminding yourself that you're taking a little time to relax and enjoy yourself. After a few minutes of spontaneous stretching, allow your body to move the way it wants. In the beginning, you will find that you repeat gestures that you have learned in yoga, a dance class, the gym, or something you saw on television. The idea is to let go of known and familiar gestures and to find out what your body wants to do at that moment. How would it express itself if you truly let it?

Unless they are trained in authentic movement, most people are unfamiliar with this way of moving; they don't have the opportunity to explore it. So, here's your chance to teach yourself to move without thinking or contriving movement. See if you can truly let your body move in unfamiliar, and maybe unexpected, ways, as if it has a mind of its own, and it does what it loves to do. If it helps, let yourself sing along or make sounds while moving. After you're finished, take a minute to experience the fun and freedom that arise from doing this exercise.

Sound Meditation

The use of breath and voice in meditation is known to calm the mind. Chanting or sounding "Om" helps us connect to the vibrational field within our body and around us. If you have a favorite chant, use a mantra, chant "Om" or use certain vowels, you are already familiar with sound meditations, but it is always good to explore new ways of sounding.

Here, I am proposing an out-of-the-box sound meditation that is very liberating. Before you start, make sure that you warn your mate, kids, or whoever lives with you, that you are going to make some strange sounds. (You may have to use your sense of humor.) Your neighbors might also need a short explanation about your practice. You can always say that you are exercising your vocal chords.

Sit comfortably, close your eyes, and take a few minutes to just relax into your body and your breath. Drop your jaw, soften your eyes, and imagine yourself sitting on a rock by a waterfall in the midst of a rainforest. You feel safe, and you know you will not be disturbed. In your imagination, start listening to the sounds of animals all around you. Then, when you're ready, begin to make sounds, responding to or imitating the sounds of the forest around you. Try out the sounds of birds, monkeys, or tigers. Some self-consciousness may creep in while doing this. See if you can overcome it. Yes, it will feel silly, and you might find yourself giggling. That's good. How many times in our adult lives do we actually take the time to sound like a bird or a monkey and feel okay about it? Enjoy the rawness of the sounds, and maybe you can forget about being a "civilized" human and become part of nature. You can continue by sounding the wind, the trees, or the waterfall. End the meditation by vocalizing the soft sound of rain, and get back to your breath and your body.

Witnessing The Energy Meditation

This is a lying down meditation. It is important that you do it when you're not overtired, because you might fall asleep. Lie down comfortably on your back, with your arms and legs spread out in what is called in yoga *Shavasana*, or the corpse pose. The lights should be dimmed, and if you want, you can put soft music on in the background. Begin by imagining yourself in a beautiful setting, a beach, a meadow, a temple, or a plush rug in an imaginary meditation room.

Add flowers, a small brook, or an ocean breeze. It is your special place, so you can put anything you like there. Before you start, remind yourself that this is your time to do nothing. You are free to be.

Now, gently suggest to your body to relax. Go over each limb, from your feet up, and repeat the suggestion. "Feet: rest, release, relax." "Ankles: rest, release, relax." And so on, all the way to your head, including your hair. Now, imagine your body slowly melting, becoming liquid, a river of energy. Next, feel your breath. Listen to 10-15 breaths, feeling the air going in and out. Imagine your breath as a gentle wind moving within the river of energy. Move to your mind, and imagine your thoughts, notions, and concepts dropping away like little raindrops into the earth. Between your eyes, where your Third Eye is, imagine a vast window opening and through it, you see an endless blue sky. Allow the sky to enter and fill your mind. Imagine your thoughts coming in and disappearing like little birds. Observe them for a second, and let them go. Feel the rhythm of your breath coming and going, the pulsation of the energy currents in your body. Relax and witness the orchestra of energy playing within you. Rest and enjoy it.

Focusing The Mind: A Sitting Meditation

Focusing the mind helps train it to dwell calmly on a specific object and stop its jumping, monkey-like movement. It cultivates the ability to gather the mind into one point (one point mind).

Start by sitting comfortably with your spine long, your neck a continuation of your spine. The chin should feel parallel to the floor, not pulled upward or tucked in. Chest and shoulders are open and relaxed. If you need to sit against the wall and use pillows, do that. If you have a comfortable chair that would accommodate you sitting straight, use that.

If you're sitting on the floor, use a small pillow under you. Cross your legs, and if need be, put two pillows under your knees so that you can relax. Create comfort, and at the same time openness and a sense of growing upward and downward at the same time.

Now, sit for a few minutes with your eyes open and feel your breath. Pay close attention to the air going in and out. Direct your thoughts, and focus on the breath. After the first few minutes, choose an object in the room: a painting, a chair, a table. Make this object the sole focus of your attention. Slowly take in every little detail, as if you are going to paint it later from memory. Notice the colors, the light and shades, the shapes, the edges, and even the energy that emanates from the object.

You might want to entertain your imagination with the question: "What would the object say if it could talk?" I have to admit to you that when I focused on my favorite rocking chair, I saw things I never saw before, even though I have been looking at it forever. I also felt renewed love and respect for it. It reminded me of my grandmother, who was big, sturdy, and so reliable, and I imagined it smiling and humming. If your mind wanders, bring it back to the object. Keep discovering and relishing the details. When you feel that you have had enough, close your eyes and see the object in your mind's eye, with all the details, then release it. Now you're ready to open your eyes and come back. Take a minute to note what happened to you as a result of this meditation.

The Four Magic "R"s

I have talked about the Four Magic "I"s *("I feel," "I think," "I need," "I want")*. These help us in communicating our feelings and thoughts. I have talked about the Four Magic "E"s (*Experience, Explore, Express, Empower*). These help us with processing feelings. I have talked about the Four Magic "C"s (*Choose, Commit, Contribute, Celebrate*).

These help you follow your life path. For the Gate of Silence, I'd like to introduce the Four Magic "R"s (*Relax, Release, Receive, Rejoice*). These help us replenish and expand. The Four Magic "R"s are deliciously refreshing and there is not much to explain about them.

1. *Relax*: We all know the importance of relaxation.
2. *Release*: What are we releasing? In this case, we are releasing worry, anxiety, over-planning, and over-thinking.
3. *Receive*: The ability to receive, be receptive, is as important and maybe more so than being active. We want to be open to receive love, abundance, healing, insights, ideas, inner guidance, and so on. The Hebrew word *kabbalah* (the Jewish mystical teaching) means "receiving." We are vessels of consciousness, and if we are open to receive, we can know the truth and be transformed.
4. *Rejoice*: Not much explanation is needed. It is nourishing to feel joy in living. Whoever can rejoice and appreciate all of life's experiences—the difficult as well as the sublime—has mastered the art of living.

Throughout the book I introduce four different sets of magic letters. For example, the Four Magic "I"s, or the Four Magic "E"s. Together, these Four Magic sets of letters, "R"s, "I"s, "C"s, and "E"s spell the acronym R-I-C-E, which symbolizes the substance of the physical life. Here, it symbolizes the spiritual and emotional substance that keeps our souls expanding and enjoying our lives.

About Prayer

What comes to my mind are the words of spiritual teacher Joel Goldsmith[7], "... understand yourself to be the instrument of God's grace, and the benefit that you can be to anyone is in proportion to your receptivity." We cannot reach the experience of being one with Spirit through our mind alone. Our emotions, our soul, and our energetic field all must be involved in that realization. When we catch a glimpse of the nature of God, the Absolute, we begin to know our oneness with it. We realize that there is nothing else other than that. It is all there, and it is all there is.

Now we can begin to relax into that oneness and stop trying desperately to reach God, as if he was the old man sitting on the cloud. Being receptive and responsive allows us to experience our unity with the One. If we're looking up to God, wanting God to do something, give us something, fix something, we are approaching from desperation, trying to influence God to do our will. The realization that we are one with It leads us to know that our true needs are understood and our highest good is being taken care of. It is then that we relax and allow ourselves to receive, and to surrender to the divine design. A different way of understanding prayer is not begging and beseeching God but being in a state of silence in which we feel united with Spirit, receptive to grace.

Aligning our will with the will of the Creator is, to me, the wisest and healthiest way to live. It leads to peace and to a greater ability to serve and contribute, since it offers us the highest point of view and the ultimate support.

Silence and Knowledge

Joel Goldsmith is one of my favorite writers/teachers. In his book, Beyond Words and Thoughts [8] (Goldsmith, 1998), Goldsmith states: "… we receive certain facets, realizations, and principles of truth which are continually flowing in, in proportion to our receptivity and openness."

Silence helps us create that open state of receptivity. When we visit the realm of inner silence through a state of meditation, we open our soul's mind to the truth that lies beyond the world of the senses and the thoughts. We learn to feel and know the truth within the heart. Slowly, we find a way to trust and surrender to it until we become it. We come to realize that we are the truth, a breathing, living expression of Spirit, beyond our body and mind. We accept the infinite as the being of every being, and we can let it function and express through us. We gladly allow its power, abundance, and grace to flow through our lives. Our prayer becomes a grateful receptivity, a listening and a communion. The only thing that's left is to become a clear channel through which grace flows and truth expresses itself.

Your Expanded Self is the individual channel through which divinity and wisdom are heard. As we learn to lead our daily lives from the spiritual understanding of our Expanded Self, we come closer to our God-like nature. Eventually, the truth begins to dawn in our consciousness. We understand that we are not the doers but the vessels of all that is true.

The Ten Commandments to Cultivating Inner Silence

1. **Commit:** Make a commitment to cultivate inner silence. We live in a very busy, noisy, fast-paced culture that is more focused on the outside "outside living" than the "inside living." Without a solid and strong commitment to stillness, we are not going to be able to swim against the common stream of rush, rush, do, do, get, get. If finding inner stillness is important to you, commit to cultivating it.

2. **Make Time and Place for Stillness:** Inner stillness is a state of being that you can take with you everywhere, but to cultivate it, we need to set up time and space for a meditative practice. Look at your schedule and your home environment and designate 15–25 minutes once or twice a day for stillness. Figure out where, how, and when you are going to be still.

3. **Practice:** Emotional commitment is a must. Setting time and place is important. But without the actual practice, nothing will be cultivated. Make it a daily practice to be still.

4. **Release the Monkey Mind:** One of the most important steps in achieving stillness is teaching yourself to detach from your Monkey Mind. Learn to observe your thoughts as they come in, acknowledge them for a second, and deliberately release them. The ability to observe your thoughts without attachment to them slowly creates a state of non-thinking, which is an inner stillness, a pause, a moment of emptiness. These moments gather and become more frequent as you practice further.

5. **Experiment:** There are a lot of different types of meditation. Experiment. There is no need to always be sitting in meditation. Moving, walking, chanting, breathing, and lying down meditations all will help you clear the mind and make your practice interesting and enjoyable. By doing a variety of meditations, you learn that meditation is a part of life and a state of being that you can call on in all situations.

6. **Be Present:** Being in the moment fully is a meditation. It helps you drop the monkey mind, breathe, and enjoy things as they are. It takes practice, as we know, since we are always in a rush to get somewhere else. Stressed and overworked, we tend to live in the imaginary future, missing our moments.

7. **Notice Your Breath:** Your breath is your best friend, your most loyal companion. Pay attention to it. Teach yourself to breathe fully, moment to moment. Catch yourself when you constrict your breath. Find a way to release it. We all need to be patient with our tendency to constrict the breath and lovingly remind ourselves to breathe.

8. **Witness:** Cultivate a way of being that is nonjudgmental and nonreactive. Judgment and reactivity cloud the mind and the heart. Do you ever wonder how life would seem if you were to have an open, more neutral way of being in it? I do, all the time, especially when I catch myself judging. I remind myself to drop it, and I find that by doing so, my breath opens up and so does my heart.

9. **Pray with Open Ears, Listening:** When in distress or confusion, we pray for clarity, resolution, or guidance. Many times we forget to stop, listen, and feel the presence handing us the guidance, the answers. Listening is receiving. Being receptive is being guided.

10. **Surrender:** This word "surrender" used to raise the hairs on the back of my neck. I, like many people, heard it as giving up and giving in. Growing up in Israel, talking about surrendering was a no-no.

    Over the years, I have learned to love and appreciate the word. Today, I experience it as an allowing, a letting be, a letting go, a widening of perspective, a state of nonresistance. It relaxes me into what is, and teaches me to trust. When I can surrender my defensive resistance, taking the appropriate action evolves naturally and effortlessly. I highly recommend experiencing some measure of surrender on a daily basis.

12

The Gate of Knowledge

*Use knowledge to enjoy creation
and share with others.*

All knowledge, art, science, philosophy, etc. investigates life, living and our understanding of reality. We, humans, seem to have an insatiable thirst for delving into the mysteries of the universe. We yearn to express its beauty and participate in its creative and ever-changing flow. The Gate of Knowledge supports your personal inquiry into the nature of reality and encourages you to make a commitment to a continuous and consistent learning, questioning, and understanding.

Have you asked yourself these questions? Even if you have, take a minute to revisit them again and write down some of your thoughts. We each have favorite areas of life that we are drawn to understand and express. Since all paths lead to the truth, much like all rivers yearn to return to the ocean, it does not matter which area you're passionate about. When you contemplate it deeply and earnestly, you touch the truth and slowly come to know it. The main thing is to keep asking, learning, and opening up to a heartfelt knowledge of self, others, and life.

The Four Questions

On our journey of discovery, we naturally ask questions. Here are four important questions:

1. **Who am I?** (What is my true essence?)
2. **Why am I here?** (What is the purpose of my life?)
3. **What's in my way?** (What is blocking me from living my truth?)
4. **How do I get there?** (What is the path that can help me live my truth?)

> **• • • Reflection Pause • • •**
> Have you asked yourself these questions? Even if you have, take a minute to revisit them again and write down some of your thoughts.

Since the beginning of time, human beings have asked themselves these questions. No matter how well defined and explored your thoughts are, this chapter may inspire more revelations, understandings, and insights. I am not attempting here to provide "the answers" to these questions, but to explore them with you. You might find this chapter to be more conceptual than the rest of the book. Try to read it using your intuition as well as your intellect.

First, I would like to share with you some ideas and concepts I enjoyed while reading the section called "Paradigm Shift" in the online *Study Guide* published by The Institute of Noetic Sciences.[9]

The *Study Guide* suggests that there are six metaphors that compose our core assumptions about the universe. These metaphors explain the different ways humans have come to understand the universe based on differing cultures. In the *Study Guide* eco-philosopher Joanna Macy[10] explores five metaphors: **world as battlefield, world as classroom, world as trap, world as lover, and world as self**; the sixth has been created by the study group from the Institute of Noetic Sciences. It is "**world as machine.**" Here are short summaries of these six metaphors.

World as Battlefield describes the notion of "good versus evil" and a world in which the forces of light battle the forces of darkness; the two forces are pitted against each other. The destiny of humankind is to fight God's battle, and ultimately to win.

World as Classroom translates the idea of "good versus evil" into a more secular understanding. In this metaphor, what counts are our immortal souls, which are being tested here. Life is a kind of moral gymnasium where you are put through certain tests so you can graduate to other arenas or levels of consciousness.

World as Trap is the view that we are being trapped by the illusion that the world as it appears is real. In this view, the struggle is to disentangle ourselves and escape from the messy-looking world by ascending to a higher spiritual plane of understanding.

World as Machine is the idea that the world is a collection of inanimate objects that interact in predictable, mechanistic ways based on mathematical laws.

World as Lover is the view that the world is a most intimate and gratifying partner. Some of the richest expressions of our erotic relationship with the world are found in Hinduism. The early goddess religions that are now being explored carry it, too, as do branches of Sufism and the Kabbalah. Even Christianity has a tradition of bridal mysticism.

World as Self is the view that the world is an interconnected whole and each individual a node in a living web of life. This perception is also now emerging in the sciences, in the realms of general theory, complexity science, and quantum physics. We are discovering that Mind is imminent in nature, extending far beyond the span of our individual conscious purpose.

> ••• **Reflection Pause** •••
>
> Ask yourself which of the above metaphors feels true to you.

How are we, collectively and individually, going to attain understanding about the nature of reality? What are we made of and why are we here? For the past 300 years, modern science has relied primarily on classical physics to tell us about the nature of reality. On the one hand, we have all benefited enormously from the technologies that science has made possible; on the other, many of us are aware that science (classical physics) cannot account for or explain our most significant personal experiences.

Experiences such as out-of-body or near-death events, telepathy, clairvoyance or remote viewing, as well as the powerful healing effects of intention and prayer are just some of the anomalies that challenge the dominant scientific explanations for how the world works.

However, we are witnessing remarkable discoveries on the frontiers of science that appear to support age-old wisdom from spiritual traditions. Gradually, purely mechanistic views are being replaced by the truly mind-boggling revelations issuing from quantum physics, systems and complexity theories, psychoneuroimmunology, and other mind-body studies in consciousness research. For decades, news from these frontier sciences has been filtering through to the general public, due in part to consciousness-raising efforts made by organizations like the Institute of Noetic Sciences.

The emerging story tells us that the universe consists not of things but of possibilities—that relationships and process are more fundamental than substance. As theologian Thomas Berry [11] puts it, "The world is a communion of subjects, not a collection of objects." It is a "world as self"—a conscious, evolving universe, in which we participate through our very thought and action. Philosopher Duane Elgin [12] puts it this way: "In regarding the universe as alive and ourselves as continuously sustained within that aliveness, we see that we are intimately related to everything that exists."

How do we attain knowledge about the nature of reality? For centuries, we were taught to suppress our subjective experience so that the senses could gather data without "hindrance" or "distortion." Nonrational ways of knowing, such as faith, intuition, spiritual insight, and body-based wisdom, have been associated with earlier stages of cultural development, and therefore considered regressive. Interestingly, in spite of itself, science's many gains and discoveries have been inspired by nonrational ways of knowing.

"The cosmic religious feeling is the strongest and noblest incitement to scientific research," said Einstein, who spoke of truths that one "feels but cannot express." And when asked how he knew a solution to a problem to be true, he replied that he "felt it in his muscles." Other scientists speak of truth that can be known through an aesthetic sense that comes about when a problem is solved with elegance and symmetry.

Women have traditionally been encouraged to receive knowledge in nontraditional ways. In ancient Greece, Italy, Egypt, and Turkey, for example, women served as oracles, or sibyls, going into a trance to reveal information about the past, present, and future. Kings and generals sought out their advice because it was so accurate and reliable.

No single way of knowing is adequate for this complex universe. Each has its own domain of expertise. It takes all our ways of knowing working in concert—rational thinking, intuition, mystical awareness, and receptive spirit—to open us to the universe.

We are being challenged to cultivate our capacities to combine rational and nonrational ways of knowing. There is no manual or blueprint to follow for changing paradigms. Needing absolute answers may be an artifact from outdated worldviews, while becoming comfortable with uncertainty may be our path to a new one.

> • • • **Reflection Pause** • • •
>
> Have you had an experience that changed, expanded, or altered your world view?

What Are We Made Of?

Quantum mechanics, the latest development in the scientific quest to understand the nature of physical reality, is a precise mathematical description of the behavior of fundamental particles. It has remained the preeminent scientific description of physical reality for 75 years. So far all of its experimental predictions have been confirmed to astounding degrees of accuracy.

Physics as a science began when Isaac Newton and others discovered that mathematics could accurately describe the observed world. Today, the Newtonian view of physics is referred to as classical physics; in essence, classical physics is a mathematical formalism of common sense.

Classical ways of regarding the world are still sufficient to explain large segments of the observable world, including chemistry, biology, and the neurosciences. Classical physics got us to the moon and back. It works for most phenomena at the human scale. It is common sense.

But it does not describe the behavior of all observable phenomena, especially the way that light and, in general, electromagnetism works.

Quantum mechanics was developed to explain the dual wave-particle nature of light and matter, and as such it provides a better way of describing the nature of physical reality. It tells us that the world of common sense reveals only a special, limited portion of a much larger and stranger fabric of reality.

What is the fabric of reality made of? To simplify, electrons can behave as both particles and waves. As waves, they have no precise location but exist as "probability fields" or energy fields. As particles, they collapse into solid objects in a particular place and time when they are being observed and/or measured. Electrons are made of subatomic particles, which have been found to consist of 99.9 percent empty space. The subatomic particles move at light speed and are actually vibrating waves of energy. The fabric of reality, therefore, is a unified field of information and energy in which everything is connected instantaneously, transcending the ordinary limits of space and time.

We can also say that the fabric of reality is a field of possibilities or a moving field of energy and consciousness collapsing into different forms as we observe it, or as we define it with our thoughts.

The startling discoveries of quantum physics invite us to entertain the possibility that things are not as they appear to be. In fact, according to quantumphysics, things are not even "things"; they are more like possibilities. Physicist Amit Goswami[13] states that "even the material world around us—the chairs, the tables, the rooms, the carpet, camera included—all of these are nothing but possible movements of consciousness." What are we to make of this? "Those who are not shocked when they first come across quantum theory cannot possibly have understood it," notes quantum physics pioneer Niels Bohr.[14]

Quantum physics theories have systematically challenged all of the assumptions of classical physics. For example, "local reality" is the reality that is governed by the laws of classical physics. In a local reality, influences cannot travel faster than the speed of light. In 1964, Irish physicist John Stewart Bell[15] showed that any model of reality compatible with quantum theory must be nonlocal. For quantum physics to work, information must travel not just faster than light, but instantaneously. Nonlocality suggests that everything in the universe is connected by information that can appear anywhere else, instantaneously.

In a quantum world, the following is now the case:

- **Reality** fades away because properties of the physical world are not fixed; the world changes in subtle ways, depending on how we wish to observe it.
- **Locality** has been replaced by nonlocality, the idea that objects that are apparently separate are actually connected instantaneously through space-time.
- **Causality** has dissolved because the fixed arrow of time is now known to be a persistent illusion, a misapprehension sustained by the classical assumptions of an absolute space and time. We now know that sequences of events depend on the perspectives (technically called the frame of reference) of the observers.

- **Continuity** has faded away because we now know that there are some discontinuities in the fabric of reality. Space and time are neither smooth nor continuous.

On July 4, 2012, scientists at the European Organization for Nuclear Research (CERN) announced that they had found a particle that behaves the way they expect the Higgs Bosom, the "God Particle," to behave. This discovery points to the intriguing possibility that the Higgs Bosom is responsible for all of the mass in the universe, hence its nickname the "God Particle." What if all particles have no inherit mass but instead gain mass by passing through a field? This field, known as a Higgs field, could affect different particles in different ways. In fact, assuming the Higgs Bosom exists, everything that has mass gets it by interacting with the all-powerful Higgs field, which occupies the entire universe.

It is interesting to note that this is exactly what the spiritual teachings of Hinduism, Buddhism, Kabalah, Sufism, Christian Science, and other religions have been telling us for centuries. They are speaking in a similar way about the nature of reality.

I would like to quote one of my favorite Hindu mantras, "SATYAM SHIVAM SUNDARAM." This translates to "Truth, Bliss, and Beauty," or as my dear teacher Shri Brahmananda Sarasvati[16] would say, "We are one with Absolute Existence, Absolute Tranquility, and Absolute Beauty." He would then add to this, "You are the ocean of awareness, and that awareness is the first and last religion, the first and last freedom."

Here are some additional quotes from different spiritual traditions, referring to the nature of reality:

First Principle of Faith: I believe with perfect faith that the Creator, Blessed be His Name, is the Creator and Guide of everything that has been created; He alone has made, does make, and will make all things. Second Principle of Faith: I believe with perfect faith that the Creator, Blessed be His Name, is One, and that there is no unity in any manner like His, and that He alone is our God, who was, and is, and will be.

— *Rabbi Moshe Ben Maimon* [17]
First two of the 13 Principles of Faith, considered to be a summary o the basic beliefs of Judaism

OM! That (the Invisible–Absolute) is whole; whole is this (the visible phenomenal); from the Invisible Whole comes forth the visible whole. Though the visible whole has come out from that Invisible Whole, yet the Whole remains unaltered. OM! PEACE! PEACE! PEACE!

— Peace Chant
Isa Upanishad, Part Of The Vedanta Texts In Hinduism

Everything you observe has its roots in the unseen world. The forms may change, but the essence stays the same. Every awesome sight will disappear, and every sweet word will fade away; but do not be dejected—for their source is eternal, growing, branching out, and giving new life and new joy. Why do you weep? The source is in you, and this whole world is springing up from it.

— (maulana) Jalal al-d i n (or Jalaluddin) rumi[18]
Sufi Mystic

The understanding of the oneness of Consciousness as our consciousness, of Life as our Life, is truth Eternal

— Joel S. Goldsmith[19]

> **• • • Reflection Pause • • •**
>
> What would it be like to feel quantum physics through the senses?

Outside of quantum physics, there are a few scientists and the occasional philosopher who focus on such things. Most of us do not spend much time thinking about quantum mechanics at all. This is natural and understandable and in most cases perfectly fine for practical purposes. But when it comes to understanding the nature of reality, it is useful to keep in mind that quantum mechanics describes the fundamental building blocks of nature (the classical world is composed of those blocks, too), whether we are able to observe them or not.

There are competing interpretations of quantum mechanics. The two that ap peal to me are "Wholeness" and "Consciousness Creates Reality":

- **Wholeness** – Einstein's protégé David Bohm[20] maintained that quantum mechanics reveals that reality is an undivided whole in which everything is connected in a deep way, transcending the ordinary limits of space and time.
- **Consciousness Creates Reality** – This interpretation pushes to the extreme the idea that the act of measurement, or possibly even human consciousness, is associated with the formation of reality. This endows the act of observation, the privileged role of collapsing the possible into the actual.

It should be emphasized that at present we are still exploring quantum mechanics, and thus there is no clear authority on which interpretation is more accurate. Both interpretations I mentioned seem to be connected in my opinion.

Experimental Tests of Mind Meeting Matter

Psychic and mystical experiences can open the doors of our consciousness to glimpses of true understanding. The cumulative evidence from the discipline of parapsychology strongly suggests that psychic phenomena do exist. There is strong evidence that we can gain information without the use of the ordinary physical senses, and in so doing, we become free of the usual constraints of space and time. The evidence remains controversial, because these effects are impossible under the rules of classical physics, but the space-time flexibility, nonlocality, and acausal connections described by quantum physics do allow for such phenomena.

The data of parapsychology provide a new perspective from which to reinterpret the various quantum realities. Bohm's "wholeness" interpretation, in which everything is ultimately interconnected with everything else, seems particularly compatible with psychic phenomena. Imagine that at some deep level of reality our brains are in intimate communion with the entire universe, as Bohm's interpretation proposes. If this is true, you might occasionally get glimpses of information about other people's minds, distant objects, the future, or the past. You would gain this information because your brain already coexists with other minds, distant objects, and everything else. From this perspective, psychic experiences may be reinterpreted not as mysterious powers of the mind, but as momentary glimpses into the quantum wholeness, the fabric of reality itself.

> • • • **Reflection Pause** • • •
>
> Have you ever experienced telepathy or any other spiritual phenomena that is difficult to explain?

Science and Mysticism

There are clearly areas of commonality between mystical experiences of unity and what physicists describe as the quantum field.

Quantum physics, with its startling revelations, has successfully awakened the world from what William Blake called "Newton's slumber." We can no longer look at a world that appears real, local, consistent, and causal and believe with full conviction that we perceive the whole of reality. Nor can we say with assurance that we know what reality we perceive ... more secrets will be revealed.

> • • • **Reflection Pause** • • •
>
> Reflection Pause: How would it change your life if you experienced reality as an open-ended conversation or dialogue?

Let's go back to our questions, "Who are we?" and," Why are we here?" Our scientific discoveries and mystical experiences reveal to us that we are part of and one with the unified field of vibration and consciousness that is the universe.

Consciousness, which can be called the One Mind, The Supreme Spirit, intelligence, or information, is imminent in nature; since we are one with this Universal Consciousness we affect reality with our thoughts, feelings, and beliefs. We are co-creating reality with the Universal Mind.

It is important that we take responsibility for the way we shape our personal experiences, and as a result the world around us. We can break our attachment to ways of thinking, feeling, and behaving that are destructive to ourselves and others. Since we are connected to the source of intelligence that is behind the movement of all energy, we are each provided with the insights needed to create our life as a unique masterpiece. Participating in the universal creation seems to be why we are here.

Gates of Power® is a method of self-healing, self-transformation, and self-actualization. The method guides you on the journey of creating your inner and outer life as a testimony of strength, creativity, and expression. It provides you with tools necessary to heal, shift, and realign your individual consciousness with the Universal One. It supports you in the process of creating the highest version of yourself and your life.

13

Creating a Personal Practice

This chapter is dedicated to supporting you in creating your own personal practice for growth, a daily discipline that will keep your focus on and commitment to your evolution: think of it as your bliss-a-plin, a practice that supports your well-being and happiness. There is a difference between knowing what is healthy and constructive for us and actually living it. Your daily discipline is what makes the difference.

A good artist, athlete, or person on a spiritual path doesn't think it is enough for them to just wish and think about their path; they practice on a daily basis. The musician spends time with his or her instrument. The dancer takes classes throughout their career every day. The singer vocalizes, and the athlete works out. The spiritually dedicated person, prays, meditates, and acts in accordance with his or her discipline. The scientist labors in the lab. The list goes on. Why do we think that personal evolution just happens? It does not.

Left to your own devices, we can stay stuck in old limited beliefs and patterns that feel comfortable and familiar. There is a tendency in most human beings to stay safe no matter how emotionally unfulfilling it is. The comfort of the known is very seductive. We all need the commitment to a daily personal practice, to gently push us forward stretching our comfort zone and facilitating change. Opening ourselves up to new possibilities, new ways of thinking, feeling, and doing is what brings us to new frontiers.

The Gates of Power ® Method emphasizes daily practice as one of the most important elements of self-transformation. All participants in the program create their practice and honor it. By practicing daily, they come to regard it as essential. In this chapter, I will offer some guidelines to help you, the reader, create a daily practice or add new elements to an existing one.

Preparation

1. Know Your Frail Point

We all have a small, medium, or what seem like large fractures in our vase (our being). We are not the fracture; we are the beautiful vase—innately whole, not less, because we have this vulnerable point within us. In fact, strengthening this vulnerability is what makes us wiser and powerful. Our vulnerability is often our biggest lesson and can be our best gift. It is our responsibility to define this emotional/psychological/spiritual frailty and to attend to it with love and dedication so that it heals and becomes our asset.

What comes to mind is the obvious case of the wounded healer who is empowered to help others by healing his or herself, or the injured athlete who now coaches other athletes about how to prevent injuries. Many of the people who contribute to others the most are able to do so because they overcame personal challenges within themselves.

Look within with great compassion and honesty, and define what causes your suffering. (I trust that reading this book has made it a little clearer.) Investigate the roots of this suffering, and make a commitment to shift and strengthen what is misaligned within you. If you feel you need professional help, get it. In this day and age, it is common and accepted. If you have just begun your self-investigation, choose intuitively what is in the way of your inner peace. Slowly but surely, you will come to understand it.

2. Create Your Inner Work Binder – Computer File

Once you have chosen your theme, understand that this theme is being reflected in all seven facets of your being, all seven Gates. Say, for example, that your theme is self-criticism. It will show up in your body, in the way you maintain your environment, finances, and so on. All of these are elements of the Gate of the Body. It will show up obviously in your Gate of Emotions. You will find that sadness, anger, fear, might be very present within this Gate. It will show up in relationships, the Gate of Dialogue, as well as the Gate of Creative Expression, Life Path, Silence, and Knowledge. In other words, everything that is happening within us is manifested and expressed in its own way, in each one of the seven Gates. In order to heal, harmonize, and empower ourselves, we need to address the theme through each one of the Gates and create a holistic comprehensive practice to realign ourselves back to wholeness.

Now get a notebook, a journal, or if you are writing on your laptop, create a new file for yourself called Personal Practice for Inner Transformation. If you are more comfortable with tangible pages my suggestion is, use a binder. (I hope you have been writing notes while reading this book.)

Write on the top of the first page in big letters, "What causes me suffering is…", then complete the statement. For example:

"What causes me suffering is … my self-criticism."

Underneath that, write a commitment statement: "I am committed to …", then complete the statement. For example:

"I am committed to … learn to value, appreciate, and accept myself."

3. Creating a Personal Practice

Start a new page and write down the first Gate: The Gate of the Body. Divide the page into two halves by creating a vertical line in the middle. On top of the left side, write: **symptoms**. On top of the right side write: **realigning actions**. On the left-hand side of the page, describe the way your theme (what is causing your suffering) affects your body, home environment, finances, and your belongings. The Gate of the Body includes our personal body as well as all physical, tangible, components of our lives. So, if I continue with my example of self-criticism as a theme, I might write on this side:

"My self-criticism affects this Gate in these ways":

1. I neglect my body: I don't go for regular checkups to the dentist, don't exercise, eat too much refined sugar in my diet, and so on.
2. I continuously criticize my looks and find faults with my appearance.
3. I neglect my home environment: my desk is cluttered, my closets are disorganized, and so on.
4. I notice a chronic tightness in my jaw, chest, and lower back.
5. I mishandle my finances.

The list can go on up to about seven symptoms. All these are possible symptoms of the self-criticism theme and some of the ways it shows up in this Gate.

I want to remind you that you have symptoms, but you are not your symptoms. These are just signs of misalignment. They are not your essence. You are your wholeness. You are listing them to take yourself back to a state of well-being. The list is meant to make it clear to you how your theme affects your Gate of the Body. It is not there to make you feel bad about yourself. It is there to empower you to shift what does not serve your well-being.

Once you finish this list, move to the right side of this page under the title Realigning Actions. Make a list of all the ways that you can take care of this Gate in a better way. Next to each symptom, write the appropriate action. For example, next to "I neglect my body," the Realigning Action would be:

1. I commit to exercising three times a week.
2. I will make an appointment this week to see my dentist.
3. I commit to limiting refined sugar in my diet.

The next page will provide a clear example of how to organize your symptom list and your Realigning Actions.

Example Theme: Self-Criticism

Gate of the Body	
Symptoms (examples)	**Realigning Actions** (examples)
1. I neglect my body. I don't exercise, eat too much refined sugar, and go for long periods with no medical checkups.	• I commit to exercising three times a week, for half an hour each time. • I am lowering the amount of refined sugar in my diet. • I will schedule an appointment to see my dentist.

2. I constantly criticize my looks and find fault with my appearance.	• I practice looking at my body, and acknowledging things I like about it.
3. I neglect my home environment. My desk is cultured, my closets are disorganized, and my refrigerator needs cleaning.	• I clear my desk. • I declutter my closets and give away what I don't need. • I throw out all expired food on a regular basis.
4. I have a chronic tightness in my jaw and my chest.	• I tune in to get a sense of the emotional stress that causes my tightness. • I also go to a chiropractor or an osteopath to get professional advice.
5. I mishandle my finances. I pay bills late. I have bad credit.	• I commit to paying bills on time. • I make it a regular habit to check and plan my budget.
6. I have a hard time falling asleep and/or staying asleep.	• I take time to self-reflect in order to find what within me is keeping me up. • I further help myself by doing yoga, meditation, relaxation techniques, drinking herbal teas, and so on.
7. I overeat when I am emotionally anxious.	• I learn to accept and embrace my emotions. • I practice sitting with my emotions compassionately before using food to numb them.

Example Theme: Self-Criticism

Gate of the Body
Committed Actions for the month of September (examples)
First Week   Make an appointment to see the dentist.
Second Week   I clean my refrigerator thoroughly.
Third Week   I start my exercise routine.
Fourth Week   I download a guided relaxation technique to help me sleep, and I try it out.

The second page of each Gate will change each month, because your committed actions will change. You will complete some, keep others, and add new ones. This page contains specific committed actions for each week of a current month. Make your committed actions realistic and attainable, and take only one action for each Gate. You will have seven committed actions for each week: one for each Gate, and that is enough. If you stick faithfully to all your committed actions, you are certain to move forward.

We all know that writing things down is very important. At the same time, our old habits are comfortable and seductive, so be ready for a clash of wills between your Expanded Self and your Defensive Self. Do not use your commitment list to be harsh toward yourself. Just keep at it with patience and diligence. You will "fall off the horse" many times; just get back on! Since this is a work-in-progress list, if you have not completed one of your commitments for whatever reason, transfer it to the next week or choose another right time to complete it. It is important to complete our commitments. When we follow through on what we promised ourselves we would do, we create a sense of inner integrity and self-respect that enhances our self-esteem. We learn to be accountable to ourselves and to others. Accountability, integrity, and committed actions strengthen our inner core and facilitate success.

The second page of each Gate will constantly change. As you complete certain commitments, you will check them off and stop for a second to feel good about it and acknowledge yourself. Some commitments will stay on the page for longer. Every month create a new page of four columns. These two pages will be duplicated for each Gate. Let's take the Gate of Emotions and follow our example.

Example Theme: Self-Criticism

Gate of Emotions	
Symptoms (examples)	**Realigning Actions** (examples)
1. My self-criticism causes me inner pain.	• I committed to learning to dissolve my pattern of self- criticism.
2. I am ashamed of my feelings.	• I learn to accept, acknowledge, and nurture my Emotional Self.
3. I repress and avoid my feelings.	• I learn to value my emotions and allow them to be and flow freely, as well guiding my Emotional Self, using the help of my Expanded Self.
4. I have a hard time expressing my thoughts and emotions to others.	• I commit to encouraging myself on a daily basis to take small risks and find ways to express my thoughts and feelings.

5. I avoid confrontations, and as a result I don't stand up for myself.	• I remind myself that I am safe and secure and I have the right to speak-up.
6. I isolate myself and I am uncomfortable in social situations.	• I start a daily routine of self-appreciating and self-accepting thoughts. I ground myself in the reality of my Expanded Self. I support my Emotional Self as well as relax my Defensive Self, which is my harshest critic. I create a sense of comfortability within myself.
7. I have a fear of intimacy.	• Through inner dialogue and compassionate self- acceptance, I learn to be intimate and loving with myself. That creates a inner sense of trust, which allows me to become intimate with others.

Example Theme: Self-Criticism

Gate of Emotions
Committed Actions for the month of September (examples)
First Week I establish a time daily to be quiet and get in touch with my feelings. I use that as part of my meditation practice.

> **Second Week**
> To my daily emotional meditation, I add a little writing in my journal to describe my feelings.

> **Third Week**
> I make a point to share with a good friend those feelings that I may otherwise find difficult to express.

> **Fourth Week**
> I sit down to have an emotional dialogue between my Expanded Self and my Emotional Self, encouraging my Emotional Self to share with me feelings that it might have avoided out of shame and fear.

I hope these two examples clarified for you this practical path that would support your emotional, physical, and spiritual empowerment. All other Gates follow the same example. By the time you are done preparing this you will have 14 pages, two for each Gate. This is a practical map for charting your transformation. You will use it for at least a few months, allowing it to help direct your committed actions and stay on the path. I suggest that you create a fifteenth page, which is a summary of all of your seven commitments.

This page will change every week. On it you will have one commitment for each Gate per week. For example:

September Committed Actions

First week

1. Body – Make appointment to go see my dentist.
2. Emotions – Establish daily quiet emotional checking.
3. Dialogue – Speak with my partner about an issue I have been avoiding.
4. Creative Expression – Go to see at the light exhibition at the Guggenheim Museum.
5. Life Path – Complete writing my business proposal.
6. Silence – Take a meditative walk and practice mindfulness.

7. Knowledge – Finish reading my book on acupuncture.

This practice will help you support and respect yourself—and as a result, others. Some of my clients call the list of commitments LATS: Loving Actions Toward Self. Use them just like that, as loving healing actions that nurture your wholeness.

4. Quiet Quality Time With Yourself

If you are involved in a committed intimate relationship with a partner, or have kids, you would not go a day without checking in with them: sharing on their feelings and concerns, supporting them, and having some fun. Your Self is your primary partner. Your Defensive Self and your Emotional Self are your inner children. You, your Expanded Self, are engaged in an intimate relationship with your inner aspects, as well as with the Great Self (the Source). It makes sense to take time daily to be with yourself and with the Self. I consider this as the most important part of my daily practice. This commitment is included in your other commitments, and actually it encompasses three commitments in one sitting:

1. A commitment to the Gate of Silence.
2. A commitment to check in with your emotions (for the Gate of Emotions).
3. A commitment to the Gate of Dialogue, since you will be dialoguing internally.

This quiet sitting with yourself allows you to receive intuitive insights about life in general, and about your life in particular. It allows you the space to create and cultivate your vision, and maybe most importantly it allows you time to recognize the witness in you, which is your essence.

In closing, I would like to remind you of the acronym RICE, which includes:

- **R** for the four magic "Rs" (supporting silence and renewal) – Relax, Release, Receive, Rejoice.
- **I** for the four magic "Is" (supporting honest communication) – I feel, I think, I need, I want.
- **C** for the four magic "Cs" (supporting focus and achievement) – Choose, Commit, Contribute, Celebrate.
- **E** for the four magic "Es" (supporting inner emotional work) – Experience, Explore, Express, Empower.

You, being a vessel of the Universal Spirit are the master and artist of your creations. It is your right and your responsibility to step into this power, and live as a contribution to yourself and others.

My spirit meets yours on the path…

14

In Their Own Words: Clients' Stories

My Mother's Daughter

I heard about Nomi from a friend who was also my voice teacher. I was a 20-something woman, who had moved to New York City to act, and I was taking voice lessons as I knew musical theater people worked more than non-musical. So, I was trying to get my voice in shape. The problem was, while my body may have been in shape, my emotional life was not. I was still a frightened child of an alcoholic inside. I had so much shame, fear, rage and self-loathing, I could barely sit still. Every time I had to hit a very high note whilst singing, I would practically pass out from the effort of trying to keep that vulnerability in. You have to be open to hit those kinds of notes. I still remember a particular voice lesson. I was doing scales and hit a note I'd never hit before, and my voice just stopped. It literally just became air, mid-note. My body was so shocked I'd let go that it shut that sound down. I couldn't handle opening up.

One day amidst warming up with the scales, I'd finally broken down and started sobbing in the middle of my lesson, overwhelmed by all the emotions I couldn't hide anymore. Between acting teachers pushing me to be "real and authentic" in the moment (a concept I could not grasp if you paid me) and my heart literally feeling like it was being pried open when I hit the high notes, I just lost it.

My vocal coach and good friend suggested Nomi to me. She didn't push; just gave me Nomi's number, and we continued with our lesson. It took a month before I got the courage to call Nomi.

Right away with Nomi, I realized she wasn't going to be like other therapists I'd been to. This would not be me talking around the issues and her asking a question here and there. This was *work*! She made it clear from the start that you don't come to her unless you're ready to do the work. And by that point in my life, I was ready to. Nomi challenged me often. She could tell right away I was a talker and needed to be taught how to feel before I spoke instead of thinking of what might be the right and correct answer. So, we did a lot of guided meditation in the beginning. It wasn't warm and fuzzy therapy. I went into the deep and scary parts of me that I never wanted to face before. The ways I'd let fear rule my life. How I'd let the people I feared as a child still rule my life's decisions. Nomi was persistent in getting me to go deeper. I couldn't talk my way out of an uncomfortable topic; I would not be allowed to shut down when I was resistant. She saw through all my tricks of avoidance. While she was tough on me, I felt safe. I felt like for the first time I was on a path that would make me feel better about myself. I wouldn't feel the need to lie, to make myself look better or make sure others were okay with who I was.

I was working all the Gates; however, the Gates of Dialogue and Emotion ruled my initial change more than anything in the beginning. Being in touch with my emotions, dealing with the feelings I had and with the conflicts in my relationships, was the biggest challenge and change of my life. Especially being with my fears, and walking through them. My relationship with my mother is the best example of how this work with those Gates changed my life.

As I said, I am the child of an alcoholic. Growing up, while I loved and worshipped my mother, I also feared her temper more than anything. The youngest of four, I felt like she would single me out as a target for her rage. At one point I felt like she would go after me because I would cry more easily than the others and not fight back. So, as I was too scared to fight back, my only rebellion was to shut down. I made myself as small as possible and learned not to talk back. To lie whenever possible to make myself look good, to get her approval, or to keep her happy with me or others, because if she got angry at one of us, all of us could eventually become the next target. While I feared her greatly, I also loved her. We had many good times together. My love of books comes from my mother the librarian. My love of the arts comes from all the times my mother took us to plays, the ballet, musicals and the symphony. She came to every tennis match, every choir performance, and every play, cheering me on all the while. But when she got angry, everything dropped away to sheer terror for me, and I would do anything or say anything to make it end. When I was young and my father was still alive, if I would get in trouble at school, I would tell him instead of my mother. While he would get angry, his response was to yell a bit and be done with it. My mother's anger would build to an epic rage that could come back again and again on the same topic on any given day. The offense would never be forgotten, and you felt you would be paying for that detention or bad grade for the rest of your life. You were just a horrible person, and that was that.

As a result, when I got older, I became totally afraid of any conflict. I was afraid that it would lead to someone not approving of me, or somehow finding out the horrible person that I was. So, I stayed a happy sun-shiny funny girl who was well liked but not well known. I had only a few close friends, whose damage seemed to mirror my own, so they could be trusted. I stayed afraid of my mother, while rebelling a bit more. Every once in a while, I would yell back and defend myself, but then feel devastated after doing so, even if I was entirely justified. I knew I wanted to move away, knowing it was my only chance to get out of my mother's claustrophobic reach and figure out who the heck I was.

When I finally got to New York, I realized that my mother's reach extended well past my hometown, and that I had taken over where my mother left off in making myself feel horrible and afraid. The bad part of my mother, the part I'd feared and so desperately needed approval from, never left me just because I had left her. I was making the same mistakes and feeling just as horrible. Also, I was trying out a career that, if I was going to be any good at it, required authenticity. I didn't know the meaning of the word.

Working with Nomi, I started to work on my relationship with my mother. I went deep into my childhood trauma and somehow found compassion for that scared little girl inside me, instead of being embarrassed and disgusted by her. I admired her ability to survive, her optimism, and her appetite for life. I learned how to nurture her, my little Emotional Self, to help her see past her fear and get her voice back. I also learned to deal with and appreciate my Defensive Self. All those years as a child, it gave me the tools to survive all the screaming and trauma. My Defensive Self has been there for me, and now I needed to be there for her. I needed to show her that we can work past fear and not let it stop us from getting the life we want and the relationships we want.

Now it helped that my mother had started to work on herself, too. She had stopped drinking and was going to AA. However, while the drinking stopped, she was still a long way from changing her behavior. So, I started to have conversations with my mother about changing the way she talked to me. Before each time I would go back to my hometown, I would have dialogues with my Emotional and Defensive Self, both at my home and also working with Nomi. Bringing my Expanded Self into situations helped me be open and vulnerable, and at the same time reminding me that I deserved to be treated better and it was okay to stick up for myself. Learning how to speak to my Emotional and Defensive selves, like they were little children inside me, made me look at how I thought of myself and how poorly I'd treated myself. I thought I'd left the bully back home, and instead she was right there inside me. So, once I started dealing with the abuser inside me, it was time to deal with the abuser at home.

The discussions with my mother at first did not go well. It's not an easy skill to master, learning to communicate honestly. Many times, it would come out as a crying snotty, angry mess. But I remember the first real moment of communication with my mother. We were in the car, and my mother said something so damaging about me, in such a careless manner, as if we were just having a normal conversation, and I snapped. Through my tears and anger, I told her exactly the effect her words had on me. It was the first time I'd ever done it or spoken about how *what she said made me feel*. It was ugly and in anger, but at least it was honest. While I still felt a little devastated by it, I have to say, it felt like a relief. Finally saying out loud what I needed to be said, speaking my truth, even if it wasn't perfect. My mother felt awful because she was finally hearing out in the open something that she probably knew but had been hiding from herself. She saw and heard the damage of her words to me.

Now, she didn't change immediately. That's not how it works. But that moment opened up so many more opportunities to talk to each other and deal with our relationship. We learned to be honest with each other. I learned about my own bad habits of speaking to her that were equally damaging to our relationship. I stopped needing to lie. It was an amazing relief not to need the lies anymore.

It's been about a decade now since I've started this work. Now my mother is my best friend, which is the greatest gift of my life. My mother used to be the person who I was very careful and guarded with. I would try to control every conversation to keep her from being upset and getting angry with me. Now she's the first person I call with good news, bad news, or just wanting to chat with my friend. We speak almost every day, ending every conversation with "I love you, heart of my heart." I know my mother as a brilliant, smart, passionate, and compassionate woman. She now knows, accepts, and appreciates the real authentic person I've become as well.

This work has given me my mother back. And I think it gave my mother her daughter back, too.

— N

Being Assertive

As a young child, I was very sick. I had croup for a few years, and my parents would always have to bring me into the bathroom and turn on the shower real hot so the steam could loosen up my cough. I was rushed to the hospital on a few occasions because I wasn't able to breathe. The feeling of being helpless was very scary to me. Because I was sick, I was a little scrawny kid. I was a very particular eater, which meant I didn't eat very much! I think this drove my parents a bit crazy. A lot of kids tried to beat me up, I was bullied, and made fun of. I didn't have a leg to stand on. Though I never felt unloved or unsupported by my parents, who were always there for me when I needed them, I was afraid. Time by myself taught me to be very independent. I would play by myself a lot as a child. Inventing games in my bedroom, riding my Big Wheel all over the neighborhood. I was happy but probably a little withdrawn and shy.

My parents decided to move to Las Vegas when I was 11 years old. They wanted some independence from their parents, and also a huge blizzard made living in the Midwest even more exhausting. I'd grown up in an idyllic neighborhood in the Midwest; I walked to grammar school and junior high, and now in Las Vegas I was put on a bus and carted off with a bunch of kids I didn't know. I didn't really have any friends for about a year. I was having a tough time. My mom suggested that I take an acting class at a local children's theater company, and suddenly I felt very much at home. It was the thing I needed, even though I did not know I did. This really set the course for my career. I was 12. I continued to be involved with theater all through high school, and got my college degree in theater. I have been making my living as an actor for the last 20 years. I feel incredibly lucky, even though I know I still have a long way to go.

In the time, I've spent working with Nomi, I'm accomplishing and learning a few key things. I'm learning to be a lot more assertive. I've always been a "people pleaser." Maybe due to the fact that I felt so weak as a kid. I didn't want to ruffle any feathers or upset anybody. Lack of assertiveness is something I struggle with and I am acknowledging within myself. I'm able to see clearly the tools with which to overcome it. With Nomi, I have pinpointed my fears and confronted my weaknesses, working on them through the Gates. I can step into my Expanded Self and see what's going on with me in a very clear and specific way. I'm learning to sit with myself at least once a day and ask, "How am I feeling?" I've created goals for myself, and once those are written down I can always see clearly what I'm working toward. I have been able to accomplish a lot of them in the last few years. Being an actor, one of my goals was to be on Broadway. I was able to do that this year. I have set other goals of writing a screenplay and creating work with my friends. All of this is possible when I open my heart to the opportunities I can create for myself.

I have learned to be healthily detached from my partner. Early on in our relationship I would get pulled into her worries and anxieties; I couldn't be a strong partner for her because I was worried and stressed out that if I said the "wrong" thing or made the "wrong" choice she would get really upset, and maybe leave. I was not comfortable with conflict. But with Nomi I've learned to express and share my feelings, and not be afraid of the consequences. Knowing that they are MY feelings they cannot possibly hurt anybody else, especially if I use the Four Magic E's—Experience, Explore, Express, Empower—to get clear about them, and then use the Four Magic I's—I feel, I think, I need, I want—to express and communicate them.

Learning assertiveness and dispelling the worry that I may disappoint my wife/ family/friend/colleagues has been at the forefront of my work with Nomi. I feel confident that the more I'm aware of it, acknowledge it, and work through it, it will become just another goal that I can check off my list.

— J.

The Me Behind the Masks

It's a very odd experience to look back on your past and feel like it happened to someone else. When you travel back in time, it's like you are spying on another person's memories. Maybe everyone feels like this. Or maybe it's a feeling accessible only to people who have changed. And when I say changed, I mean a deep internal metamorphosis of sorts. This is what happened to me.

I have been in therapy on and off since I was eight. I experienced my first therapy session with a school counselor, who declared she was going to try and help me with the abusive teasing I found myself a victim of. Although I wanted to believe her, my miniature, jaded eight-year-old self did not have any faith in her. She, as expected, did not help me to miraculously shed my identity as scapegoat.

I switched schools, feeling after those three years that there was something inherently wrong with me.

My following encounter with therapy began when I had starved myself to a dangerously low weight at age 14 and was on the verge of hospitalization. A few years after my struggle with anorexia nervosa, my angry, suicidal Defensive Self reared her head again, and I began to drink. And not experiment with alcohol typical teenager style, but blackout every weekend style. Finally, my parents intervened and sent me to a therapist who specialized in substance abuse. What I really needed at that time was to cry. To bawl my eyes out about how I would have to leave my beautiful, tortured, drug addict boyfriend, which would feel like heart-wrenching abandonment, and about how I would no longer be able to escape through the poison that scorched my throat. I didn't feel like I could cry with my therapist. When I broke up with my boyfriend I did not have a therapist, and I felt as though I was crawling out of my skin. I had never been so depressed. My boyfriend had been the only addiction I could get away with, and I found the courage to leave him when I got sober.

When I walked into Nomi's office I was skeptical. I didn't want to cry anymore about my boyfriend, and I didn't want to be confronted about my stuff and about how I was being a victim of my life (which I was). Anyway, I liked her right away. I expected a broad, tall woman with a deep voice, but I walked into the little red room and a petite, pale woman with a single streak of fire engine red in her hair introduced me to a process that would help me to transform myself from a dark, melancholy, self-destructive girl into a self-aware, intuitive, brave soul.

Before I started seeing Nomi, I never understood why sometimes I would be carefree, excited, and hopeful and the next, impulsive, spiteful, and deceptive. I thought for a long time that I was bipolar. Nomi helped me to understand that we all have three unique selves. We have our Emotional Self: the young, vibrant one who likes to play and be creative, but is also often vulnerable and neglected. We have our Defensive Self, strong, protective, and shrewd, yet highly controlling and manipulative. And finally, we have our Expanded, serene, intuitive, and grounded, but often seemingly out of reach. Our actions, our words, and the course of our lives depend on our three selves working in harmony. I imagine my Emotional Self as a Teletubby, my Defensive Self as Cruella Deville, and my Expanded Self as Gandalf from Lord of the Rings. If the root of my problems wasn't obvious before, it is now. Through the intense self-exploration journey

I experience in my work with Nomi, I learned about all of my selves. I learned how to have a dialogue with my different selves. For example, when my Defensive Self comes up, often she is telling me that I am too fat. Then I have to bring my Expanded Self into the picture and gently correct my Defensive Self, explaining that I am strong now and that health is most important. I have learned to listen patiently to the desires and feelings of my selves without judging their fluctuations or criticizing their drastic differences. I have learned through my work with Nomi, to be open to reliving my darkest moments so that I can see the brightest. Sometimes that means lying on the floor, crying hysterically, bringing Nomi back with me to resolve my old hurts. I feel lighter, more present, more loving of myself when I do this deep work. I have come to the realization that I don't have to run away from my feelings and turn to addictions, but that I can sit with my pain and, therefore, grow. I make commitments as a part of my work with Nomi weekly, that help me to strengthen my relationships, get in touch with myself, and explore more things the world has to offer and I can be a part of. My life has expanded in so many directions, because I have learned that fear was trembling under so many of my feelings, constricting my Expanded Self from realizing my life's purpose. Fear is an illusion that binds us, and courage is ultimately what liberates us. I learned through my meditations with Nomi that each part of my body has a story to tell, feelings to share. I learned that as Nomi often says, "We create our realities." Through these lessons, I was able to make decisions about my life that have led me to a place of peace. At this point, I've done my best to surprise Nomi. I've worn dark makeup that hides my big brown eyes, I've chopped all my hair off, I've gotten a tattoo, I've been sad, I've been hysterical, and I've been calm. But I don't think Nomi will ever be shocked. She always knows what my next move is and what is behind it.

— L.

Conquering Fear

My name is Moshe, and I have lived in New York for the past 10 years. A short time after I moved to New York from Israel—or I can say I ran away from the life that I didn't like—I met Nomi. I'd like to tell you a little bit about myself. I grew up as an abused child. My dad was heavily addicted to drugs, and he used to hit me often. I was afraid of not only him but of other members of my family that also used to treat me like I was nothing and beat me. My uncle, for example, used to beat me often. I lived in fear all the time that I did something wrong and would receive more beatings. Being afraid was a big part of my life. I used to wish that something would take me way and stop the suffering that was a part of my life every minute.

In spite of my past, I tried to have as normal a life as possible. I finished high school and served in the army. I had a good job, but something within me did not let me relax. And that was my fear. I always found a different issue to be afraid of. After I moved to New York, I found out that my fears came with me, too.

Ten years ago, I met Nomi and started my healing process with her. We started to work with my fears, and we went back to my childhood. We relived, analyzed, and discovered things that I was not aware of. Piece by piece, I struggled to find healing and forgiveness for my dad and other family members. It was a difficult process. My heart contained tremendous pain from the past. It was not easy to find a place of forgiveness, but I have learned to do that. I also learned to build my personality as an adult and as someone that has something to offer to this world, and most importantly, as someone who knows how to love and be loved.

Today I know how to dialogue with my fears. I know how to use my voice. I don't let negative people be part of my life, and I have a great relationship with my partner as well as with my family. I have created a successful professional life. I know how to use my voice and fight for my rights for a better life. Thank you, Nomi, for the Gates that we went through together.

— M.

Healing The Healer

I met Nomi two years ago, on the street in front of my holistic center in Peekskill. At the time, I was struggling to manage two businesses, accruing debt by the minute. My personal training business was doing well, but the other business, a holistic fitness center, was not. I had grandiose ideas, bigger than myself but with only myself to make them live. Nomi told me that she was a self-actualization coach and counselor. She told me about the method she had developed, the Gates of Power ®. We thought it would be perfect for the studio. To say the least, I was interested. Nomi suggested I try it for myself before recommending it to others. So, on January 28, 2012, I started My Journey.

At the time, I was making inappropriate decisions, feeling unfocused, not finding the words to clearly articulate my vision, and feeling that I was losing control over my life. In the first year of working with Nomi and moving through the Gates of Power ®, I learned how to clearly understand and identify my symptoms as well as their root causes. I learned to uncover the underlying trauma, which was the fear of being slapped down whenever asserting myself.

There are three parts to all of us, a trinity. All religions speak of this, as do all other psychotherapeutic modalities. But Nomi has put it into a clear and real system that captures the concept with simplicity and without a hierarchy. We simply are made up of our Emotional Self, Defensive Self, and Expanded Self. All three are important and must earn to work together. We learn to develop our Expanded Self in order to observe and coach the other two aspects. This helps us fulfill our life's purpose.

I am a healer, but if I don't heal myself I will crumble. It is hard, but this is the only program that I know of that gets to the root. In my case, the root is a feeling of humiliation when being myself. My theme is to clearly express myself to myself and others without the fear and the sense of humiliation. As I learn to trust myself and always express love with integrity, honesty, and compassion to those around me, I connect to my purpose, to the world, and to my life. Without this expression, I am disconnected from what I am doing and where I am going. Now, as I am writing this down, I am realizing that this is the missing piece. Developing my Expanded Self helps me to calm the fear that comes up when I start to speak about my feelings and coaches my Defensive Self when she wants to procrastinate and vacillate from one thing to another.

Nomi is relentless, yet compassionate and loving. My journey is ongoing, and my life is transforming with the unconditional love she brings. There is no other style of therapy that gets to the root of real trauma and coaches you back to wholeness with the kind of love and support that I feel only the Gates of Power® provides. We all have a purpose in this life, a gift, a cause, something to learn and something to give. With Gates of Power ®, you too can find and live the life you were meant to have.

— D.

Beyond Addictions

Addictions to gambling, alcohol, sex, food, media, and a very vicious self-loathing— this is what I brought with me when Nomi and I started working together. I had lived most of my life in the throes of these addictions—I was running away from the pain of the lost years of life in which I lived in failure, starting at the age of 10. I was smoking, drinking and gambling at 10 years old and already failing in school.

I started booking bets in high school and started dealing pot when I graduated. I was introduced to street hookers by some friends at the age of 18, and for the next 12 years went to many street hookers in Manhattan. Over those same 12 years, I gambled away any money I made and drank alcohol to squelch the pain of my life. I lived in a little room in my mother's apartment, where I paid no rent, never bought food, and rarely talked to my mother. I worked in a junkyard and often picked through garbage looking for scrap metal to sell for money.

But ... these behaviors were a manifestation of something much deeper for me that went beyond the external acting out of these addictions. That much deeper issue was self-hatred, plain and simple. I couldn't stand myself, and the addictions became a way for me to escape the pain of my own self-loathing.

I also resented the world and everyone I met. I isolated myself in a cocoon of hostility and resentment and protected myself from intimacy, connection, and love, because it was too painful to get hurt and too painful for me to look at my life and what I had become. Deep down I wanted more out of life, but the thing about addiction is that it can baffle and trick one into thinking that there is no other alternative to life except the life one has now.

I can't say why I started to work with Nomi or what brought me to my senses. What I do know is that I could not take any more misery. I had reached my breaking point. All of the loneliness, the gambling losses, the depression from drinking, the empty sexual encounters with the hookers, and most of all, the dreams that were slowly becoming nothing more than memories, had all taken their toll.

Nomi and I started working together, and she provided what I needed most: listening and love. See? I was never able to tell people, whether it was family or "friends" (all my friends were addicts too) what was really going on with me. I kept all my feelings and thoughts bottled up inside of me and was just looking for someone to tell it all to. I came to Nomi filled with shame, hostility, resentment, anger, sadness, and self-loathing ... and underneath all of that was a scared little soul that was quivering at the thought of actually living life because the only associations I had with life were failure, pain, and misery.

A small pearl of kindness was provided to me by Nomi...I made a commitment to see her every week but often would sit and not talk to her. I was difficult to work with—I had been hurt so often, mostly by my own actions, but also by an abusive family as a child, that it was hard for me to trust her. I was uptight, hostile, and resented using money to see her that I could have been gambling with. But … I persisted and as time went by I started talking more openly about myself and my addictions, confessing my behaviors to her. She listened and observed and never gave me advice and most of all did not judge me. I grew to trust this person who would not judge but only witness what I was saying and encouraged me to feel and to accept myself.

The seed of self-appreciation had been planted. It was a dry seed that needed much watering, but here is what happened. The first thing I did was stop the gambling, drinking, and acting out with prostitutes. I learned that these were all forms of self-punishment due to my self-hatred, and stopping these external behaviors would at least help me deal with what was going on inside of me—the internal stuff that needed to be dealt with.

As Nomi and I continued to work together, she introduced me to the concept of the three selves: The Expanded, The Defensive, and the Emotional.

For most of my life, my Defensive Self was running the show, guarding and protecting me from any sort of emotional pain that life sometimes brings. It was also protecting me from my own feelings of self-loathing through instant gratification (gambling, drinking, and sexual actions) that gave me the illusion that I was "living the good life." The addictions provided a "pleasurable" escape from my own reality. The bigger problem with this was that it seemed that this was who I was and would always be.

Through working with Nomi, I was able to identify two other aspects of myself: my Expanded Self and my Emotional Self. My Expanded Self became the guide, the leader, the one who would have to "fight" the urges and powerful self-destructive habits of my Defensive Self. Through stillness and sitting with the urges, they slowly started loosening their grip on me. I started to find the third aspect of my selves, the Emotional Self, and was able find its voice.

It turned out that my Emotional Self is a very kind, creative, gentle, poetic, humorous, intense, emotional, and talented entity that was simply buried under all the acting out of my Defensive Self. As I started to shed the cloak of my Defensive Self and give my Emotional Self permission to express its humanity, my life started to change.

The hostility that kept me from people started lifting, the fear that kept me paralyzed no longer gripped me, and the self-hatred that drove me to the addictions slowly turned to self-appreciation and self-acceptance.

I now own a successful entertainment company and make my living as a professional clown who has performed on military bases, in prisons, on the streets of New York City, at Lincoln Center in New York, and at thousands of events throughout New York. I have appeared on national television as a clown, as well as on Comedy Central, I have studied classical guitar, and am currently learning to play the piano.

I have also become a very entertaining, over-the-top stand-up comedian and would like to quote a fellow comedian who said, "Every time he sees me perform, I make him laugh so hard, he cries."

I now see life and enjoy the small things that make it rich. I see dogs walk and laugh. I look into a dog's sad eyes, and I am moved deeply. I see the sky and am in awe. I see the beauty of nature and how each leaf contributes to the majesty of trees.

I feel compassion for the people who pick through garbage and ask for money. I know where they are at, and I know they don't have to be that way. I allow my heart to break for them. I laugh freely and loudly, cry when I am moved, and am slowly learning to love humanity (very slowly!)

Nomi has been a friend, a guide, and a trustworthy ally in my struggle to reclaim my true and authentic self.

— M.

Transforming a Broken Heart

Gates of Power® techniques have helped me on every level of my life. I came to work with Nomi and Gates of Power® after being beaten down emotionally and dumped. I was in a long-term relationship that I thought was solid and committed. I felt we were better together than apart, so when my partner announced to me out of the blue that he was leaving, I was stunned. It was a devastating shock. I was shattered, and my sense of self-esteem crumbled. I felt emotionally bruised beyond repair. I felt that I had been betrayed. I felt that I had done something wrong... The feeling of loneliness was unbearable. I experienced an extreme amount of grief, without an actual death.

I needed help to start my single life over again and to find a way to feel okay being with me. I needed help in rebuilding my confidence. With Nomi, I learned to affirm that I am better than "okay." I learned to release and allow my emotions of grief, disappointment, and anger to dissolve. I learned to be there for myself in my dark moments.

Today, I am back to my amazing self, thanks to Nomi and the Gates of Power®. As I was introduced to the different Gates I learned to take care of myself physically, emotionally, spiritually, mentally, and creatively. I learned better ways to set up 38 important commitments, and also to say no. I learned to express my emotions and deal with my defenses in a more expanded way. This was so great because I finally felt heard. The healing came with the work. I now see the gift that it has been for me to no longer be in that long-term relationship. I have grown stronger and more in touch with my needs and feelings. I know now what is good for me. I reconnected with my spiritual practice. I have been able to focus again on my business and steer it toward more success. I am looking forward to meeting a man that appreciates and respects all that I have to give. A man that is not afraid of all that life has to offer. I have learned through the techniques of Gates of Power® that I matter.

Nomi, thank you.

— P.

A Hopeful Journey...

When I first met Nomi, over 20 years ago, I was lost, broken, empty, and scared. My life had come to a point where I was a mere shell of a person. I had a job that was destroying my very soul. I was lost. I was afraid. I was alone.

When I met Nomi, she reminded me that in life we have a journey and a purpose. Nomi helped me see myself better than I ever could, to see the inner beauty that lies within. She has enhanced my life and has helped me love the man I have become.

One of my favorite sayings is, "When the student is ready the teacher appears." For me, my spirit was ready, and my angel appeared, and that angel was Nomi. I was introduced to her through a friend, and from that moment, my life has never been the same. After my first session, I felt that there was finally someone that was there for *me*, someone to help me to tackle my most painful memories and help me see a light, a light that was dimmed by the rest of the world.

For the past several years Nomi and I looked at it all: my childhood, my relationship with my parents, my siblings, and friendships. She guided me so that there was no stone left unturned. Nomi would challenge me to stay in the moment and allow my feelings to reveal themselves. She taught me not just to feel, but to feel it all. She introduced me to my little boy, the little boy inside that was hidden and scared. She had me challenge my Defensive Self—the part of me that was pinning me and keeping me down. We would often celebrate my Expanded Self, all the while nurturing and loving my Emotional Self, the part of me that's pure, sweet, and authentic.

Finally, after all these years, I can look in the mirror and like what I see. I have learned how to make healthy promises to myself and be loyal to all of my Gates, the Gates that create me: a loving, kind, authentic man.

— L.

Ellie's Story: Finding My Strength

When I came to Nomi, the façade I wore was all I knew of myself. I was a person driven to have people love me, willing to do pretty much anything to get that love. I had no idea how I had become this person or why I was compelled to do things that were harmful and unworthy of me.

My history of sex abuse came almost immediately to the foreground. Nomi lovingly and carefully created a space safe enough for me to completely break the façade and see the utter despair that lay beneath. Painstakingly, we chipped away and uncovered the core of who I was at that time. I was a broken spirit. It was impossible for me to love from this place. All I knew was that I was starving, empty, and I NEEDED!!! It did not sometimes matter how I filled that need, whether it was through sex addiction, alcohol, or food. These were my three "drugs of choice." If one became too painful I just switched to another.

Using the tools of the inner dialogue between my Emotional Self, my Defensive Self, and my Expanded Self, I began…

I can honestly say that at that time, I HAD NO Expanded Self. The idea of parenting myself was not only foreign to me, my resistance was powerful. I wanted others to parent me. My thought was, "I didn't get what I needed from my parents, so I should get it now in whatever form I could find." Mostly, my choice was inappropriate men. Attaching myself to them, I turned them into my savior and expected them to meet my needs and make me feel better about myself. This was my one and only plan for filling the void.

Well, food was the other. I used food as my best friend and my worst enemy. Struggling between the latest crash diets and flipping into bingeing till I was sick. The level of self-disgust was torturous and never-ending. Alcohol was the numbing tool to escape the pain.

Little by little, and ever resisting, I stumbled my way into communicating with the childlike self inside me who was so very broken. Tears fell endlessly, month after month. Heartbroken, I told Nomi that I felt as if I couldn't love … that I was incapable. At that point, I had not yet developed my own compassionate Expanded Self. I could see my broken little child in a clear image as a prisoner hiding in a corner under a bench in as small a space as possible. The need to hide from further hurt was my motivating feeling. When I saw her in my mind, I felt nothing but numb and was reluctant to try to help.

Meanwhile, my Defensive Self would observe and criticize, "Get up!" "Stop crying" "Grow up" "Nobody will love you like this." I would look at my emotionally broken inner child and not be able to find one iota of compassion. It was disgusting and repulsive to me. I was at war with myself.

Then one day, my Expanded Self showed up. At first, the need of my Emotional Self was overwhelming, and I felt that I had no ability to help her. Nomi said to just observe, to just sit in the presence of my broken inner child. I started communicating with this child. Not really knowing how to help her, I finally physically put myself in my mind and body in a position to simply lie down next to her and tell her, "I see you. I may not know how to help you right now, but I am here and I am not going anywhere."

This was the moment where my true healing began. The trust was developed between my broken Emotional Self and my GOOD parent: me. The negotiations began with my Defensive Self in order to relieve her of the fear, to stop her dictatorship, and to have my Expanded Self take the reins as a true parent and leader.

This was years ago now, and although there are certainly some chronic neurosis and habits that I continue to negotiate, I now have the tools to walk through my life with confidence. My career has taken a giant leap forward, as I now am willing to lead. My relationships have sometimes been challenging as I have changed … but they are always leading me toward better and better friendships. I have a meaningful intimate marriage that continues to grow. Most importantly, I am not being led by my neurosis and need. I use the techniques of the Gates of Power® Method to help me daily when these needs surface. I have the confidence that I will be able to survive any tidal wave that life may throw at me. I learned to be committed to all my Gates and nourish them. Thank God for Nomi and her amazing patience in guiding me through this process, which lives within me and instructs me daily.

About the Author

Nomi Bachar, a holistic spiritual counselor is a self-healing, selfactualization expert and coach. She is the director of White Cedar Institute for Expanded Living LLC and the creator of the Gates of Power ® Method. The Gates of Power ® Method is an experiential, creative, and spiritual method that assists participants in reaching holistic integration, empowerment, and fulfillment. Ms. Bachar has been working with individuals, couples, and groups for the last 26 years, as well as lecturing and facilitating workshops.

Alongside her counseling and training, Ms. Bachar has an extensive back ground as a multidisciplinary performing artist. Her artistic background includes acting, dance, choreography, producing, and writing. In the last few years, she has made a choice to dedicate herself to empowering people through the Gates of Power ® Method. Her mission and passion is this exploration and expansion of human potential and the ways it can be achieved through transformation, creativity, and leading a life of contribution.

About the Gates of Power® Program

Note: *The Gates of Power ® Method is copyrighted, registered, and protected by Orrick, a law firm for intellectual property.*

The Gates of Power ® Method is a comprehensive curriculum that supports and maximizes the process of self-transformation and self-actualization, leading to empowerment. The curriculum includes seven levels that can be completed in three stages. The seven levels of the program build upon each other. Participants need to complete each level before moving to the next one. Each level includes discussions, interactive processes, and experiential exercises from each of the seven Gates. On completion of the Gates of Power ® curriculum, participants who so choose may graduate into the leadership program, which trains them to facilitate alongside a Gates of Power ® certified coach. Ms. Bachar offers individual and couples counseling, as well as lectures, presentations, and workshops for interested organizations. For more information visit *www.gatesofpower.com*

Bibliography

Bell, John S. *Collected Papers on Quantum Philosophy.* Cambridge, UK: Cambridge University Press, 1988.

Bernay-Roman, Andy. *Deep Feeling, Deep Healing: The Heart, Mind, and Soul of Getting Well.* Jupiter, FL: Spectrum Healing Press, 2011.

Berry, Thomas. *Religions of India: Hinduism, Yoga, Buddhism.* New York: Colombia University Press, 1992.

Bohr, Niels Henrik David. *The Philosophical Writings of Niels Bohr.* Woodbridge, CT: Ox Bow Press, 1999.

Eddy, Mary B. *Science and Health With Key to the Scriptures.* CreateSpace Independent Publishing Platform, 2012.

Elgin, Duane. *Voluntary Simplicity: Toward a Way of Life That Is Outwardly Simple, Inwardly Rich.* New York: Harper, 2010.

Farhi, Donna. *The Breathing Book: Good Health and Vitality Through Essential Breath Work.* New York: Holt, 1996.

Goldsmith, Joel S. *Beyond Words and Thoughts.* Camarillo, CA: De Vorss & Co/ Acropolis Books, 1998.

Goswami, Amit. *Physics of the Soul: The Quantum Book of Living, Dying, Reincarnation and Immortality.* Newburyport, MA: Red Wheel/Weiser/ Conari/Hampton Roads Publishing, 2001.

Keleman, Stanley. *Emotional Anatomy: The Structure of Experience.* Westlake Village CA: Center Press, 1986.

Laitman, Rav Michael. *The Path of Kabbalah.* Toronto, Canada: Bnei Baruch, Laitman Kabbalah, 2005.

Lowen, Alexander. *The Betrayal of the Body.* Alachua, FL: Bioenergetics Press, 2005.

Macy, Joanna. *Word as Lover, World as Self: Courage for Global Justice and Ecological Renewal.* Berkeley, CA: Parallax Press, 2007.

Maimonides. *Ethical Writings of Maimonides.* Mineola, NY: Dover Publications, 1983

Mishra, Rammurti S., and Shri Brahmananda Sarasvati. *Fundamentals of Yoga: A Hand book of Theory, Practice and Application.* New York: The Julian Press, 1987.

Myss, Caroline. *Anatomy of the Spirit: The Seven Stages of Power and Healing.* New York: Crown/Harmony Books, 1997.

Rosenberg, Marshall B. *Nonviolent Communication: A Language of Life.* Encinitas, CA: Puddledancer Press, 2003.

Rūmī, Jalāl ad-Dīn M. *The Essential Rumi, New Expanded Edition.* New York: HarperOne, 2004.

Thich Nhat Hanh. *No Death, No Fear: Comforting Wisdom for Life.* New York: Penguin/Riverhead Books, 2003.

Endnotes

1. Keleman, Stanley. *Emotional Anatomy: The Structure of Experience.* Westlake Village CA: Center Press, 1986.
2. Lowen, Alexander. *The Betrayal of the Body.* Alachua, FL: Bioenergetics Press, 2005.
3. Myss, Caroline. *Energy Anatomy.* Boulder, CO: Sounds True, 2001. Audiobook.
4. "Shri Brahmananda Sarasvati," *Ananda Ashram*, www.anandaashram.org/Founder
5. Farhi, Donna. *The Breathing Book: Good Health and Vitality Through Essential Breath Work.* New York: Holt, 1996.
6. Rosenberg Marshall B. *Nonviolent Communication: A Language of Life.* Encinitas, CA: Puddledancer Press, 2003.
7. Wikipedia contributors, "Joel S. Goldsmith," *Wikipedia, The Free Encyclopedia, http://en.wikipedia.org/w/index.php?title=Joel_S Goldsmith&oldid=556961640* (accessed September 27, 2013).
8. Goldsmith, Joel S. *Beyond Words and Thoughts.* Acropolis Books, 1998.
9. "Study Guide," *The Institute of Noetic Sciences and Captured Light, http://media.noetic.org/uploads/files/Bleep_Study_Guide.pdf*
10. "Macy, Joanna," *Joanna Macy and Her Work*, http://www.joannamacy.net
11. "Berry, Thomas," *Thomas Berry*, http://www.thomasberry.org/Biography
12. "Elgin, Duane," *Duane Elgin*, http://duaneelgin.com/
13. "Goswami, Amit," *Amit Goswami*, http://www.amitgoswami.org/about/
14. Wikipedia contributors, "Niels Bohr," *Wikipedia, The Free Encyclopedia, http://en.wikipedia.org/w/index.php?title=Niels_Bohr&oldid=574614591* (accessed September 27, 2013).
15. Wikipedia contributors, "John Stewart Bell," *Wikipedia, The Free Encyclopedia, http://en.wikipedia.org/w/index.php?title=John_Stewart_Bell&oldid=565298291* (accessed September 27, 2013).

16. "Shri Brahmananda Sarasvati," *Ananda Ashram*, www.anandaashram.org/Founder
17. Wikipedia contributors, "Maimonides," *Wikipedia, The Free Encyclopedia*, http://en.wikipedia.org/w/index.php?title=Maimonides&oldid=569619147 (accessed September 27, 2013).
18. Wikipedia contributors, "Rumi," *Wikipedia, The Free Encyclopedia*, http://en.wikipedia.org/w/index.php?title=Rumi&oldid=572199235 (accessed September 27, 2013).
19. Wikipedia contributors, "Joel S. Goldsmith," *Wikipedia, The Free Encyclopedia*, http://en.wikipedia.org/w/index.php?title=Joel_S._Goldsmith&oldid=556961640 (accessed September 27, 2013).
20. Wikipedia contributors, "David Bohm," *Wikipedia, The FreeEncyclopedia*, http://en.wikipedia.org/w/index.php?title=David_Bohm&oldid=566920462 (accessed September 27, 2013).

www.ingramcontent.com/pod-product-compliance
Lightning Source LLC
Chambersburg PA
CBHW050520170426
43201CB00013B/2023